Study Guide to Accompany
PHYSIOLOGICAL PSYCHOLOGY
by Robert Graham

Study Guide to Accompany
PHYSIOLOGICAL PSYCHOLOGY
by Robert Graham

LESLIE E. FISHER
Cleveland State University

with the assistance of
Gregory E. Fisher

Wadsworth Publishing Company
Belmont, California
A Division of Wadsworth, Inc.

© 1990 by Wadsworth, Inc. All rights reserved. No part of this book may be reproduced, stored in a retrieval system, or transcribed, in any form or by any means, electronic, mechanical, photocopying, recording, or otherwise, without the prior written permission of the publisher, Wadsworth Publishing Company, Belmont, California 94002, a division of Wadsworth, Inc.

Printed in the United States of America   49

1 2 3 4 5 6 7 8 9 10—94 93 92 91 90

ISBN 0-534-10105-4

CONTENTS

Preface **vi**

Chapter 1   Sampling Physiological Psychology: A Preview **1**
Chapter 2   Cells of the Nervous System **15**
Chapter 3   The Basic Plan of the Nervous System **33**
Chapter 4   Conduction and Transmission **59**
Chapter 5   Exploring the Nervous System Through Science **81**
Chapter 6   Vision **101**
Chapter 7   Auditory and Chemical Senses **137**
Chapter 8   The Somatic Senses **169**
Chapter 9   The Production and Sensing of Movement **191**
Chapter 10   Sleep and Attention **223**
Chapter 11   The Control of Ingestion **243**
Chapter 12   Sexuality and Reproduction **267**
Chapter 13   Emotion and Stress **289**
Chapter 14   Learning **311**
Chapter 15   The Hippocampus in Learning and Memory **337**
Chapter 16   Memory **349**
Chapter 17   Brain Dysfunction **369**
Chapter 18   Neuropsychology of Cortical Function **401**

Pre-Exam Answers **433**

PREFACE

Welcome to the study of physiological psychology. I hope that as the term progresses you will catch some of the interest and enthusiasm for this area that Dr. Graham has managed to capture in the pages of your text. A strong motivational state is half the battle in mastering this material. The other half requires your active participation in the learning process. The passive reading of the assignment, combined with the underscoring of what seems to be important, will not adequately prepare you to perform well on exams or allow you to retain the material for future reference. This second goal is especially important. As the course develops, you will discover that understanding the new material depends, in large part, on how well you understand the earlier assignments.

By this point in your education, you undoubtedly have some well-established study habits, but I would like you to think about trying something a little different this term. Begin by reading the chapter, not for detail but for a familiarity with what the chapter is all about. Don't waste time underscoring or taking notes during this first reading. It is important that you complete this task before the professor begins lecturing on the material. Such familiarity with the chapter should enable you to better understand and retain the lecture material while taking fewer and much clearer lecture notes.

Now you are ready to use your study guide, which has been designed to guide your active study of the material presented in the text. Each chapter has been divided into three sections: read-write-review, pre-exam quiz, and concept flash cards.

The read-write-review section of each chapter has been broken down into more manageable study units. At the beginning of each of these units you will find a statement like the following: "Read pages 000-000 and summary statements 0-00, pages 000-000, then answer each of the following questions in this section." This time read the indicated text material for both detail and understanding. When you have finished, close the book and answer each of the questions in the corresponding study unit. It is important that you try to answer the questions without resorting to the text. If you are unable to answer a particular question you can return to the text and read the appropriate section again. The page or pages on which each question is answered are listed at the end of each question. Once you have read the section, set the book aside and write the answer from memory. If you are not able to remember an answer a short time after reading the information in the book, you cannot expect to remember it when you take the exam.

Once you have finished a study unit put things away and take a break. In the beginning you may feel as though you could do another unit without a break; however, it is important that you establish the habit of taking a break early in the term. When the material becomes more difficult, and it will, looking forward to the break will serve as a motivator.

At the end of each chapter in this study guide you will find a set of concept cards. These cards contain most of the terms listed in the chapter glossaries of your text. These terms compose the vocabulary of the physiological psychologist, and a mastery of these terms is essential to your understanding of the field. These cards are simple to use. Cut them out, put them in a pile, and test yourself. If your definition is incomplete or incorrect put that card in a second pile that you will go through again until you are satisfied that you have it mastered. If you want more information about the concept than appears on the card you can go to the textbook page or pages listed on the card.

The pre-exam quiz should be used as a final check on your preparation. Take the quiz as you would take an exam, and then turn to the answers in the back of your workbook to check your performance. If you miss a question go back to the appropriate page or pages in the text and restudy the material.

As with most such endeavors, the preparation of this study guide has been a collaborative effort, and I would like to take this opportunity to thank some of the people who helped to bring this effort to fruition. For providing me with an excellent text from which to work, I would like to thank Dr. Robert Graham. Thanks to Kenneth King, the psychology editor at Wadsworth Publishing Company for bringing me into the project; to Stacey Pollard, assistant editor, who helped to keep me on course; and to Donna Linden, production editor, who made sure the final product never strayed. Finally, I wish to thank Gregory Fisher, who word-processed the entire manuscript and tolerated my many last minute changes.

Leslie E. Fisher
Cleveland, Ohio 1990

CHAPTER ONE
SAMPLING PHYSIOLOGICAL PSYCHOLOGY: A PREVIEW

READ-WRITE-REVIEW

Read pages 1-9 and summary statements 1-10 on page 15, then answer each of the following questions in this section.
---

1. During your recent brain surgery Dr. Hacknslash, your surgeon, stopped cutting long enough to determine where he was. To do this he simply electrically stimulated a brain tissue site and simultaneously observed the resultant pattern of neural activity and your overt response, a report of a pleasurable feeling. Clearly this is an example of the link between mind and brain. From a philosophical point of view this link can be interpreted in one of two ways. List and define each of these positions. (2-3)

    a. Using the above example, interpret the relationship from each of the two viewpoints. (2-3)

    b. Describe the more modern position of interactional dualism. (3)

    c. How does parallelism differ from interactional dualism? (3)

    d. Of the philosophical positions dualism and monism, which is adopted by most scientists? (3)

2. What is reductionism? (3)

    a. Distinguish between molar and molecular explanations. (3)

    b. Reductionism poses what major problem for the psychologist? (3)

3. For each of the contributors to the understanding of brain function listed in Column A, locate the contribution made in Column B.

Column A	Column B
____ Bernstein (4)	a. "animal electricity"
____ Galvani (4)	b. brain is composed of individual cells called "neurons"
____ Muller (4)	c. concluded that all nerve impulses are qualitatively the same, their effect due to where in the brain they travel
____ Ramon y Cajal (4)	d. described how neurons generate electrical currents called nerve impulses
____ Sherrington (4)	e. microscopic structure of brain tissue
	f. synapses and reflex arcs
____ Waldeyer (4)	g. The Organization of the Brain

1

4. With the formation of the International Society for Neuroscience in 1969, the field of neuroscience was formally established. What two disciplines came together in the formation of this new field? (5)

   a. Neuropsychology is a branch of what field of psychology? (5)

   b. Neuropsychology deals with what? (5)

   c. Cognitive neuroscience represents the joining of forces from what three disciplines? (5)

   d. What is it that cognitive neuroscience studies? (5)

5. List the basic symptoms in Tourette syndrome. (5-6)

   a. A drug that helps to reduce the frequency of the symptoms associated with Tourette syndrome belongs to what class of drugs? (6)

   b. How do these drugs produce their effects? (6)

   c. What reason is there to believe that dopamine may not be the only chemical involved in Tourette syndrome? (6)

   d. Data suggest that another chemical involved in Tourette syndrome is ____. (6)

   e. What is a neurotransmitter? (6)

   f. What evidence, both human and animal, is there to suggest that the cingulate gyrus plays a role in Tourette syndrome? (6-7)

   g. What is an obsessive-compulsive disorder and how might it be related to Tourette syndrome? (7)

6. What is a neurotransmitter system? (8)

   a. Which of the neurotransmitter systems may be involved in obsessive-compulsive disorders? (8)

   b. What is an obsession? A compulsion? (8)

   c. What is dexamethasone and how did it play a role in determining what neurotransmitter substance may be involved in obsessive-compulsive behavior? (9)

   d. What is a neurotransmitter antagonist? (9)

Read pages 9-15 and summary statements 11-13 on pages 15-16, then answer each of the following questions in this section.
---

1. At what point in your life did you have all the nerve cells you will ever have? (9)

    a. Suppose that at age 10 you had a severe sinus infection that, because it went untreated, spread to the surrounding brain tissue, where it formed a localized brain abscess. By the time this was treated and brought under control several thousand brain neurons had been destroyed. The doctor told your parents not to worry; you were young and those lost cells would grow back in a couple of months. Is he right? Give a reason for your answer. (9)

    b. What makes the transplanting of tissue from a donor to a recipient difficult? (9)

    c. How can this be minimized? (9-10)

    d. Is this problem true of all body tissues or are there exceptions? (10)

    e. What makes brain-tissue transplants especially difficult? (10)

    f. Who is responsible for carrying out the first brain-tissue transplant experiments and when were they done? (10)

2. Describe a case of Parkinson's disease. (10)

    a. What is the immediate cause of the movement problems seen in Parkinson's disease? (10)

    b. What neurotransmitter is employed by these neurons? (10)

    c. What is the current standard therapy for Parkinson's disease? (10)

    d. Why does this therapy eventually become ineffective? (11)

    e. Why is it difficult to test brain-tissue transplant techniques as a therapy for Parkinson's disease? (11)

    f. What two solutions have been found for this problem? (11-12)

    g. Identify some of the major problems that researchers will have to face once they begin using human patients. (12-13)

3

PRE-EXAM QUIZ

Multiple-Choice
Select the choice that best completes the stem in each question and indicate your selection in the appropriate space to the left of the question.

_____ 1. The philosophical view that the mind is simply the functioning of the brain is
   a. interactional dualism
   b. monism
   c. parallelism
   d. position taken by most scientists today
   e. more than one of the above

_____ 2. His research led him to believe that all nerve impulses are qualitatively the same and that the resultant sensations produced by the stimulation of a particular neuron depends on that area of the brain to which it travels. He is
   a. Ramon y Cajal
   b. Muller
   c. Sherrington
   d. Hebb
   e. none of the above

_____ 3. The branch that examines the effects of brain damage on the patient's behavior is
   a. neurophysiology
   b. cognitive neuroscience
   c. neuropathology
   d. neuropsychology
   e. psychobiology

_____ 4. The drug _____, which belongs to the class of drugs called _____, is considered to be the best therapy for Tourette patients.
   a. dexamethasone; antidepressant
   b. clomipramine; antidepressant
   c. dopamine; antipsychotic
   d. haloperidol; antipsychotic
   e. MPTP; hallucinogen

_____ 5. Studies of which of the following brain areas suggest that it is the dysfunctional brain center in Tourette syndrome?
   a. substantia nigra
   b. cingulate cortex
   c. caudate nucleus
   d. brain stem
   e. none of the above

_____ 6. The neurotransmitter system that appears to be involved in the production of obsessive-compulsive disorder is one that uses _____ as its neurotransmitter.
   a. dopamine
   b. GABA
   c. serotonin
   d. norepinephrine
   e. none of the above

_____ 7. Which of the following makes brain-tissue transplant so difficult?
   a. in order for transplanted brain tissue to react normally it would have to be capable of forming the billions of highly specific connections to make it functional
   b. immune system activity will almost always bring about rejection of transplanted tissue if it comes from an outside donor
   c. donated brain tissue cannot be kept alive in most recipients because there is no way to provide it with an adequate blood supply
   d. all of the above are major problems in brain-tissue transplant
   e. none of the above are major problems in brain-tissue transplant

_____ 8. The loss of nerve cells in the brain region called _____ is the immediate cause of the motor problems seen in Parkinson's disease.
   a. cingulate cortex
   b. striatum
   c. substantia nigra
   d. brain stem
   e. none of the above

_____ 9. Which of the following substances has been shown to mimic the cellular destruction of Parkinson's disease almost perfectly?
   a. 6-hydroxydopamine
   b. serotonin
   c. 1-methyl-4-phenyl-1,2,3,6-tetrahydropyridine
   d. clomipramine
   e. haloperidol

_____ 10. Recent brain-tissue transplant experiments designed to demonstrate that this was a reasonable therapeutic technique in treating Parkinson's disease have identified some problems, among which are
   a. that dendrites of the transplanted cells do not appear normal
   b. that the transplanted cells survive but do not produce the dopamine necessary to function normally
   c. that when striated neurons were transplanted into the striatum of normal hosts the brain appeared to shrink, suggesting that the graft resulted in the loss of millions of cells
   d. that the transplant appears to be perfectly normal but there is no change in the progression of the disease
   e. more than one of the above

True/False

_____ 1. The typical physiological psychologist is most probably an interactional dualist and a reductionist.

_____ 2. One who holds the position of parallelism would contend that the mind and brain are completely independent of each other.

_____ 3. The notion that the whole is greater than the sum of its parts would lead its advocate to search for a more molecular explanation rather than a molar explanation for a phenomenon.

_____ 4. The basic symptom in Tourette syndrome is the tic.

_____ 5. One of the effects of haloperidol is to increase the sensitivity of neurons to dopamine.

_____ 6. Because the brain contains no pain receptors it is possible to perform brain surgery using only a local anesthetic for the scalp.

_____ 7. An obsession is a repetitive, purposeful and intentional behavior performed in response to a compulsion or according to certain rules or in a stereotyped fashion.

_____ 8. The brain and spinal cord apparently are exempt from the immune process.

_____ 9. Because of legal problems in applying fetal-tissue techniques to humans, some researchers have implanted tissue from the patient's own pituitary gland in the treatment of Parkinson's disease.

_____ 10. Early results of brain-tissue transplants as a means of treating Parkinson's disease in the United States have been disappointing.

1.1

antipsychotic

(6)

1.2

axons

(10)

1.3

cingulate cortex

(6)

1.4

cognitive neuroscience

(5)

1.5

compulsion

(8)

1.6

coprolalia

(6)

1.7

dendrites

(14)

1.8

dexamethasone

(9)

1.9

doctrine of specific nerve energies

(4)

1.10

dopamine

(6)

1.6

A tic characteristic of Tourette syndrome. It takes the form of a compulsion to utter obscenities or vulgar phrases.

1.1

A class of drugs used to treat schizophrenia. They affect the activity level of a system of nerve cells within the brain that are stimulated by the chemical neurotransmitter, dopamine.

1.7

Long, branch-like extensions from the center of a neuron on which the synaptic connections are formed.

1.2

The long fibrous extensions of neurons that carry nerve impulses to other nerve cells.

1.8

A drug that turns off the endocrine response to stress in normal people but not in some patients who suffer from depression or obsessive-compulsive disorder.

1.3

A part of the brain related to emotions that may be malfunctioning in Tourette syndrome.

1.9

Muller's doctrine that all nerve impulses are qualitatively the same regardless of the type of information they carry.

1.4

A discipline that uses the information-processing ideas of computer science to understand the relation between brain events, thinking, and language.

1.10

A neurotransmitter employed by a system of nerve cells involved with producing patterns of movements.

1.5

Repetitive, purposeful, and intentional behaviors that are performed in response to an obsession, or according to certain rules or in a stereotyped fashion.

Copyright 1990 by Wadsworth, Inc.

1.11

dualism

(2)

1.12

haloperidol

(6)

1.13

interactional dualism

(3)

1.14

molar

(3)

1.15

molecular

(3)

1.16

monism

(3)

1.17

MPTP

(12)

1.18

nerve impulse

(4)

1.19

neuron

(4)

1.20

neuron doctrine

(4)

1.16

The view that the mind and brain are one--that the mind is simply the functioning of the brain. This is the position most neuroscientists accept.

1.11

Philosophical position that holds that the mind and body are two different phenomena. The body is a biological mechanism that obeys physical laws, whereas the mind is the nonphysical, spiritual soul.

1.17

A contaminating chemical found in "street drugs" that brings about the death of nigrostriatal neurons.

1.12

One of the antipsychotic drugs, currently the best therapy for Tourette patients.

1.18

Electrical events occurring in neurons when they are active.

1.13

A philosophical position that holds that the brain can cause changes in the mind and vice versa.

1.19

A nerve cell

1.14

Refers to the holistic view of a phenomenon, which avoids reductionism.

1.20

Waldeyer's doctrine that the brain was composed of individual cells, which he called neurons.

1.15

Refers to explanations that are reductionistic, i.e., that analyze wholes into their parts to see how the parts interact.

Copyright 1990 by Wadsworth, Inc.

1.21 neuropsychology (5)

1.22 neuroscience (5)

1.23 neurotoxins (11)

1.24 neurotransmitter (6)

1.25 neurotransmitter antagonists (9)

1.26 neurotransmitter system (8)

1.27 nigrostriatal neurons (10)

1.28 obsession (8)

1.29 obsessive-compulsive disorder (6-7)

1.30 Parkinson's disease (10)

1.26

A group of cells all using the same neurotransmitter.

1.21

A branch of clinical psychology that examines the effects of brain damage on patient behavior.

1.27

Cells that connect the substantia nigra with the striatum.

1.22

A new science that combines our knowledge of the biology, psychology, and chemistry of the nervous system.

1.28

Recurrent, persistent ideas, thoughts, images, or impulses that the individual does not wish to experience.

1.23

Nerve poisons.

1.29

A psychiatric syndrome in which the person feels compelled to perform meaningless acts.

1.24

A chemical secreted by a neuron at its synapse to excite the neurons it contacts.

1.30

An incurable brain disorder that slowly erodes a person's ability to control the voluntary muscles.

1.25

A drug that blocks the action of a neurotransmitter at the synapse.

Copyright 1990 by Wadsworth, Inc.

1.31 parallelism (2-3)	1.36 striatum (10)
1.32 reductionism (3)	1.37 substantia nigra (10)
1.33 reflex arcs (4)	1.38 synapse (4)
1.34 serotonin (8)	1.39 Tourette syndrome (5)
1.35 6-hydroxydopamine (11)	

1.36

Part of the brain that normally receives impulses from the substantia nigra. The striatum malfunctions in patients with Parkinson's disease.

1.37

An area of the upper brain stem that is important to muscle control. This area is damaged in patients with Parkinson's disease.

1.38

A point at which one neuron contacts and communicates with another neuron.

1.39

A collection of brain-damage symptoms, the most outstanding of which is tics.

1.31

A form of philosophical dualism that holds that the mind and brain are completely independent of one another; they act simultaneously on the same stimuli and responses.

1.32

A strategy for developing explanations of phenomena by analyzing them into components at a more molecular level.

1.33

A circuit composed of neurons that connects a receptor organ with muscles to produce an automatic response to a stimulus.

1.34

A sleep-related neurotransmitter that may also be involved in obsessive-compulsive disorder.

1.35

A neurotoxin that can kill cells using dopamine as a neurotransmitter.

Copyright 1990 by Wadsworth, Inc.

CHAPTER TWO
CELLS OF THE NERVOUS SYSTEM

READ-WRITE-REVIEW

Read pages 20-26 and summary statements 1-4 on page 45, then answer each of the following questions in this section.

---

1. What is the basic building block of an organism? (20)

    a. Put together a group of cells having similar functions and you have what? (20)

    b. Several types of these (answer to a) combined to do a particular job becomes what? (20)

    c. A collection of these (answer to b) is what? (20)

2. What are the three divisions of the generalized cell? (20-21)

3. Describe the composition of the cell membrane. (21-22)

4. How does the cell nucleus exert its control? (23)

5. What functions do each of the following organelles perform within the cell?

    a. mitochondria (24)

    b. rough endoplasmic reticulum (23)

    c. Golgi complex (24)

    d. filaments and microtubules (24)

Read pages 26-32 and summary statements 5-6 on page 45, then answer each of the following questions in this section.

---

1. Define metabolism. (26)

    a. Distinguish between anabolism and catabolism. (26)

    b. What does the body use to create adenosine triphosphate (ATP)? (26)

c. What form does the energy stored in sugar take when it is transferred to ATP? (27)

d. The response of muscle cells and nerve cells to a sudden disruption in blood supply will differ in what way? Why will this difference occur? (27)

e. What happens to the ATP molecule when energy is expended? (27)

f. Precisely where are most ATP molecules created? (27)

g. What is an enzyme and what does it do? (27)

2. Proteins, the building blocks of the body, consist of what? (27)

3. Describe the deoxyribonucleic acid (DNA) molecule. (29)

   a. What is accomplished during the process of transcription? (30)

   b. What is a condon? (30)

   c. What is the role of messenger RNA (mRNA) in the process of translation? (31)

   d. What is the role of transfer RNA (tRNA) in the process of translation? (31)

   e. In what structural way do the DNA and RNA molecules differ? (30-31)

Read pages 32-39 and summary statements 7-12 on pages 45-46, then answer each of the following questions in this section.
---

1. What are the two most important cell types in the tissue of the nervous system? (32)

2. The diagram below is that of a typical nerve cell together with an enlargement of the terminal and synapse. Immediately below the diagram is a series of six statements, identified as a-f, which describe the various structures. Read each statement and identify the structure by name, and then locate and label it on the diagram.

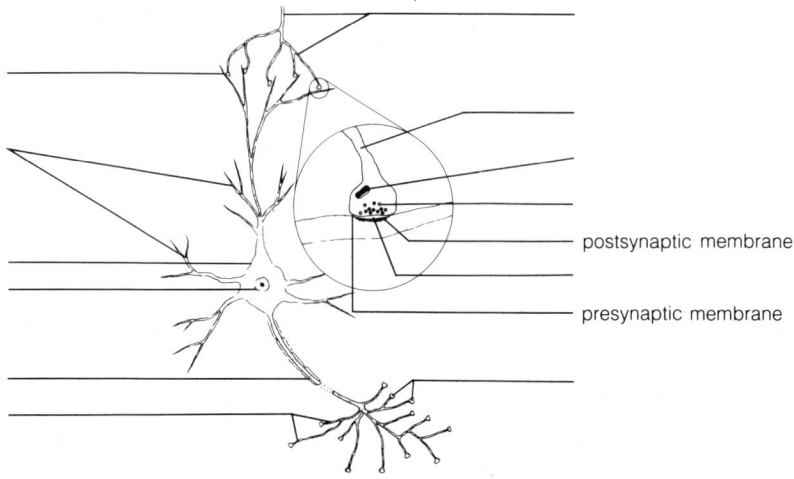

   — postsynaptic membrane
   — presynaptic membrane

   a. Swellings at the end of the branching structure. (33-34)

b. Relatively short processes designed to receive messages from other neurons. (33-34)

   c. The junction between two neurons. (33-34)

   d. The white fatty covering provided by Schwann cells or oligodendroglia. (35-34)

   e. The location of the cell nucleus. (33-34)

   f. Structure that carries information away from the soma to other neurons. (33-34)

   g. Branch like structures found at the end of the axon. (34)

3. Distinguish between Golgi type I and Golgi type II neurons. (33)

4. What are the five major types of glial cells and where in the nervous system is each located? (33)

   a. What is a nerve fiber? (35)

   b. Distinguish between Schwann cells and oligodendrocytes. (35, 37)

   c. List five functions of the astrocyte cell. (35-36)

   d. What is the function of the microglia and where are they located? (36)

   e. Where are ependymal cells found and what are they? (37)

5. What is the function of the blood-brain barrier? (37-38)

   a. What makes up this blood-brain barrier? (37-38)

   b. What is the area postrema and where is it located? (38)

Read pages 39-45 and summary statements 13-14 on page 46, then answer each of the following questions in this section.
---

1. In terms of tissue preparation how does one "fix a brain"? (39)

   a. What is paraffin used for in tissue preparation? (39)

   b. What is a microtome used for? (39)

2. What are the two basic problems in visualizing neurons? (39)

3. The Golgi-Cox method stains what part of the neuron? (40)

4. What is the Nissl stain used for? (39-40)

5. Why is the electron microscope capable of resolving much finer detail than is the light microscope? (41)

a. In the transmission electron microscope what is used to focus the beam of electrons? (41)

b. What causes the light-dark variations that can be seen in an electron micrograph of brain tissue? (41)

c. In the transmission electron microscope, at what are the images directed? (43)

6. List and define the three features of a synapse which were defined through the use of an electron microscope. (43)

    a. What dendritic feature was clarified through the use of the electron microscope? (43)

7. What is the major advantage of the scanning electron microscope? (43)

    a. What makes this possible? (43)

PRE-EXAM QUIZ

Multiple-Choice
Select the choice that best completes the stem in each question and indicate your selection in the appropriate space to the left of the question.

_____ 1. In what part of the cell are oxygen and glucose converted into energy and stored as adenosine triphosphate molecules?
   a. nucleus
   b. mitochondria
   c. Golgi complex
   d. rough endoplasmic reticulum
   e. ribosomes

_____ 2. Cell bodies but not dendrites or axons are stained using
   a. myelin stain
   b. Nissl stain
   c. Golgi-Cox stain
   d. heavy metal stains
   e. none of the above

_____ 3. Poisons that enter the bloodstream at the intestinal level are able to leave the blood at a particularly leaky area of the blood-brain barrier called the _____ and stimulate the vomiting center of the brain.
   a. cristae
   b. neuropil
   c. telodendria
   d. area postrema
   e. none of the above

_____ 4. The part of the neuron that contains the neurotransmitter substances is called a(n)
   a. dendritic spine
   b. mitochondrion
   c. synaptic vesicle
   d. postsynaptic thickening
   e. none of the above

_____ 5. Cells with similar functions combine into groups called
   a. organs
   b. systems
   c. tissues
   d. organisms
   e. none of the above

_____ 6. Phagocytosis in the central nervous system is accomplished by
   a. microglia
   b. ependymal cells
   c. Schwann cells
   d. astrocytes
   e. oligodendroglia

_____ 7. Formalin is used to
   a. stain the membrane of a neuron
   b. embed brain tissue
   c. fix brain tissue to stop further tissue degeneration and to initiate the hardening
   d. stain both the axon and the dendrites but not the soma of the neuron
   e. stain specimens for viewing under a scanning electron microscope

_____ 8. The role of messenger RNA in translation is to
   a. copy the information on the parent DNA molecule
   b. carry the amino acids to the ribosome where the protein is assembled
   c. serve as the assembly template for the new protein
   d. carry the code out of the nucleus to the rough endoplasmic reticulum
   e. more than one of the above

_____ 9. What chemical processes will be allowed within a cell and thus what the cell's structure and function will be is controlled by the
   a. cell cytoplasm
   b. cell membrane
   c. cell nucleus
   d. rough endoplasmic reticulum
   e. none of the above

_____10. The blood-brain barrier is formed by a combination of
   a. oligodendroglia and astrocytes
   b. astrocytes and endothelial cells
   c. endothelial cells and ependymal cells
   d. ependymal cells and astrocytes
   e. Schwann cells and microglia

_____11. Instead of directing a beam of electrons to the retina of the eye, the transmission electron microscope directs the electron beam to a
   a. magnetic field
   b. condensing lens
   c. scanning circuit
   d. cathode ray screen
   e. none of the above

_____12. The structural difference between Golgi type I and Golgi type II neurons lies in the
   a. number of dendrites the axon possesses
   b. length of the axon of the neuron
   c. number of connections the neuron makes with other neurons
   d. number of axons the neuron possesses
   e. type of neurotransmitter employed by the neuron

_____13. The hollow, tubular-shaped connections through the membrane that allow the passage of some substances but not others from extracellular to intracellular fluid or from intracellular to extracellular fluid are composed of
   a. cholesterol
   b. phosphates
   c. bases
   d. lipids
   e. none of the above

_____ 14. Filaments and microtubules make up the _____ of a cell.
   a. membrane   d. protein synthesis
   b. cytoplasm   e. cytoskeleton
   c. energy system

_____ 15. The rate at which the chemical reactions of the body take place can be sped up by specialized protein molecules called
   a. deoxyribonucleic acids   d. enzymes
   b. amino acids   e. ribonucleic acids
   c. ribosomes

True/False

_____ 1. Cholesterol is one of the lipids involved in the membrane of a cell.

_____ 2. One of the several functions of the mitochondria is to form the secretion vesicles.

_____ 3. Because they are capable of storing glucose in the form of glycogen, neurons are able to continue to function for some time after their blood supply is cut off.

_____ 4. Sugar phosphate groups form the sides of the DNA molecule ladder, and the rungs are formed by pairs of bases.

_____ 5. The little rigidity the cell has can be attributed to the cell membrane.

_____ 6. Oligodendroglia cells provide myelin for only a single axon.

_____ 7. The Golgi-Cox method stains axons but not somas or dendrites.

_____ 8. Electron micrography employs stains that make all the cells in a specimen visible.

_____ 9. The process by which the base, thymine, in DNA is replaced by uracil is called translation.

_____ 10. The passage of a molecule over relatively long distances within a cell is accomplished by the vesicles created by the Golgi apparatus.

_____ 11. Although there are only 20 common amino acids, they make up thousands upon thousands of different protein combinations.

_____ 12. The myelin sheath provides the axon with an insulation that is important in the conduction of an impulse.

_____ 13. Transmission electron micrography provides the viewer with a three-dimensional view of the specimen.

_____ 14. Synaptic spines are found on some axons.

_____ 15. An organism is composed of tissues with various functions.

2.1 adenosine triphosphate (ATP)	2.6 astrocyte
(26)	(35-36)
2.2 amino acid	2.7 axon
(27-28)	(33)
2.3 anabolism	2.8 blood-brain barrier
(26)	(37-38)
2.4 anoxia	2.9 catabolism
(36)	(26)
2.5 area postrema	2.10 cell
(38)	(20)

2.6

A star-shaped central nervous system glial cell. Among their several functions these cells provide structural support and isolate the neurons from one another. They also help form the blood-brain barrier.

2.7

The single elongated process of a neuron that conducts impulses away from the soma of the cell and toward its telodendria and terminals, which synapse on other neurons, muscles, or glands.

2.8

A barrier produced by the astrocytes and endothelial cells that form the walls of the capillaries in the brain; this barrier permits the passage of only certain substances.

2.9

The collection of destructive reactions that destroy chemicals in order to extract energy.

2.10

The basic anatomical unit of the organism.

2.1

A chemical composed of three phosphate groups attached to a molecular fragment called adenosine. The energy stored in sugar is transferred to the ATP in the form of chemical bonds between the atoms of the molecule.

2.2

The building blocks of proteins.

2.3

That series of constructive reactions that builds chemicals needed by the body.

2.4

A lack of oxygen.

2.5

The leaky area in the blood-brain barrier that is located below the cerebellum next to the cells that make up the brain-stem center that controls vomiting.

Copyright 1990 by Wadsworth, Inc.

2.11 condon

(30)

2.12 cristae

(27)

2.13 cytoplasm

(23)

2.14 cytoskeleton

(24)

2.15 dendrite

(33)

2.16 dendritic spine

(43)

2.17 deoxyribonucleic acid (DNA)

(23)

2.18 embedding

(39)

2.19 ependymal cell

(37)

2.20 filaments

(24)

2.16

Small bud-like structures found on the surface of some dendrites, on which the terminals from other neurons synapse.

2.17

A long complex molecule consisting of two interconnected strands in the form of a double helix. The two sides of this molecule are composed of sugar phosphate groups that are connected by pairs of four bases. It contains the genetic information of the organism.

2.18

One of the processes in tissue preparation by which the tissue is either frozen or placed in a paraffin block.

2.19

Cells that form the lining of the fluid-filled cavities of the brain.

2.20

Protein strands that run through the cytoplasm and help to make up a part of the cytoskeleton.

2.11

Found on the messenger RNA molecule it is the sequence of three consecutive bases required to specify each amino acid in the creation of a protein.

2.12

Multiple folds of membrane found within the mitochondria. Adenosine triphosphate molecules are created on these folds of the membrane.

2.13

The thickened, semiliquid substance contained in the interior of a cell.

2.14

Provides what rigidity a cell possesses. It is a network of proteins, filaments, and microtubules that runs through the cytoplasm of the cell.

2.15

A many-branched process attached to the soma that receives impulses from other neurons and carries them to the soma.

Copyright 1990 by Wadsworth, Inc.

2.21

fixing

(39)

2.22

glucose

(26)

2.23

glycogen

(27)

2.24

Golgi complex

(24)

2.25

Golgi-Cox method

(40)

2.26

Golgi type I

(33)

2.27

Golgi type II (interneurons)

(33)

2.28

messenger ribonucleic acid (mRNA)

(31)

2.29

metabolism

(26)

2.30

microglia

(36)

2.26

Neurons that have long axons that are designed to carry impulses over long distances in the nervous system.

2.27

Neurons that have extremely short axons or no axons at all and are designed to form microcircuits within the various areas of the brain and spinal cord.

2.28

A molecule that carries the genetic code in the form of a condon to the ribosomes on the rough endoplasmic reticulum where it will serve as a protein assembly template.

2.29

The collection of chemical reactions that make up our physiological life processes.

2.30

A central nervous system glial cell, the main function of which is to clean up an area of tissue that has suffered damage.

Copyright 1990 by Wadsworth, Inc.

2.21

The first step in the preparation of tissue. It involves soaking the tissue in a chemical called formalin to stop all tissue degeneration and begin the hardening process.

2.22

The term for blood sugar.

2.23

An altered form of glucose that most cells, except nerve cells, are capable of storing.

2.24

An organelle composed of a network of pancake-flat, hollow storage vessels, formed from lipid bilayer membrane, that grows continually, shedding portions of itself in the form of little spheres called secretion vesicles.

2.25

A membrane stain that colors both somas and dendrites of the neuron.

2.31

microtome

(39)

2.32

microtubule

(24)

2.33

mitochondria

(24)

2.34

myelin sheath

(35)

2.35

nerve fiber

(35)

2.36

neuroglia (glial)

(33)

2.37

neuron

(33)

2.38

neuropil

(33)

2.39

Nissl stain

(39-40)

2.40

nucleolus

(23)

2.36

The supportive cells of the nervous system.

2.37

A nerve cell.

2.38

A dense thicket of cell fibers (axons and dendrites) in which the somas of the neurons are embedded.

2.39

A neural tissue stain that colors cell bodies but not axons or dendrites.

2.40

A cytoplasmic inclusion within the nucleus of a cell where ribosomes are produced.

2.31

A machine that is used to cut embedded or frozen tissue into thin slices called sections.

2.32

An organelle through which molecules that need to be transported relatively long distances within a cell are piped. They also make up a part of the cytoskeleton.

2.33

An organelle that has a double membrane around it and contains a few strands of its own unique DNA and a few ribosomes. It is here that the cell's energy is developed and stored in the form of ATP molecules.

2.34

A wrapping found on certain axons that provides the axon with a certain amount of insulation from other neurons.

2.35

An axon together with its sheath of Schwann cells.

Copyright 1990 by Wadsworth, Inc.

2.41

oligodendroglia (oligodendrocyte)

(37)

2.42

organ

(20)

2.43

organelle

(23)

2.44

organism

(20)

2.45

phagocytosis

(36)

2.46

phospholipid molecule

(21)

2.47

ribosome

(23)

2.48

rough endoplasmic reticulum

(23)

2.49

Schwann cell

(33)

2.50

section

(39)

2.46

The type of molecule that makes up the bilayered membrane of the cell. It consists of a phospho-"head" and a lipid-"tail".

2.47

Formed in the nucleolus of the cell by combining RNA with proteins. These ribosomes find their way to the surface of the rough endoplasmic reticulum where proteins are manufactured.

2.48

An organelle that consists of many folds of membrane dotted with ribosomes. It is the site of protein formation.

2.49

A glial cell in the peripheral nervous system that provides the myelin sheath for peripheral neurons.

2.50

A thin slice of embedded or frozen tissue made by a microtome.

2.41

A central nervous system glial cell that provides the myelin sheaths for axons within the brain and spinal cord.

2.42

Composed of several types of tissue, organized to perform some vital function to the whole animal. Examples are heart, lungs, and brain.

2.43

The microscopic organ-like structures within a cell.

2.44

The complete animal.

2.45

The process by which certain glial cells, microglia for example, engulf and digest debris left by dead neurons and glia.

Copyright 1990 by Wadsworth, Inc.

2.51

soma

(33)

2.52

sugar phosphate group

(29)

2.53

synaptic cleft

(43)

2.54

synaptic vesicle

(43)

2.55

telodendria

(33)

2.56

terminal

(33)

2.57

tissue

(20)

2.58

transcription

(30)

2.59

transfer ribonucleic acid (tRNA)

(31)

2.60

translation

(31)

2.56

The swelling at the end of each telodendria. It contains synaptic vesicles and mitochondria.

2.51

The cell body of the neuron.

2.57

Composed of a group of cells with similar function, which in turn combine to make up an organ.

2.52

Molecules that form the sides of the DNA molecule.

2.58

The process by which RNA is created from a parent DNA molecule.

2.53

The widening of the intercellular space between the terminal ending of the presynaptic element and the postsynaptic element.

2.59

Tiny scraps of ribonucleic acid that capture free-floating amino acids in the cytoplasm and bring them to the appropriate condon site on the messenger RNA found on the ribosomes, thus adding to a growing protein chain.

2.54

Small spheres found primarily in the axon terminals and synapses. They contain the neurotransmitter chemicals.

2.60

The process of converting the genetic code into amino acids.

2.55

A tree-like structure consisting of tiny branches formed as the axon divides repeatedly at its end.

Copyright 1990 by Wadsworth, Inc.

CHAPTER THREE
THE BASIC PLAN OF THE NERVOUS SYSTEM

READ-WRITE-REVIEW

Read pages 50-61 and summary statements 1-5 on page 103, then answer each of the following questions in this section.
---

1. A number of directional terms are commonly used in discussing the anatomy of the nervous system. See how many of the following you can get right.

   TERMS
anterior	dorsal	medial	rostral
caudal	inferior	peripheral	superior
central	lateral	posterior	ventral

   _____ a. toward the head with reference to the whole nervous system. (50)

   _____ b. away from the core of the nervous system. (50)

   _____ c. toward or on the back side. (50)

   _____ d. in reference to the brain, toward the front end. (50)

   _____ e. toward the side. (50)

   _____ f. toward the rear of the brain. (50)

2. What are the two basic divisions of the nervous system? (52)

3. What is a nerve? (52)

   a. Differentiate between a nerve and a neuron. (52)

   b. Differentiate between a nerve and a tract. (52)

   c. What is a ganglion? (59)

   d. When distinguishing neural fibers based on where they are coming from and where they are going to, it is possible to identify two types of fibers. Identify and define each. (53)

   e. Differentiate between cranial and spinal nerves. (53)

   f. Distinguish between the autonomic and somatic fibers in terms of the types of organs served. (53)

4. While cutting a path through the dense underbrush for you and your hunting party, you lose control of your blade and accidentally cut your left leg. Immediately you apply a tourniquet to stop the bleeding but it is already too late. You have little feeling in your foot and almost no motor control. The doctor tells you that in addition to having cut tissue and a major blood supply, you have also severed most of the fibers of a major nerve branch.
    You are completely immobilized and then carried back to civilization and a hospital. While you're laying there recuperating indicate in some detail what is happening at a neural fiber level. (55-56)

    a. What is a neuroma? (56)

    b. Would you get the same results if the knife had damaged brain tissue? (55)

5. Distinguish between gray matter and white matter in the brain and spinal cord. (58-59)

    a. The "real work" of the nervous system is carried out in which type of matter? (58)

    b. Explain. (58-59)

6. Differentiate between a nucleus and a ganglion. (59)

Read pages 62-66 and summary statement 6 on page 103, then answer each of the following questions in this section.
---

1. What is a reflex? (62)

    a. Give three examples of a reflex. (62)

    b. What is a reflex arc? (62)

2. Below is a diagram of a cross section of a spinal cord showing a reflex arc. Below the diagram are five statements that identify the structures seen in the diagram. Identify the structure described by the statement and then label the structure on the diagram using just the letter of the statement.

    a. Carries impulses from the cord to the muscle or gland. (64)

    b. Connects with the back side of the cord. (62)

34

c. Swelling that contains a nerve cell body that is peculiar in that it has one long fiber that serves as both axon and dendrite. (62)

   d. The soma of the motor neuron is located here. (62)

   e. Connects afferents with efferents. (63)

3. Where would you find the cell bodies of those fibers making up the autonomic nervous system? (65)

   a. The sympathetic chain ganglia are composed of what? (65)

   b. What feeds into the sympathetic chain ganglia? (65-66)

   c. Distinguish between a preganglionic and postganglionic fiber. (66)

   d. How is coordination achieved in the sympathetic nervous system? (66)

   e. What are the two parts of the autonomic nervous system? (66)

   f. How do they differ in terms of function? (66)

Read pages 66-72 and summary statements 7-10 on pages 103-104, then answer each of the following questions in this section.
---

1. Locate verbally the brain stem. (66)

   a. What are the three major parts of the brain stem? (66)

   b. The afferents of cranial X, the vagus nerve sends information where? (66)

   c. What are the functions of the nucleus of tractus solitarius? (66-67)

2. What are the major structures of the pontine region? (68)

3. Describe the two components of the cerebellum. (68)

   a. What is the function of the cerebellum? (68-69)

   b. Describe the main connecting route between the two hemispheres of the cerebellum. (69)

4. A midsagittal view of the brain stem would show two bumps on the dorsal side of the midbrain. What is the top pair called? (71)

   a. Describe the three levels of this pair of structures. (71)

   b. What is the bottom pair called? (71)

   c. Together these two pairs of structures serve what function? (72)

5. Locate verbally the reticular formation. (72)

   a. What is its function? (72)

6. Trace the flow of the cerebrospinal fluid through the ventricles of the brain, beginning with the most superior ventricle. (72)

   a. What functions does the cerebrospinal fluid serve? (72)

Read pages 72-79 and summary statements 11-13 on page 104, then answer each of the following questions in this section.

---

1. What is the single sense modality that does not pass through the thalamus on its way to the cortex? (72)

2. What are the two pathways through which the hypothalamus exerts control over the internal environment? (74)

   a. How does the hypothalamus obtain information concerning the conditions of the visceral organs? (74)

   b. The hypothalamus employs the autonomic nervous system to exert its neural control over the internal environment. Describe the connection between the hypothalamus and the sympathetic and parasympathetic nervous systems. (74-76)

3. Distinguish between endocrine and exocrine glands. (76)

4. The diagram below locates the various endocrine glands of the body. Below the diagram are a series of statements, each of which describes the function of one of these glands. For each statement identify the gland and then label it appropriately on the diagram using the letter of the statement.

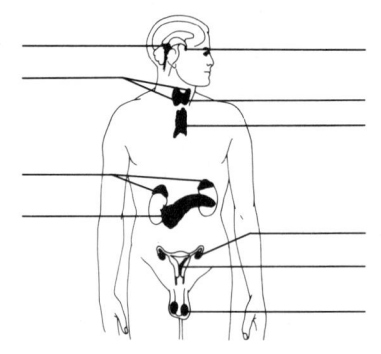

   a. Secretes a hormone that enables glucose and fats to get into cells where they can be used. (77)

   b. Secretes a hormone that sets the base level for your metabolism. (77)

   c. Consists of a core and a medulla with the former secreting hormones that act on the visceral organs in the same manner as the sympathetic nervous system. (77)

   d. The master gland of the system. (76)

e. Secretes the reproductive hormones. (77)

   f. Secretes a hormone that controls calcium concentration in the blood. (77)

5. Where are the hormones oxytocin and vasopressin made? (79)

   a. In which part of the pituitary are they stored? (79)

   b. What causes the anterior pituitary to secrete its hormones? (79)

Read pages 79-84 and summary statements 14-15 on page 104, then answer each of the following questions in this section.

---

1. What are the major nuclei that make up the corpus striatum? (79)

   a. Which two of these nuclei function as a unit and are commonly referred to as the striatum? (79)

   b. What role does the corpus striatum play in complex movements? (80-82)

2. What are the seven major parts of the limbic system? (82)

   a. Describe the anatomical connection that would explain how the limbic system might be involved in many of the same functions as the hypothalamus. (82-83)

   b. Explain why it is necessary for both the hypothalamus and the limbic system to be involved in emotional behavior. (84)

Read pages 84-92 and summary statements 16-18 on page 104, then answer each of the following questions in this section.

---

1. Describe the cellular structure of the neocortex. (84)

2. Gyri, fissures, and sulci abound on the surface of the cortex and have been used by anatomists as landmarks. Describe each. (85)

3. Below is a diagram of the cerebral cortex, lateral view. Immediately below the diagram are a series of statements describing the functions of some of the cortical areas. Identify the area being described and then label the area on the diagram using the identifying letter of the statement.

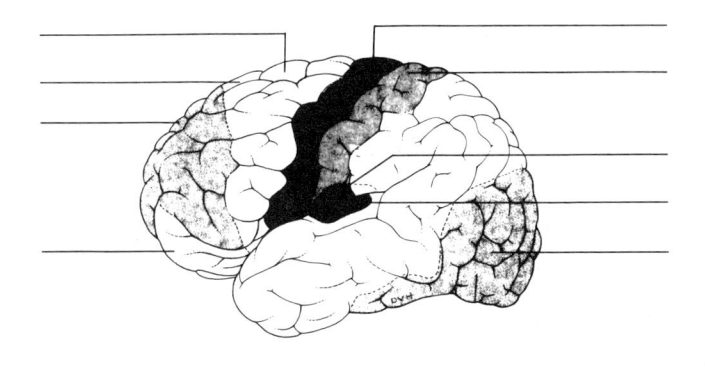

37

a. It appears to control sequences of movements. (91)

   b. It is devoted to the processing of visual information. (87)

   c. Memories of lengthy behavior sequences are probably stored here. (91)

   d. Information from taste receptors eventually winds up here for processing. (88)

   e. It is associated with intentions to act rather than the actions themselves. (91)

   f. Information from the skin, muscles, and joints are blended and processed here. (88-90)

   g. Damage to this area would result in an inability to recognize any sound sequences. (88)

   h. It creates fine precision movements. (91)

Read pages 92-103 and summary statements 19-21 on pages 104-105, then answer each of the following questions in this section.
---

1. Humans belong to the phylum Chordata, subphylum Vertebrata, class mammalian, order primate. Describe that characteristic that gives us membership in each of these categories. (94,96)

2. What characteristic was necessary to move organisms from the water and onto the land? (94)

   a. What still tied amphibians to a water environment? (94)

   b. What features did the reptile develop that allowed it to become a full-time land dweller? (94)

   c. What probably happened to move some reptiles into the air? (96)

3. What characteristic makes the therapsid unique among reptiles? (96)

   a. What is unique about the duck-billed platypus? (96)

   b. What makes it possible for mammals to nurture their young inside their bodies for weeks or months? (96)

   c. What is the advantage for the developing young to be able to stay inside the mother's body for this long period of time? (96)

   d. What part of the developing young benefits most from this added development time? (96)

4. What are the five major groups of primates? (96)

5. Bilateral symmetry and encephalization are both characteristics that are found in the human nervous system. Define these characteristics. (98)

a. At what level are the origins of these characteristics found? (98)

6. What possible explanation can be given for the fact that such vital functions as heartbeat, respiration, and blood pressure are controlled at the brain stem level? (100)

   a. At what level is the thalamus clearly developed? (100)

   b. At what level is the limbic system clearly seen? (100)

   c. When do we see the development of the neocortex? (100)

7. What can be said about the apparent redundancy in the function we see in the brain parts of the vertebrate brain? (100)

8. How is the link between the hypothalamus and hippocampus related to the evolution of the temporal lobes? (102)

PRE-EXAM QUIZ

Multiple-Choice
Select the choice that best completes the stem in each question and indicate your selection in the appropriate space to the left of the question.

_____ 1. The only sensory system that does NOT send information to the thalamus is
   a. smell
   b. hearing
   c. vision
   d. taste
   e. skin senses

_____ 2. Which endocrine gland secretes a hormone that sets the base level for metabolism?
   a. posterior pituitary
   b. pancreas
   c. thyroid
   d. adrenal medulla
   e. adrenal cortex

_____ 3. Which of the following senses does NOT project to the somatosensory in the postcentral gyrus of the cortex?
   a. thermoreception
   b. gustation
   c. kinesthesia
   d. mechanoreception
   e. more than one of the above

_____ 4. It is a large fiber tract composed of axons of cortical neurons. It is a major communication link between the two hemispheres at the cortical level. It is the
   a. cingulate gyrus
   b. corpus callosum
   c. fornix
   d. septum
   e. hippocampus

_____ 5. A cluster of cell bodies with related functions and lying within the central nervous system is called a
   a. nucleus
   b. tract
   c. nerve
   d. fiber
   e. ganglion

39

_____ 6. Cell bodies of the primary afferent neurons are located at the
       a. receptor   d. ventral root ganglion
       b. ventral horn   e. none of the above
       c. dorsal horn

_____ 7. Which of the following best describes the cerebellum?
       a. it functions to localize visual and auditory stimuli relative to the body
       b. it controls the arousal level of the entire nervous system
       c. it aids the cortical circuits by storing plans for movement
       d. it smooths movements by giving them the precise amount of force and
          determining exactly when muscle contractions should end to obtain
          greatest accuracy
       e. more than one of the above

_____ 8. Which of the limbic system structures is functionally a part of the
       reinforcement system?
       a. nucleus basalis   d. cingulate gyrus
       b. amygdala   e. hippocampus
       c. nucleus accumbens

_____ 9. You have just eaten a big Sunday dinner and all you want to do is lay down
       and take a nice long nap. This response is most probably due to the
       activity of the
       a. medulla oblongata   d. sympathetic nervous system
       b. corpus striatum   e. parasympathetic nervous system
       c. limbic system

_____10. It is one of the most critical regions in the brain because it controls such
       vital life functions as heart rate and respiration. It is the
       a. corpus striatum   d. cerebellum
       b. medulla oblongata   e. corpus callosum
       c. pons

_____11. Most of the information about conditions in the visceral organs comes to the
       hypothalamus by way of its connections with the
       a. pons   d. thalamus
       b. cerebral cortex   e. superior and inferior colliculi
       c. nucleus of tractus solitarius

_____12. The hormones oxytocin and vasopressin are produced by the
       a. posterior pituitary   d. anterior pituitary
       b. parathyroid   e. hypothalamic nuclei
       c. pancreas

_____13. Which of the following best describes the function of the intact limbic
       system?
       a. it stores motivational and emotional memories and memories for events
       b. it initiates and controls both motivational and emotional responses
       c. it selects the proper variation of each voluntary movement that best
          fits the momentary context of posture and ongoing behavior
       d. it monitors and coordinates the activities of the autonomic nervous
          system
       e. more than one of the above

_____14. In the spinal cord the gray matter is _____ relative to the white matter.
       a. superior   d. inferior
       b. central   e. anterior
       c. peripheral

_____ 15. The most important contribution mammals made to the evolutionary process was the fact that they were the first animals to
   a. develop lungs
   b. develop mammary glands to nurse their young
   c. leave the water and live on land
   d. give birth to their young
   e. none of the above

True/False

_____ 1. In most people, language functions are primarily found in the right hemisphere.

_____ 2. The role of the convolutions of the cortex seems to be one of increasing cortical mass without making it necessary to increase skull size.

_____ 3. Before one of the anterior pituitary hormones can be secreted it must be induced by an appropriate releasing factor secreted by the hypothalamus.

_____ 4. The cerebellum has a primary role in motor behavior and as such receives no sensory input.

_____ 5. The connection between the two hemispheres of the cerebellum is the corpus callosum.

_____ 6. The earliest version of our brain stem seems to have evolved from the fish.

_____ 7. The axon of a damaged tract can regenerate.

_____ 8. The lateral ventricles are connected by a thin tube called the cerebral aqueduct.

_____ 9. All spinal nerves are mixed.

_____ 10. An afferent nerve carries impulses from the central nervous system to the muscles and glands.

_____ 11. Interneurons serve to connect muscles and glands.

_____ 12. Exocrine glands deliver their secretions directly to the point where they are used, whereas endocrine glands deliver their secretions via the bloodstream to their point of use.

_____ 13. The corpus striatum, lying between the thalamus and the cortex, consists of the caudate nucleus, the putamen, and the globus pallidus.

_____ 14. Sulci and fissures are groves in the neocortex separating one gyrus from another.

_____ 15. The cell bodies of efferent spinal neurons lie in the ventral horn.

3.1

adrenal cortex

(77)

3.2

adrenal medulla

(77)

3.3

amygdala

(89)

3.4

anterior pituitary

(79)

3.5

autonomic fibers

(53)

3.6

bilateral symmetry

(98)

3.7

brain stem

(66)

3.8

central nervous system

(52)

3.9

cerebellum

(68)

3.10

cerebral aqueduct

(72)

3.6

A bodily arrangement in which each side is a mirror image of the other side.

3.7

The region between the superior portion of the spinal cord and the superior portion of the midbrain.

3.8

The division of the nervous system, that is composed of the brain and spinal cord.

3.9

A motor structure on the dorsal side of the pontine region that uses sensory input to determine both the timing and the force of movements.

3.10

Thin tube through which cerebrospinal fluid passes on its way from the third to the fourth ventricle.

Copyright 1990 by Wadsworth, Inc.

3.1

The outer part of the adrenal gland, which secretes mineralocorticoids and glucocorticoids.

3.2

The central core of the adrenal gland, which secretes the hormones adrenalin and noradrenalin. These hormones act on the visceral organs in the same way as the sympathetic nervous system.

3.3

That part of the limbic system that is vital to the acquisition of memories, especially those dealing with which stimuli should be approached and which should be avoided.

3.4

That part of the pituitary that manufactures, stores, and secretes six hormones. Four of these act on other endocrine glands to control their output.

3.5

Fibers connecting the central nervous system (hypothalamus) to the visceral organs.

3.11

cerebral cortex

(59)

3.12

chordata

(94)

3.13

cingulate gyrus

(84)

3.14

class

(94)

3.15

corpus callosum

(87)

3.16

corpus striatum

(79)

3.17

cranial nerves

(53)

3.18

dorsal horn

(62)

3.19

dorsal root

(62)

3.20

dorsal root ganglion

(62)

3.16

A group of three nuclei, the caudate nucleus, the putamen, and the globus pallidus. These nuclei select the proper variation of each voluntary movement that best fits the posture and ongoing behavior.

3.17

The 12 pairs of nerves that emerge from the brain. They can be sensory, motor, or mixed.

3.18

Dorsal area of gray matter in the spinal cord. Primary afferent fibers terminate here.

3.19

Bundle of spinal nerve fibers that connects with the back side of the cord and contains the afferents from the skin, muscles, and joints.

3.20

The swelling on the dorsal root that contains the cell bodies of primary afferent neurons.

3.11

The surface covering of the cerebral hemisphere, which is composed of gray matter.

3.12

A phylum that contains all animals having a nerve cord running down the back.

3.13

A part of the limbic system that together with another structure, the parahippocampal gyrus, collects sensory information and funnels it to the hippocampus.

3.14

In classifying animals, it is a division of subphyla.

3.15

A large fiber tract that acts as a major communication link between the two hemispheres at the cortical level.

Copyright 1990 by Wadsworth, Inc.

3.21

dura mater

3.26

fourth ventricle

(72)

(72)

3.22

encephalization

3.27

ganglion

(98)

(59)

3.23

endocrine system

3.28

gonads

(76)

(77)

3.24

exocrine system

3.29

gyrus

(76)

(85)

3.25

fissure

3.30

hypothalamus

(85)

(74)

3.26

Part of the brain's ventricular system that is found in the pontine region of the brain stem.

3.27

Small group of cell bodies having a similar function and located outside the central nervous system.

3.28

Endocrine glands that secrete the reproductive hormones, estrogen, testosterone, and progesterone. They are responsible for creating secondary sex characteristics, masculinizing or feminizing the brain, and controlling the sequence of events in pregnancy.

3.29

The hill portion of each convolution.

3.30

A group of nuclei lying just ventral to the thalamus that control the internal environment of the body including food intake, temperature, and water balance; reaction to stress and emotional reactions are also controlled by the hypothalamus.

Copyright 1990 by Wadsworth, Inc.

3.21

A tough, heavy membranous sac that separates the brain from the inside of the skull. It also holds in the circulating cerebrospinal fluid after it leaves the ventricular system.

3.22

The establishment of a front end with a central neural controller and a concentration of receptors.

3.23

A group of glands that secrete chemicals called hormones into the bloodstream to be carried to where they will be used.

3.24

A group of glands that deliver their secretions directly to the point where they are to be used.

3.25

Very large, deep sulcus. Many of these are used by anatomists as boundaries between large segments of the cortex called lobes.

3.31

inferior colliculi

3.36

longitudinal fissure

(71)

3.32

kinesthesia

(87)

3.37

mammalian class

(88)

3.33

lateral fissure

(96)

3.38

medulla oblongata

(85)

3.34

lateral ventricles

(66)

3.39

midbrain

(72)

3.35

limbic system

(70)

3.40

module (minicolumn)

(82)

(84)

3.36

Largest fissure of the cortex. It runs the length of the cortex, separating the brain into right and left hemispheres.

3.37

Class of Vertebrata that were the first to give birth to their young rather than lay eggs.

3.38

Region of the brain stem just superior to the spinal cord. Contains nuclei that control vital life functions.

3.39

Most superior region of the brain stem. In lower vertebrates it contains the neural circuits for some basic, unlearned behaviors. The superior and inferior colliculi are found in the midbrain in humans.

3.40

A set of cortical circuits that performs some function. Each module occupies a very small vertical cross section stretching over the six cortical layers.

Copyright 1990 by Wadsworth, Inc.

3.31

The lowest pair of colliculi located on the dorsal side of the midbrain. This pair controls the localization of auditory stimuli with respect to the body.

3.32

A sensory system, the receptors of which are located in the muscles and joints. Information from these receptors makes it possible to keep track of where all the body parts are located in space at any one moment.

3.33

Grove running up the lateral surface of each hemisphere. It provides a boundary for the temporal lobe.

3.34

Two cavities, one in each hemisphere, that begin in the frontal lobes, extend back under the parietal lobes, send an offshoot into the occipital lobes, and then curl around the temporal lobe.

3.35

System of interconnected structures that form a ring around the central core. This system stores both the motivational memories and the emotional memories as well as memories for events.

3.41

motor

(53)

3.42

neocortex

(84)

3.43

nerve

(52)

3.44

neuroma

(56)

3.45

nucleus

(59)

3.46

orbitofrontal area

(91)

3.47

order

(96)

3.48

parasympathetic nervous system

(66)

3.49

pons

(69)

3.50

pontine region

(68)

3.46

Cortical area by which memories of lengthy behavioral sequences are passed on to the motivation area of the cortex.

3.41

Nerve fibers that conduct impulses from the central nervous system to the muscles and glands.

3.47

A subdivision of class.

3.42

Composes the majority of the cerebral cortex. It has a six-layered structure and is composed entirely of gray matter.

3.48

Branch of the autonomic nervous system that generally controls internal responses that occur during periods of rest and digestion.

3.43

A bundle of axons clustered together and found in the peripheral nervous system.

3.49

A large bridge of connecting fibers on the ventral side of the pontine region which serves as the main connecting link between the cerebellar hemispheres.

3.44

A tangled ball of axon tendrils that results when an injured nerve attempts to regenerate across a wide gap within a zone of injury where most axons have no sheath.

3.50

Area superior to the medulla and inferior to the midbrain. It is composed of the pons, cerebellum, and a variety of smaller structures.

3.45

Small group of cell bodies having related functions and located within the central nervous system.

Copyright 1990 by Wadsworth, Inc.

3.51 posterior pituitary (79)

3.52 prefrontal area (91)

3.53 premotor area (91)

3.54 primary afferent fiber (62)

3.55 primate (96)

3.56 reflex (62)

3.57 releasing factor (79)

3.58 reticular formation (72)

3.59 sensory (53)

3.60 sensory projection system (74)

3.56

A simple unlearned response consisting of a fairly fixed pattern of muscle contractions that is automatically elicited by a particular kind of stimulus because of the existence of genetically determined connections within the nervous system.

3.57

A hormone-like hypothalamic chemical that is carried from the hypothalamus via the portal veins to the anterior pituitary where it causes the release of a specific anterior pituitary hormone.

3.58

Group of neurons that runs through the core of the spinal cord and brain stem, controlling the intensity of responses and adjusting the amount of impact that any stimulus will have on the rest of the brain.

3.59

Nerve fibers that conduct impulses from receptor organs to the central nervous system.

3.60

The neural route from the receptors to the cerebral cortex where conscious perception can take place.

3.51

That part of the pituitary gland that stores and secretes both oxytocin and vasopressin.

3.52

Cortical area that apparently stores memories of lengthy sequences, which makes possible imagining future possibilities and planning.

3.53

Cortical area that appears to control the sequences of movement.

3.54

Sensory cells with receptor endings in the skin, muscles, joints, and internal organs. They have a long fiber that functions as both an axon and a dendrite with a cell body located in the dorsal root ganglion.

3.55

Order that contains five major groups, prosimians, new-world monkeys, old-world monkeys, apes, and humans.

Copyright 1990 by Wadsworth, Inc.

3.61

septal nucleus

(84)

3.62

smooth muscle

(53)

3.63

somatic nervous system

(53)

3.64

somatic senses

(88)

3.65

spinal nerves

(53)

3.66

striate muscles

(53)

3.67

sulcus

(85)

3.68

superior colliculi

(71)

3.69

supplementary motor area

(91)

3.70

sympathetic chain ganglia

(65)

3.66

All so-called striped muscles, they are found in the legs, arms, and trunk and are under conscious control. For this reason these muscles are also termed voluntary muscles.

3.67

A "crack" or "grooves" on the cortical surface which separates one gyrus from another.

3.68

The top pair of colliculi located on the dorsal side of the midbrain that controls the localization of visual stimuli with respect to the body.

3.69

Cortical area that appears to be associated with the motivation to act.

3.70

A string of interconnected ganglia that contains the cell bodies of neurons whose axons join spinal nerves. The chain lies just outside the spinal column and belongs to the sympathetic nervous system.

Copyright 1990 by Wadsworth, Inc.

3.61

Part of the limbic system that may be the repository of memories concerning the appropriate levels of emotion to display in any situation.

3.62

Flat white sheets of muscle tissue found in the viscera. These muscles are almost all contracted reflexively.

3.63

Fibers that connect the central nervous system to the body with the exception of the viscera. Somatic sensory fibers conduct information from the skin, joints, and tendons, whereas motor fibers stimulate the striate muscles.

3.64

A group of senses whose receptors lie in the skin and the internal organs. The senses are mechanoreception, thermoreception, and nociception.

3.65

Pairs of nerves that emerge along the spinal cord. Spinal nerves are mixed nerves.

3.71

sympathetic nervous system

3.76

ventral horn

(66)

3.72

thalamus

(62)

3.77

ventral root

(72)

3.73

third ventricle

(62)

3.78

Vertebrata

(72)

3.74

thyroid gland

(94)

3.79

viscera

(77)

3.75

tract

(53)
---

(52)

3.76

Area of gray matter in the spinal cord where the cell bodies of motor neurons are located.

3.77

The bundle of spinal nerve fibers that connects with the ventral side of the spinal cord and contains the efferent fibers.

3.78

A subphylum containing those chordates that have spinal columns.

3.79

The internal organs including the heart, stomach, lungs, blood vessels, and glands.

3.71

The branch of the autonomic nervous system that generally controls responses that occur during periods of strenuous activity.

3.72

A large group of nuclei that lie to the immediate right and left of the third ventricle. They are important in relaying sensory information from receptors to the sensory cortex and from the cortex to other parts of the brain.

3.73

Part of the brain's ventricular system, this cavity lies along the midline in the same plane as the longitudinal fissure.

3.74

Endocrine gland that secretes the hormone thyroxine, which sets the base level for your metabolism.

3.75

Consists of a bundle of axons inside the central nervous system.

Copyright 1990 by Wadsworth, Inc.

CHAPTER FOUR
CONDUCTION AND TRANSMISSION

READ-WRITE-REVIEW

Read pages 110-123 and summary statements 1-11 on pages 145-146, then answer each of the following questions in this section.

---

1. What is a nerve impulse? (110-111)

    a. What are the two principles governing a nerve impulse? (111)

    b. What is the difference between the current in a lamp cord and that in a nerve impulse? (111)

    c. Solid matter is composed of particles called _____ (111), which, in turn, are made up of _____ (111). They are composed of nuclei and _____ (111), which carry a(n) _____ (111), charge. Located within the nuclei are _____ (111), and _____ (111). The nucleus contains a(n) _____ (111) charge. The charge of an atom is _____ (112).

2. When discussing a "potential" why is it necessary to speak of it as existing between two points? (113)

    a. How is the strength of the potential related to the strength of the current when released? (113)

    b. Potentials are measured in what units? (113)

    c. What is the resting membrane potential? What value does this potential take? (114)

    d. The cell membrane is said to be semipermeable. What is meant by this? (115)

    e. What is the sodium/potassium pump, and what role does it play during the resting potential? (117)

3. Locate the axon hillock. (119-120)

    a. What is its importance in the discharge of a nerve impulse? (121)

    b. When a current disturbs the membrane, what happens to the sodium ions? (121)

c. What is referred to when the nerve impulse is described as a succession of transmembrane ion currents? (121)

d. The nerve impulse is said to be self-propagating. What is meant by this? (122)

e. The influx of sodium ions causes the outside of the axon to become negative. What happens to offset this change in charge and why? (117)

f. An impulse causes the inward movement of sodium ions while the potassium ions move outward. What happens to restore these ions to their starting point? (117)

4. What are the four factors that play an important role in how the ions will be distributed between the inside and outside of a neuron, and what role is played by each? (114-117)

5. What occurs at the ion level across the axon membrane when the sodium equilibrium potential is reached? (117)

a. What occurs at the level of the forces acting on the sodium ions as the sodium equilibrium potential is reached? (117, 119)

b. What is the measured value of the sodium equilibrium potential? (117)

c. What occurs at the ionic level across the axon membrane as it moves toward the potassium equilibrium? (119)

d. What is the measured value of the potassium equilibrium potential? (119)

6. What is the current in a stimulating electrode? (121)

a. Exactly how does this current bring about a depolarization of the membrane? (121)

b. The stimulating electrode current opens only the gates under the electrode or nearby. What opens the gates in the parts of the membrane not depolarized directly by the electrode? (121)

c. This type of current consists of a flow of what? (121)

d. Compare the speed of this current flow to that of the transmembrane current. (121)

e. The nerve impulse is said to be self-propagating. How do the two currents work together to produce this characteristic? (121-122)

f. What is meant when we say that the conduction of a nerve impulse is nondecremental? (122)

7. What are the nodes of Ranvier? (122)

a. How are these nodes related to the conduction of a nerve impulse? (122-123)

b. What are the advantages of this type of conduction? (123)

Read pages 123-129 and summary statements 10-15 on page 146, then answer each of the following questions in this section.
---

1. For what can an oscilloscope be used? (124)

a. Describe the cathode ray tube of the oscilloscope. (124)

b. Why is an electron beam employed in an oscilloscope? (124)

c. What is a stimulator and for what is it used? (124)

d. In studying the nerve impulse and its characteristics the giant axon of the squid is often employed. Why is it used instead of a human neuron? (124-125)

2. When is the axon membrane said to be polarized? (126)

a. What does it mean to say that an axon membrane is polarized? (126)

b. What causes depolarization of an axon membrane potential? (126-127)

3. What is the axon threshold? (127)

a. What is the relationship between excitability and threshold? (128)

4. When does the absolute refractory period occur? (128)

a. What voltage is required during this absolute refractory period to reach the axon threshold? (128)

b. How would you describe the absolute refractory period in terms of ion channels and ions? (128)

c. When does the relative refractory period occur? (128)

d. What voltage is required during the relative refractory period to reach the axon threshold? (128)

e. What is the size of the axon potential during the refractory period? (128)

f. How is stimulus intensity coded? (128)

Read pages 129-140 and summary statements 16-22 on pages 146-147, then answer each of the following questions in this section.

---

1. List and identify the three components of a synapse. (129-130)

    a. In which of these components would you find the vesicles, assuming no neural activity? (130)

    b. What is contained within these vesicles? (130)

    c. What two events are necessary before the vesicles can release their contents? (130-131)

2. What is the relationship between a neurotransmitter molecule and its particular receptor site? (132)

    a. What is meant by the term "binding"? (132)

    b. Assuming that the neurotransmitter causes the postsynaptic membrane's sodium channels to open, what postsynaptic event occurs? (132-133)

3. What is an excitatory postsynaptic potential? (133)

    a. What is the difference between the membrane channels through which excitatory postsynaptic potentials and nerve impulses flow? (133)

    b. This difference in membrane channels produces what important difference between excitatory postsynaptic potentials and nerve impulses? (133-134)

4. Define summation. (135)

    a. In the neuron, where does summation occur? (135)

    b. What is the difference between excitation and facilitation? (136)

5. Describe the series of reactions that occur in the cyclic AMP messenger system from the time the transmitter substance binds with the receptor site until a membrane channel is opened. (136)

6. How do inhibitory postsynaptic potentials differ from excitatory postsynaptic potentials? (137)

   a. How do $GABA_A$ receptors produce IPSPs? (138)

   b. How do $GABA_B$ receptors produce IPSPs? (138)

7. List three advantages a nervous system that produces postsynaptic potentials has over one that would not have that capability. (139-140)

Read pages 140-145 and summary statements 23-25 on page 147, then answer each of the following questions in this section.
---

1. List and identify five ways in which drugs can affect the nervous system through action at the synapse. (140-145)

   a. How does curare interfere with acetylcholine at neuromuscular junctions to produce a flaccid paralysis? (141)

   b. What is this principle called? (141)

   c. What other drug does the same thing to dopamine at its receptor sites? (141)

   d. Both curare and <u>Clostridium botulinum</u> create a flaccid paralysis--by affecting the activity of acetylcholine at the neuromuscular junction. How do they differ in producing this effect? (142)

   e. David's doctor prescribed reserpine for him and now he no longer hears Supercreature warn him about the pending invasion of the little green creatures from planet Zork. Explain to David's parents how this drug works. (142)

   f. Indicate and describe briefly two ways in which a neurotransmitter is normally removed from the synaptic gap once it has served its purpose. (142)

   g. What effect do MAO inhibitors have on the neurotransmitter norepinephrine, and how is this accomplished? (143)

63

h. Why does a drug such as cocaine serve as a stimulant? (145)

9. What two substances are employed in the synthesis of acetylcholine? (145)

   a. From where do these substances come? (145)

   b. Synthesis of the catecholamine neurotransmitters begins with what amino acid? (144)

PRE-EXAM QUIZ

Multiple-Choice
Select the choice that best completes the stem in each question and indicate your selection in the appropriate space to the left of the question.

_____ 1. Membrane channels in the axon are said to be _____ regulated; dendrite/soma membrane channels are _____ regulated.
   a. voltage; transmitter
   b. voltage; voltage
   c. transmitter; transmitter
   d. transmitter; voltage
   e. none of the above

_____ 2. The tendency for ions to move apart from one another so that they fill all the available space with the greatest possible distance between each particle is called:
   a. electrostatic rejection
   b. osmosis
   c. profusion
   d. diffusion
   e. none of the above

_____ 3. Which of the following flows during the depolarization of the axon?
   a. transmembrane current
   b. electrostatic current
   c. electric current
   d. electrotonic current
   e. more than one of these

_____ 4. During the relative refractory period
   a. a second impulse may be initiated by a normal strength test shock
   b. a second impulse may be initiated by a weaker than normal strength test shock
   c. a second impulse may be initiated by a greater than normal strength test shock
   d. a second impulse may not be initiated no matter how strong the test shock
   e. none of the above are true of the relative refractory period

_____ 5. Botulinum toxin produces its effect at the neuromuscular junction by the mechanism of
   a. receptor blocking
   b. transmitter depletion
   c. reuptake blocking
   d. release blocking
   e. enzyme deactivation

_____ 6. When a substance such as table salt is placed in water it breaks down into
   a. molecules
   b. nuclei
   c. ions
   d. atoms
   e. none of the above

_____ 7. At which of the following points in the neuron is a nerve impulse initiated?
   a. dendrite   d. axon
   b. soma   e. any of the above
   c. axon hillock

_____ 8. When the axon is in the resting state both the electrostatic force and diffusion pressure would dictate that
   a. the potassium ion would move to the outside of the axon
   b. the chloride ion would move to the inside of the axon
   c. the potassium ion would move to the inside of the axon
   d. the sodium ion would move to the inside of the axon
   e. the chloride ion would move to the outside of the axon

_____ 9. During the action potential, it is the _____ that allows the re-establishment of the resting potential.
   a. outward movement of the potassium ions
   b. inward movement of the chloride ions
   c. outward movement of the sodium ions
   d. outward movement of the chloride ions
   e. inward movement of the potassium ions

_____ 10. For the neurotransmitter substance to be released into the synaptic cleft
   a. calcium gates must open to allow the influx of calcium ions into the presynaptic terminal
   b. chloride ions must bind to the membranes of the vesicles in the presynaptic terminal
   c. nerve impulse must arrive at the terminal
   d. chloride ions must bind the vesicles to the membrane of the presynaptic terminal
   e. more than one of the above

_____ 11. Which of the following is not true of EPSPs?
   a. it is conducted with decrement
   b. the membrane channels it uses are transmitter regulated
   c. it is self-propagating
   d. it occurs in the dendrite and/or soma of the neuron
   e. more than one of the above

_____ 12. In the cyclic AMP cascade, we have an example of a(n)
   a. effect of hyperpolarization   d. second messenger system
   b. summation   e. none of the above
   c. facilitation

_____ 13. Drugs such as cocaine and the amphetamines serve as _____ because _____
   a. depressant; they block neurotransmitter receptor sites
   b. stimulant; they attract the enzyme that deactivates the neurotransmitter
   c. stimulant; they block the reuptake of the neurotransmitter
   d. depressant; they deplete the amount of neurotransmitter available by attacking the presynaptic vesicles
   e. none of the above

_____ 14. The synthesis of the catecholamines begins with the amino acid
   a. CoA   d. tryptophan
   b. tyrosine   e. L-DOPA
   c. tyramine

_____ 15. The making of decisions and the ability of synapses to vary in strength can be attributed to which of the following?
   a. strength of the initiating stimulus
   b. amount of neurotransmitter released
   c. existence of postsynaptic potentials
   d. existence of myelin and the nodes of Ranvier
   e. none of the above

True/False

_____ 1. Even though the axon membrane is semipermeable, the large protein anions are trapped inside the axon.

_____ 2. The potential inside the axon is negative.

_____ 3. Acetylcholinesterase is an enzyme necessary in the synthesis of acetylcholine.

_____ 4. According to the all-or-none law, if an axon fires at all, it will fire at full strength.

_____ 5. A nerve impulse is only conducted in one direction--toward the telodendria.

_____ 6. It is impossible for a current to flow between two points until a potential has been established between them.

_____ 7. A neurotransmitter binds with a receptor site to cause the sodium channels in the postsynaptic membrane to open, which in turn sets off a nerve impulse.

_____ 8. Transmembrane ion currents, not electronic currents, flow down the length of the axon from cell body to telodendria.

_____ 9. The binding of the neurotransmitter GABA with either a $GABA_A$ or a $GABA_B$ receptor site will produce an IPSP.

_____ 10. During the resting state the axonal membrane is relatively impermeable to the sodium ion.

_____ 11. A membrane potential of -70 is the sodium equilibrium potential.

_____ 12. The action potential can be described as a shift from depolarization through polarization to depolarization again.

_____ 13. Excitability is the reciprocal of the axon threshold.

_____ 14. The rate at which a neuron can fire is limited by the duration of the absolute refractory period.

_____ 15. The transmembrane ion current is much slower than the electrotonic current.

4.1

absolute refractory period

(128)

4.2

acetyl coenzyme A (acetyl CoA)

(145)

4.3

acetylcholine (Ach)

(138)

4.4

acetylcholinesterase (AchE)

(144)

4.5

action potential

(119)

4.6

all-or-none law

(111)

4.7

axon hillock

(121)

4.8

axon threshold

(127)

4.9

binding

(132)

4.10

calcium channels

(130)

4.6

If an axon fires at all, it will fire at full strength. Each axon has only one size nerve impulse, and stronger stimuli simply produce more frequent impulses.

4.7

The initial segment of the axon. It is here that impulses are born.

4.8

The least amount of electrical stimulation (in millivolts) required to trigger an action potential. The opposite of excitability.

4.9

The chemical reaction in which the transmitter molecule reacts with the channel protein. As a result the protein molecule is twisted a little more, opening up the ion channel through its center.

4.10

Channels that open in response to the arrival of an impulse in the terminal. This allows calcium to enter the terminal where it does its job of linking vesicle to membrane.

Copyright 1990 by Wadsworth, Inc.

4.1

A short period of nonexcitability that occurs in the early part of the action potential. During this time the ion channels are already open and cannot be re-opened.

4.2

One of the substances from which Ach is made.

4.3

A neurotransmitter substance found at neuromuscular junctions.

4.4

An enzyme that terminates the activity of acetylcholine by destroying it in the synapse.

4.5

Sometimes referred to as a spike potential, a shift from polarization through depolarization to repolarization. It is the sequence of voltage charges seen at any one point on a neuron membrane when a nerve impulse passes through.

4.11 catecholamines

(142)

4.12 chlorpromazine

(141)

4.13 cholinergic synapse

(144)

4.14 curare

(141)

4.15 cyclic AMP cascade

(136)

4.16 decremental conduction

(134)

4.17 depolarization

(126)

4.18 diffusion

(115)

4.19 electrostatic attraction

(116)

4.20 electrostatic repulsion

(115)

4.16

A decrease in amplitude of a current as it flows away from its source. The electrotonic currents of EPSPs conduct decrementally.

4.17

A decrease in polarization either through the removal of charges from the situation or by the coming together of unlikely charges to cancel out one another.

4.18

Tendency for identical particles in solution to move apart from one another so that they fill all the available space with the greatest possible distance between each other.

4.19

The tendency for particles with unlike charges to attract one another.

4.20

The tendency for particles with identical charges to repel one another.

Copyright 1990 by Wadsworth, Inc.

4.11

A subclass of monoamine transmitters that includes epinephrine, norepinephrine, and dopamine.

4.12

A drug that is used to gain some relief from the symptoms of schizophrenia. It blocks receptor sites for the transmitter dopamine.

4.13

Synapses that use the neurotransmitter acetylcholine.

4.14

A paralytic drug that has its effect at the synapses that connect the motor neurons of the peripheral nervous system to the muscle fibers they control.

4.15

The neurotransmitter binds with an enzyme that converts a molecule of ATP to cyclic AMP, which then floats in the intercellular fluid until it randomly contacts a channel and a molecule of kinase. When cyclic AMP binds to the kinase, the channel opens.

4.21 electrotonic current (121)

4.22 equilibrium point (116)

4.23 excitability (127)

4.24 excitation (136)

4.25 excitatory postsynaptic potential (EPSP) (133)

4.26 facilitation (136)

4.27 electrode (111)

4.28 flaccid paralysis (141)

4.29 GABA$_A$ receptor (138)

4.30 GABA$_B$ receptor (138)

4.26

A condition that occurs when a nerve impulse arrives at a synapse. The resultant EPSP adds to the existing summated potential without providing enough additional voltage to push the axon over its threshold.

4.27

A conductor that is designed to carry an electric current to or away from some part of the body.

4.28

A condition in which striate muscles cannot contract and stay limp all of the time. It is due to the loss of the stimulus because of damage to the peripheral motor neuron.

4.29

A receptor that is connected directly with a chloride channel. It is the receptor for gamma-amino-butyric acid.

4.30

A receptor that can open potassium channels. This receptor either is directly connected to the ion channel or communicates with it indirectly by a second messenger and protein kinase.

Copyright 1990 by Wadsworth, Inc.

4.21

A type of current that flows during depolarization, which consists of a flow of electrons, jumping from one ion to the next very much like electrons in an electrical wire move from one molecule of copper to the next.

4.22

Point at which the electrostatic and diffusion forces are balanced by each other.

4.23

The reciprocal of the threshold voltage.

4.24

A condition that occurs when a nerve impulse arrives at a synapse. The resultant EPSP adds to the existing summated potential to boost it above threshold and fire the axon.

4.25

The triggers for nerve impulses, they are small transmembrane currents of inward-flowing sodium ions and outward-flowing potassium ions that occur at the postsynaptic membrane.

4.31	4.36
gamma-amino-butyric acid (GABA)	ion
(137)	(112)
4.32	4.37
inhibition	ion channels
(137)	(115)
4.33	4.38
initial segment	MAO inhibitors
(121)	(143)
4.34	4.39
hyperpolarization	monoamine oxidase
(137)	(142)
4.35	4.40
inhibitory postsynaptic potential (IPSP)	monoamines
(136)	(142)

4.36

An unbalanced (charged) particle that results from a molecule breaking apart.

4.37

Special protein molecules in the cell membrane through which some of the ions can pass and some cannot.

4.38

A class of antidepressant drugs that indirectly increases the supply of norepinephrine by slowing down its destruction by monoamine oxidase.

4.39

An enzyme that destroys monoamine neurotransmitters by breaking them down into basic molecular components.

4.40

A class of neurotransmitter substances that includes serotonin and the catecholamines.

Copyright 1990 by Wadsworth, Inc.

4.31

A neurotransmitter that binds with two types of receptors, both of which produce IPSPs.

4.32

The occurrence of IPSPs at the initial segment.

4.33

The segment of axon closest to the cell body. It is also called the axon hillock.

4.34

An increase in polarization, it serves as the basis of inhibition.

4.35

The triggers for nerve impulses. They are small transmembrane potentials that occur when potassium channels are opened and some of the potassium ions are able to flow out. The additional positive ions on the outside increase polarization of the membrane, making it harder to depolarize the initial segments and fire the axon.

4.41

neuromuscular junctions

(141)

4.42

neurotransmitters

(130)

4.43

nodes of Ranvier

(122)

4.44

nondecremental conduction

(122)

4.45

one-way conduction

(111)

4.46

oscilloscope

(124)

4.47

polarized

(126)

4.48

potassium equilibrium potential

(119)

4.49

potential

(113)

4.50

protein kinase (PKC)

(136)

4.46

Electronic instrument for displaying voltage changes on a cathode ray tube screen.

4.47

Term describing a membrane with a resting potential across it. It simply refers to the fact that there is some separation of charges so that there are more positive charges on one side and more negative charges on the other.

4.48

Potential reading across the axon membrane when the force of electrostatic repulsion is strong enough to balance the diffusion pressure and the outward flow of potassium ions stops. In the axon of the mammal this is -70 mv.

4.49

Term referring to the separation of charges between two places: the positive charges in one place and the negative charges in another place.

4.50

A molecule that normally holds an ion channel in the closed position.

4.41

Synapses that connect the motor neurons of the peripheral nervous system to the muscle fibers they control.

4.42

The chemicals that are stored in and released by the vesicles into the synapse, diffuse across it, and trigger activity in the postsynaptic neuron.

4.43

Bare (nonmyelinated) spots between glial cells. They are the only places on a myelinated fiber where transmembrane currents can be elicited.

4.44

A characteristic of a nerve impulse, the impulse shows no decrement (does not decrease) as it travels.

4.45

Under normal conditions, a nerve impulse is only conducted in a particular direction--toward the telodendria.

Copyright 1990 by Wadsworth, Inc.

4.51 receptor site

(132)

4.52 relative refractory period

(128)

4.53 resting potential

(114)

4.54 reuptake

(142)

4.55 saltatory conduction

(123)

4.56 self-propagating

(122)

4.57 semipermeable

(115)

4.58 sodium equilibrium potential

(117)

4.59 sodium/potassium pump

(117)

4.60 spike potential

(127)

4.56

Characteristic of a nerve impulse that explains how this impulse moves down the axon. Each individual current provides the disturbance that triggers the next current in the neighboring section of the axon.

4.57

Property of the membrane that refers to the fact that the membrane is selective about which ions it allows to pass.

4.58

Potential reading across the axon membrane when the diffusion pressure causing sodium ions to move into the axon is balanced by the electrostatic forces that resist the entrance of the sodium ions. In the axon of a mammal this is +30 mv.

4.59

A "mechanism" of the membrane that consists of a series of chemical reactions that pick up sodium from inside the cell and transport it through the membrane. This pump gathers potassium ions from the extracellular fluid outside the cell and transports them to the inside.

4.60

The sequence of voltage changes seen at any one point on an axon membrane when a nerve impulse passes through.

4.51

Sites on the postsynaptic membrane formed by the outside portions of the long protein molecules that makes up a membrane channel. They are shaped like a specific molecule of neurotransmitter.

4.52

Period of time following the absolute refractory period during which it becomes progressively easier to produce a section action potential before the axon has completely recovered from the first.

4.53

Period during which the axon is not conducting an impulse. At this time the membrane potential is -70 mv.

4.54

Process in which the action of a neurotransmitter is terminated by bringing back the transmitter molecules into the terminal.

4.55

The jumping of the action potential from one node of Ranvier to another in a myelinated axon.

Copyright 1990 by Wadsworth, Inc.

4.61

summation

(135)

4.62

synapse

(130)

4.63

synaptic cleft (gap)

(130)

4.64

transmembrane ion currents

(119)

4.65

transmitter regulated

(133)

4.66

vesicles

(130)

4.67

voltage regulated

(133)

4.66

Tiny, bubble-like structures that are always present in the terminal. They act as storage "bottles" for chemicals called neurotransmitters.

4.61

A process whereby the electrotonic currents from different EPSPs can add together.

4.67

Characteristic of membrane channels that are held closed by a voltage between the inside and the outside of the membrane and opened when depolarization occurs. Such channels are found in the membrane of the axon.

4.62

An area that includes parts of the two connecting cells plus the gap between them.

4.63

The fluid-filled space between the presynaptic and postsynaptic cells. It is hardly more than a few molecules wide.

4.64

Term that points out that there is no single current that flows down the axon but rather a succession of many individual currents that flow through the membrane.

4.65

Characteristic of membrane channels found in the dendrites and soma. Such channels are opened by a neurotransmitter.

Copyright 1990 by Wadsworth, Inc.

CHAPTER FIVE
EXPLORING THE NERVOUS SYSTEM THROUGH SCIENCE

READ-WRITE-REVIEW

Read pages 152-160 and summary statements 1-3 on page 191, then answer each of the following questions in this section.
---

1. The clinical observation data on people with damage to a part of the brain are carried out in modern science by what kind of psychologist? (153)

    a. What are some of the reasons why the data from such clinical observations are less reliable then those that come from true experiments? (153)

2. What is the difference between the lesioning technique and the ablation techniques? (154)

    a. Describe the aspiration technique. (155)

    b. Why is this technique employed when the lesion is limited to the cortex? (155)

3. The development of what instrument in 1827 by whom was necessary before it could be demonstrated that animals actually do generate electrical currents in nerves and muscles? (155)

    a. Who were the two scientists who were responsible for a series of experiments involving the electrical stimulation of the cortex of dogs? (155)

    b. What structure were they responsible for locating? (155)

    c. What problem did Wilder Penfield try to circumvent using electrical brain stimulation? (156)

    d. What areas of the cortex did Penfield map? (157)

4. The technique of electroencephalography had its beginnings with the work of whom? (157)

    a. What is the role of the EEG amplifier in the recording of electrical brain activity? (157)

    b. When employing normal electrodes, how is this electrical brain activity finally presented to the researcher? (157)

    c. List and identify the two dimensions along which EEG waves vary. (158)

d. What entire field of research was built on EEG methodology? (158)

Read pages 160-169 and summary statements 4-5 on page 191, then answer each of the following questions in this section.
---

1. Describe what would be seen in a stereotaxic brain atlas. (160)

    a. What is done to the animal to make the measurements found in the stereotaxic brain atlas meaningful? (160)

    b. In implanting electrodes in the brain below the cortex, how is the barrier of the skull circumvented? (160)

    c. What is done to keep the electrode in place for a period of time? (162-163)

    d. Why would a researcher prefer to use an electrolytic lesioning technique to destroy the amygdala rather than trying to accomplish the task with a scalpel? (164)

    e. How is tissue destroyed using an electrolytic lesioning technique? (164)

2. Describe the basic logic of a lesioning experiment. (164)

    a. What is a neurotoxin? (164, 166)

    b. What is 6-hydroxydopamine and what is it used for? (166)

    c. What delivery system is used with such chemicals? (166-167)

    d. Why have glutaminergic neurons been the target of a considerable amount of neurotoxin research? (167)

    e. List two neurotoxins that are specific to glutaminergic neurons. (167)

    f. What is the relationship between "neurotoxins" and an "animal model"? (167)

Read pages 169-174 and summary statements 6-7 on page 191, then answer each of the following questions in this section.
---

1. What is the advantage gained by using the "signal averaging" technique? (170-171)

    a. Describe what is done using this technique. (171)

    b. Describe the rationale behind the use of this technique. (171)

82

c. A sensory evoked potential consists of a series of waves. From what are these waves derived? (171)

2. In recording from single neurons what kind of electrodes are used and of what are they made? (174)

   a. List and identify the two types of single neuron recording. (174)

   b. How can a single subcortical neuron be located? (174)

Read pages 174-182, and summary statements 8-10 on page 191, then answer each of the following questions in this section.
---

1. The brain is organized in different ways at different levels. Describe these three levels of organization. (174)

2. What determines the function of any single neuron? (174-175)

   a. What is stained by the Nauta-Gygax method? (175)

   b. What metal salt is employed in the Nauta-Gygax method? (175)

   c. From previous research studies you have hypothesized that a motor pathway exists between nucleus A and nucleus B. Using the Nauta-Gygax stain, how would you provide support for your hypothesis? (175)

   d. What is a tritiated molecule? (176)

   e. How can such molecules be used to trace a suspected pathway between two nuclei? (176)

   f. What is horseradish peroxidase? (176)

   g. How can horseradish peroxidase help in tracing a pathway between two nuclei? (176)

   h. Distinguish between anterograde and retrograde tracing and identify the horseradish peroxidase and autoradiographic techniques in this respect. (176)

3. What is a neurotransmitter system? (176)

   a. List four techniques that can be employed to determine what type of neurotransmitter substance is employed by a specific neuron. (177)

   b. The oldest of these techniques, histofluorescence, is used to identify those neurons that employ which class of neurotransmitters? (177)

   c. What is used to covert this type of neurotransmitter into fluorescing compounds? (177)

d. Describe the method of reuptake autoradiography. (177)

e. What is the major limitation of this procedure? (177)

f. What information can be obtained using the receptor labeling technique? (177)

g. What is the difference between in vivo and in vitro? (177)

h. A virus has entered your body. If we could find that virus, what would we find on its surface and what are they? (177)

i. What are antibodies and what do they do? (177-178)

j. What are "designer" antibodies? (178)

k. List the steps in the immunohistochemical method. (178)

4. What advantage do methods such as regional cerebral blood flow technique, 2-deoxyglucose autoradiography, and voltage sensitive dye technique have over such techniques as the immunohistochemical method and the horseradish peroxidase method? (178)

   a. What rationale underlies the use of the regional cerebral blood flow technique? (178)

   b. What is "Xenon" and what is its function in the regional cerebral blood flow technique? (178, 180)

   c. What role does the computer play in the regional cerebral blood flow technique? (180)

   d. In autoradiographic research designed to reveal brain function, why is 2-deoxyglucose preferred to normal glucose that has been tagged with a radioactive carbon atom? (180)

   e. The use of voltage sensitive dye technique is limited to what area of the brain? (181)

   f. Explain how the voltage sensitive dye technique works. (181)

Read pages 183-189, appendix pages 192-194 and summary statements 11-12 on page 191, then answer each of the following questions in this section.
---

1. Computerized axial tomography and positron-emission tomography are examples of what class of techniques? (183)

   a. What are the difficulties with using the regular x-ray to obtain information about the brain? (183)

   b. Explain in some detail how computerized axial tomography is able to provide the researcher with a three-dimensional view of the brain. (183-184)

c. What are radioactive isotopes and what function do they have in positron-emission tomography? (185)

d. What is the major advantage of computerized axial tomography over positron-emission tomography? (185)

e. What is the major advantage of positron-emission tomography over computerized axial tomography? (187)

f. In the nuclear magnetic resonance method, the subject is placed within a strong magnetic field. Why? (187)

g. What is resonance, and what is the effect of this phenomenon on those magnetizable nuclei in the brain? (187)

h. Explain how the nuclear magnetic resonance image is produced. (187)

i. Using the nuclear magnetic resonance method, how might the researcher study brain chemistry? (187)

2. On what are the current federal government guidelines for animal research based? (187)

   a. According to these federal government guidelines, what must each research institution do to provide a mechanism for the enforcement of these rules? (187-189)

   b. What is the composition of an animal care and use committee and what is its function according to these federal guidelines? (189)

PRE-EXAM QUIZ

Multiple-Choice
Select the choice that best completes the stem in each question and indicate your selection in the appropriate space to the left of the question.

_____ 1. A lesioning technique that employs a fine-tipped pipette attached to a suction hose is called
    a. electrolytic lesioning   d. chemical lesioning
    b. aspiration   e. none of the above
    c. ablation

_____ 2. He was responsible for the development of electroencephalography. He is
    a. Eduard Hitzig   d. Paul Broca
    b. Roberts Bartholow   e. Leopoldo Nobili
    c. Hans Berger

_____ 3. Driving electrodes, even very thin ones, will have which of the following effects?
   a. will produce no brain tissue damage
   b. will produce some tissue damage but the damage will be so small that it rarely will produce any behavioral result
   c. will produce some tissue damage, which will, in turn, produce some very definite behavioral results
   d. will produce a good deal of tissue damage, which in turn will produce no very definite behavioral results
   e. none of the above are true

_____ 4. Electrolytic lesioning produces tissue damage by using
   a. a neurotoxin to destroy the nerve cell bodies
   b. an alternating electric current that permanently deactivates the neurons in the area without damaging the tissue
   c. a series of very fine knife cuts
   d. a direct current that produces enough heat to destroy the surrounding tissues
   e. none of the above

_____ 5. Glutamate is a
   a. strong antibiotic
   b. neurotransmitter
   c. membrane stain
   d. neurotoxin
   e. more than one of the above

_____ 6. What is actually averaged in the signal averaging technique?
   a. the several waves that appear in response to a stimulus
   b. only the initial wave that appears in response to a stimulus
   c. the voltage at a number of points following stimulus presentation
   d. the strength of the stimuli presented
   e. nothing is averaged using this technique

_____ 7. The _____ are a group of transmitters built around or from a basic molecule called _____.
   a. cholinergic; choline
   b. catecholamines; DOPA
   c. glutamines; gamma-amino-butyric acid
   d. endorphins; tryptophan
   e. none of the above

_____ 8. Which of the following is used in the construction of microelectrodes?
   a. tungsten
   b. platinum
   c. silver
   d. tin
   e. gold

_____ 9. The Nauta-Gygax method employs a(n) _____ salt to selectively stain _____.
   a. iron; cell bodies
   b. silicon; axons
   c. silver; degenerating axons
   d. iron; degenerating axons
   e. silver; telodendria and dendrites

_____ 10. The autoradiography method employs a(n) _____ molecule to emit radiation.
   a. magnetized
   b. stained
   c. tritiated
   d. any untreated
   e. none of the above

_____ 11. The histofluorescence technique will not work with which of the following?
   a. acetylcholine
   b. serotonin
   c. norepinephrine
   d. dopamine
   e. more than one of the above

_____12. Which of the following best describes the legacy of the 1984 University of Pennsylvania neurosurgery labs incident?
   a. some scientists continue to carry out research that is not in compliance with federal government guidelines
   b. animal-rights activists do not operate within the law
   c. animal-rights activists were provided with so much emotionalized publicity that the possibility of working out the best compromise between human and animal need has been put in serious danger
   d. medical science cannot progress in certain areas if scientists are not allowed to carry out their experiments using animal subjects
   e. none of the above

_____13. All viruses and microorganisms have on their surfaces protein molecules called _____, which allow our immune systems to identify and destroy them.
   a. antibodies   d. antigens
   b. tritium   e. none of the above
   c. antihistamines

_____14. The major difference between computerized axial tomography and positron-emission tomography has to do with
   a. whether or not the picture produced is three-dimensional
   b. whether or not a computer is used
   c. whether or not it can be used on living subjects
   d. from where the radiation originates
   e. none of the above

_____15. Which of the following is not one of the techniques used to map cortical functions?
   a. 2-deoxyglucose autoradiography   d. voltage-sensitive dye
   b. histofluorescence   e. more than one of the above
   c. regional cerebral blood flow

True/False

_____ 1. The clinical observations of neuropsychologists are rarely as reliable as data obtained from true experiments.

_____ 2. Aspiration is a technique used to remove large sections of the brain other than the cortex.

_____ 3. Unlike Dr. Bartholow in 1874, researchers today do not employ human patients as subjects in electrical stimulation studies.

_____ 4. Brain waves are emitted not only by the cortex but also by the deep brain structures.

_____ 5. The wave recorded by the EEG pen represents an increase and decrease in voltage at one point on the scalp that is an algebraic summation of current fields from millions of individual neurons.

_____ 6. To make certain that during stereotaxic surgery the rat does not move its head, the head is positioned by being clamped at three points, the ear canals, the nose, and the scalp.

_____ 7. If you have properly secured the rat's head in the stereotaxic instrument and if you have properly read the brain atlas, then you are certain of where the electrode tip is even though you cannot see it.

_____ 8. In the sensory evoked potential the large wave at the beginning represents sensory cortical activity, whereas the smaller waves represent subcortical activity as the sensory input from the receptors is received.

_____ 9. The development of "animal models" of the brain damage produced by a disease is one of the uses developed for neurotoxins.

_____ 10. Single cell, intracellular recording eventually kills the neuron whose activity is being recorded.

_____ 11. It is possible to organize the brain into systems according to the neurotransmitter employed.

_____ 12. Horseradish peroxidase is an enzyme that can be used in an anterograde tracing technique.

_____ 13. One of the major drawbacks to the use of receptor labeling is that some chemicals used in this method are unable to cross the blood-brain barrier.

_____ 14. The problem with using normal glucose made radioactive in autoradiography is that the animal uses glucose molecules at such a high rate that glucose does not stay in the cell long enough for the procedure to be accomplished.

_____ 15. The picture produced by computerized axial tomography has less resolution than that produced by positron-emission tomography and therefore is less clear.

5.1

ablation

(154)

5.2

amplitude

(158)

5.3

animal care and use committee

(189)

5.4

animal model

(167)

5.5

Animal Welfare Act

(187)

5.6

anterograde tracing

(176)

5.7

antibodies

(178)

5.8

antigens

(177)

5.9

aspiration

(155)

5.10

auditory evoked potential

(169)

5.6

A pathway tracing technique that relies on the cell to transport the radioactive-labeling molecules from the soma out to the ends of the axons.

5.7

Proteins manufactured by the body, each of which is designed to bind with a specific antigen. An organism carrying that antigen is marked by the antibody for destruction by cells of the immune system

---

5.8

Protein molecules found on the surfaces of all viruses and microorganisms that the body's immune systems use to recognize and destroy them.

5.9

A technique employed when the lesion is to be limited to the cortex. A small length of glass tubing drawn to a finely polished tip is attached to a suction hose and inserted into a hole in the pia so that the cortical tissue can be sucked out.

5.10

A large brain wave response to an auditory click stimulus recorded from an electrode over the auditory cortex. It represents the voltage changes in the cortex as a burst of impulse enters it from the auditory nucleus of the thalamus.

Copyright 1990 by Wadsworth, Inc.

5.1

The surgical removal of a very large part of the brain for the experimental purpose of determining how the loss of that part affects behavior.

5.2

The height of the EEG wave, which represents the amount of energy involved.

5.3

A committee that must be established by each research institute to oversee all animal research projects to make certain they are in compliance with the federal regulations set forth in the government publication Guide for the Care and Use of Laboratory Animals.

5.4

A reproduction in experimental animals of the type of brain damage generated by a disease. It is typically the first step by the clinical researcher toward the development of a real understanding of the disease process.

5.5

Federal regulations governing the care of animals. This law was inspired by the lobbying of various animal welfare groups. These regulations form the basis for the federal government's guidelines for animal research.

5.11

autoradiographic method

(176)
5.12

averaged evoked potentials

(171)
5.13

catecholamines

(166)
5.14

clinical observation

(153)
5.15

computerized axial tomography (CAT)

(183)

5.16

electroencephalograph (EEG)

(157)
5.17

electrolytic lesion

(164)
5.18

excitotoxins

(167)
5.19

extracellular microelectrode technique

(174)
5.20

frequency

(158)

5.16

An instrument for recording the brain's electrical activity.

5.17

Brain damage produced by a direct electrical current that heats and eventually destroys the tissue through which it passes.

5.18

A group of neurotoxins, ibotenic acid and kainic acid, that excite neurons in many areas of the nervous system probably because they fit into glutamic receptor sites.

5.19

A recording technique in which the electrode is positioned as close as possible to the soma or fiber of the neuron without penetrating the membrane of the cell. Technique leaves the cell intact and is used when a long recording session is required.

5.20

The number of repetitions of an EEG wave in 1 second.

Copyright 1990 by Wadsworth, Inc.

5.11

A pathway-tracing technique in which some chemical essential to neurons is made radioactive so that it can be located after it has been incorporated into brain tissue. Afterwards, the animal is sacrificed, brain tissue is sectioned, and the sections are coated with photographic emulsion and exposed to film.

5.12

Recordings that are the result of the signal averaging technique.

5.13

A group of transmitters built around or from a basic molecule called DOPA. The simplest is dopamine, which can be converted to norepinephrine and then to epinephrine.

5.14

One method of gathering data about brain function. It involves the study of people with brain damage.

5.15

A technique that involves taking dozens of separate x-ray pictures through the head at dozens of different angles and then combining the results with a computer to produce a three-dimensional picture of the brain.

5.21 glutamate (167)	5.26 immunohistochemical method (177)
5.22 histofluorescence (177)	5.27 intracellular microelectrode technique (174)
5.23 horseradish peroxidase technique (HRP) (176)	5.28 in vitro autoradiography (177)
5.24 ibotenic acid (167)	5.29 in vivo (177)
5.25 immune system (177)	5.30 isotope (185)

5.26

A cell-marking technique in which an antibody is created that has been combined chemically with either a fluorescing dye or horseradish peroxidase. The brain tissue is then exposed to the antibody long enough for it to bind to the substance being located.

5.27

A recording technique in which microelectrodes are used to penetrate the membrane of a single neuron and record the cell's own electrical impulses. Such a recording is of short duration because the technique damages the cell and it eventually dies.

5.28

A technique in which the experiment is conducted on tissue removed from the body and pieces of brain tissue are exposed to the labeled chemical. It is then subjected to autoradiography.

5.29

The tissue remains within the living animal.

5.30

One of a variety of forms of a chemical element, each having a different number of neutrons and protons in the nuclei of its atoms.

5.21

A likely candidate for a neurotransmitter in a number of places in the nervous system including the hippocampus. In larger doses it is a powerful neurotoxin.

5.22

A technique in which brain tissue slices are exposed to formaldehyde or glyoxylic acid, and monoamine neurotransmitters are converted into fluorescing compounds, thus revealing their location in brain tissue with a ghostly yellow-green glow.

5.23

A pathway-tracing technique in which the enzyme HRP is injected into an area of gray matter where it is taken up by the terminals and telodendria entering the area. It arrives at the soma. The experimenter then sections the brain and exposes sections to a chemical that reacts with HRP so that the cells containing HRP stain brown or blue against a black background.

5.24

A neurotoxin, related to glutamate, that is found in mushrooms and is used to kill glutaminergic neurons.

5.25

A set of chemical reactions and specialized cells that are designed to fight off infections and tumors.

Copyright 1990 by Wadsworth, Inc.

5.31 kainic acid	5.36 neurotoxin
(167)	(164, 166)
5.32 lesioning	5.37 nuclear magnetic resonance (NMR)
(154)	(187)
5.33 microelectrode	5.38 photon
(174)	(185)
5.34 Nauta-Gygax method	5.39 positron
(175)	(185)
5.35 neuropsychologist	5.40 positron-emission tomography (PET)
(153)	(184)

5.36

A substance that poisons nerves.

5.37

A technique that uses the fact that some types of atomic nuclei act as magnets. When a patient is placed in a strong magnetic field all these nuclei will orient in the same direction. When these nuclei absorb radio wave energy they are knocked out of alignment but return to their regular alignment by shedding this energy, which is used to make NMR pictures

---

5.38

Particles of electromagnetic radiation.

5.39

A particle like an electron but with a positive charge.

5.40

One of the newest techniques in radiology in which the brain is made temporarily radioactive by injecting a radioactive isotope labeled material that will be taken up by the brain cells, where it is then used in the PET scan.

Copyright 1990 by Wadsworth, Inc.

5.31

A neurotoxin, related to glutamate, that is found in seaweed and is used to kill glutaminergic neurons. It selectively lesions cell bodies within the injected region while leaving alone the axons and telodendria, although this selectivity is not perfect.

5.32

A surgical method used in the study of brain function in which a relatively small area of the brain is damaged or destroyed. The area of damage is called a lesion.

5.33

Exceptionally thin electrodes made of glass tubes filled with a conductive solution of ions and drawn to a microscopic tip or a very fine tungsten wire insulated down to the tip.

5.34

A staining technique that employs a silver salt to selectively stain degenerating axons.

5.35

One who is trained in gathering together all clinical observations with the goal of attempting to derive from them an explanation of function.

5.41 radioactive isotope (185)

5.42 receptor labeling (177)

5.43 regional cerebral blood flow technique (178)

5.44 retrograde tracing (176)

5.45 reuptake autoradiography (177)

5.46 signal averaging (171)

5.47 6-hydroxydopamine (6-OHDA) (166)

5.48 stereotaxic brain atlas (160)

5.49 stereotaxic instrument (160)

5.50 tritiated molecule (176)

5.46

A technique used to enhance the auditory evoked potentials while diminishing the size of the other brain wave activity. It uses the fact that whereas evoked potential occur in only one direction, random activity can occur in either direction. The voltages are algebraically added across a number of records.

5.47

A neurotoxin used to selectively destroy neurons that secrete one of the catecholamine neurotransmitters.

5.48

A book of calibrated drawings or photographs of an average-sized animal's brain that provides measurements to be used to place an object in a particular location within an animal's brain, using a stereotaxic instrument.

5.49

A laboratory instrument used to hold the animal's head firmly in a fixed position so that a carrier, once properly placed according to the measurements provided in the stereotaxic brain atlas, can lower a wire electrode, glass tube, or other object into a particular location within an animal's brain.

5.50

A molecule in which tritium has been substituted for its hydrogen atoms.

Copyright 1990 by Wadsworth, Inc.

5.41

An isotope that, as it begins to disintegrate because of an unstable balance of neutrons and protons, also begins to emit radiation.

5.42

A technique that involves marking receptor sites with radioactive molecules using the autoradiographic technique.

5.43

A method that can reveal the activity levels in various parts of the human brain during the execution of behavioral tasks based on the fact that increased activity in a brain region brings with it increased blood flow. A small amount of radioactive gas, Xenon, once inhaled by the subject is carried by bloodstream to the brain, and its location is monitored by radioactive detectors attached to a computer.

5.44

A pathway-tracing technique in which the chemical used in the process is transported from telodendria to soma.

5.45

Radioactive molecules of a transmitter substance are injected into an area of gray matter to be taken up by any terminal in that area that uses that transmitter. The brain is sectioned and coated with photographic emulsion. Terminals that took up the labeled transmitter substance will photograph themselves.

5.51

2-deoxyglucose (2-DE) autoradiography

(180)

5.52

voltage-sensitive dye

(181)

5.51

A method to detect activity levels in various parts of the brain. With increased brain activity comes an increased need for glucose. The radioactive 2-DE is injected immediately before stimulus is presented or the task begins. More of it is taken up by the active brain tissue, and it is detected by autoradiography.

5.52

Used in a technique that is designed to reveal the function of various cortical areas. This dye is placed on the general area of the cortex that should be involved in the task or in responding to a stimulus. It fluoresces when the action potentials and postsynaptic potentials of the neurons pass through it.

Copyright 1990 by Wadsworth, Inc.

CHAPTER SIX
VISION

READ-WRITE-REVIEW

Read pages 198-202 and summary statements 1-2 on page 246, then answer each of the following questions in this section.
---

1. What makes an object in your visual field become visible? (198)

    a. How would an object appear if it were able to absorb all light? (198)

    b. How would an object appear if it reflected all light? (198)

    c. What determines the color of an object? (198)

2. What is the electromagnetic spectrum? (199)

    a. What part of this spectrum can be seen by the human eye? (199)

    b. What other part or parts of the electromagnetic spectrum are we capable of sensing and with what sense or senses? (199)

3. Below is a diagram that represents a cross section of the eye.

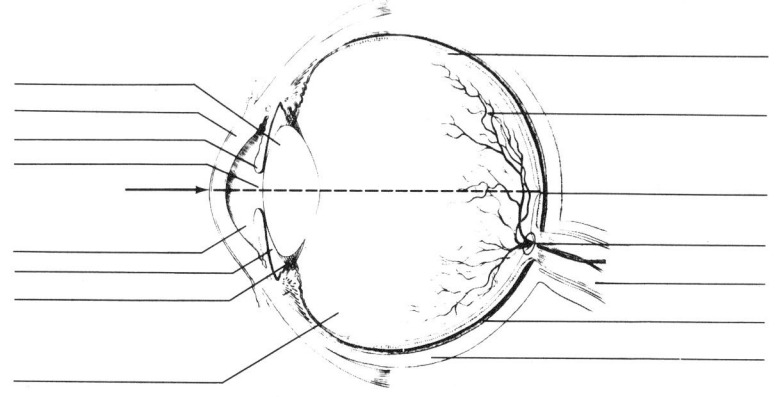

    Below you will find a series of statements that identify the various structures of the eye. Identify the structure described, locate it on the diagram, and label it.

    a. Changing its shape allows for focusing on near vs. faraway objects. (201)

    b. This is the point of clearest vision on the retina. (202)

    c. It is composed of axons of the ganglia cells. (204)

    d. It is the rounded, transparent part of the sclera. (200-201)

    e. This layer contains the blood supply that feeds the photoreceptor cells. (203)

101

f. This ring of muscles controls the size of the hole that allows light into the inner chamber of the eye. (201)

   g. It contains the rods and cones. (202)

   h. This tough membranous sac encloses the eyeball. (200)

4. Three conditions produce difficulties in focusing. List the three conditions and describe the precise cause of each. (201-202)

Read pages 202-212 and summary statements 3-10 on pages 246-247, then answer each of the following questions in this section.
---

1. Describe the arrangement of cells on the retina. (202)

   a. Describe the connections of these cells in the retina in such a way as to explain how the activity of the receptors gets to the optic nerve. (202-204)

   b. Which of the retinal cells produces all-or-none action potentials? (203)

   c. What is the disadvantage of having the receptors at the front rather than the back of the retina? (203)

2. What is the photochemical substance in the rod? in the cones? (204, 206)

   a. Explain how the closing of the sodium channels in the receptor cells by transduction works to bring about the release of neurotransmitter substance by the receptor cell. (204)

   b. Identify the two types of bipolar cells. (206)

3. For a colored surface to appear red, what must happen at the stimulus level? (206)

   a. Based on different opsins, how many different cones exist? (206)

   b. To understand the Young-Helmholtz theory we must begin with what assumption? (207)

   c. According to the Young-Helmholtz theory, how are different patterns of light absorption dealt with by the cones? (207)

4. What is the basis for considering the retina as a dual-functioning system? (207-208)

a. Poor visual acuity results in a loss of what? (208)

b. Describe how a straight black line on a plain white sheet of paper appears to someone with poor visual acuity. (208)

c. Rods are to brightness and operating under low levels of illumination as cones are to _____ and _____. (208)

d. What part of the retina must an image fall on if it is to be perceived with the greatest clarity and sharpness? (208)

e. Why are cone circuits so much better at producing acuity than are rod circuits? (209)

5. Sensitivity is inversely related to what? (209)

a. Why on a moonlit night are all surfaces achromatic? (209)

b. What is dark adaptation? (209)

6. Describe the distribution of rods and cones across the surface of the retina. (210)

a. Explain what this has to do with night vision. (210)

7. Our retina is nature's solution to the problem of providing an eye that is capable of being able to resolve tiny visual detail while still being able to see well enough to get around on a dark night, despite the fact that these two functions are to some extent mutually incompatible. How does the retina serve as a compromise? (210)

8. In order to perceive a boundary or contour we must first be able to detect what? (210)

a. Describe the retinal circuitry that allows such perception. (211-212)

b. Such a perception will serve as the raw material for the perception of what? (212)

Read pages 212-220 and summary statements 11-13 on page 247, then answer each of the following questions in this section.
---

1. According to the classic model of vision, of what did the visual projection system consist? (212)

a. According to this model, at what point in the visual projection system did the visual experience become conscious? (214)

b. According to this model, what was the function of the retina? (214)

c. According to this model, what was the function of the lateral geniculate nucleus? (214)

2. What ability is lost in the patient that suffers from visual agnosia? (214)

   a. Damage to what part of the visual projection system appears to produce visual agnosia? (214)

   b. What implications were drawn from this finding concerning the role of the structure? (214)

   c. Connections between this structure and Brodmann's areas 18 and 19 suggested that this structure merely _____, whereas areas 18 and 19 _____. (214)

   d. What important visual connections are made with the inferotemporal cortex? (214)

   e. What is the function of the inferotemporal cortex? (214)

3. Research such as that of Schneider (1967) using hampsters, of Weiskrantz (1975) using monkeys, and of Poeppel suggested that even after extensive cortical damage to the visual area, some visual capability still remains. On the basis of findings like these, Trevarthan (1968) proposed the idea of a(n) _____ _____ to replace the classic viewpoint. (217)

   a. According to this model, there were two pathways that simultaneously processed the retinal output in parallel with one another. List these two pathways and identify the kind of information processed by each. (217)

   b. How can you account for the results of the "blindsight" subjects' inability to locate objects perfectly? (217)

   c. Trevarthan proposed the existence of two types of vision. On what anatomical feature did he base this? (217)

   d. List the two forms of vision proposed by Trevarthan and the type of analysis visual information analyzed by each. (218)

4. Distinguish between X- and Y-cells in the retina of the cat, on the basis of receptive field size, receptive field location, and types of information processed. (218-219)

   a. How is the X- and Y-cell division maintained at the lateral geniculate nucleus level? (219)

   b. What is the relationship of X- and Y-cells in the geniculostriate system? (219)

   c. In the retinotectal system? (219)

5. Another name for the retinotectal pathway may be the _____ pathway. (219)

   a. The superior colliculi projects to which major thalamic center? (219)

   b. Visual location information is projected from the thalamic nucleus to three major cortical areas. Identify each of these areas. (219)

6. The dual-projection theory concentrates its attention on pathways that end in the cortex. What fact does this focus ignore? (219)

   a. What is the key structure in the collicular pathway to the cortex? (219)

   b. This structure projects to what three cortical areas? (219)

7. What is the function of the frontal eye fields? (219)

   a. Where are the frontal eye fields located? (219)

   a. Why are the functions of the brain stem visual nuclei not considered to be duplicated by the frontal eye fields? (219)

Read pages 220-232 and summary statements 14-19 on pages 247-248, then answer each of the following questions in this section.
---

1. The majority of visual processors in the primate are located where? (220)

   a. Identify V1, V2, V3, and V4. (220)

   b. Mishkin (1983) has proposed that there are two major pathways that relate to important aspects of vision. What are these pathways and with what aspect or aspects of vision is each associated? (220-221)

2. The object vision pathway's analyzers extract what three types of information? (221)

   a. List two V1 cell types that function as edge analyzers and in each case describe the characteristics of a stimulus that would produce maximal firing. (222)

3. Compare the edge analyzers in V1 with the form analyzers in V2. (224)

   a. How does this help to explain why the visual analyzers occupy the entire posterior end of the cerebrum? (225)

   b. At what point in the visual projection system has enough information been extracted from the stimulus so that whole forms can now be identified and discriminated? (225)

c. Actually this area can be divided into two parts, each serving different roles. Identify the two parts and their roles. (225)

4. Using macaque monkeys, Desimone and colleagues (1984) found some rather unique cells referred to as "grandmother cells." What is a "grandmother cell"? (225)

   a. Where were these cells found? (226)

   b. To what type of stimuli did these cells respond? (227-228)

   c. What reason does Desimone offer to explain why these stimuli seemingly violate the apparent rule of organization of the visual brain? (228)

5. At what point in the visual system is the output from the two retinas melded together to form a single visual perception? (228)

   a. The binocular cells in this structure evidence ocular dominance. What does this mean? (228)

   b. Describe the receptive fields of a binocular cell in the visual cortex. (228)

   c. What is stereopsis? (229)

   d. Why does stereopsis occur? (229-230)

6. As I focus on my finger at arm's length in front of me, and then continue to focus on the finger as I move it to my nose, what do the eyes have to do to maintain my fixation? (230)

   a. What is this movement called? (230)

   b. If you now moved your finger back to its first location while maintaining your focus, an opposite set of movements would occur. What is this set of movements called? (230)

   c. What does the brain use to determine the distance from the eye to the object? (231)

   d. Explain the difference between near and far disparity. (231)

   e. What is stereo blindness? (232)

Read pages 232-246 and summary statements 19-25 on pages 248, then answer each of the following questions in this section.
---

1. At what level of the visual projection system is the trichromatic representation dropped in favor of three opponent processes? (232)

106

a. List and describe briefly the three types of opponent process cells. (232-233)

b. What are the characteristics of the color processing cells of the lateral geniculate? (233)

c. What are center-surround, double-opponent RF cells and where are they found? (233)

d. Describe the phenomenon of color constancy. (234)

2. Using the chemical [^{3}H] proline technique, Hubel et al. (1982) discovered what about the cytoarchitecture of V1? (235)

   a. Where are blobs found? (236)

   b. What are the characteristics of the blob cells? (236)

   c. What is the ice-cube model of Hubel et al. (1982)? (237)

   d. Describe the organization of the area V1 in terms of Hubel's ice-cube model. (237-238)

3. Where are end-stopped cells found in great abundance? (238)

   a. From where do these end-stopped cells receive their input? (238)

   b. What characteristics are unique to end-stopped cells? (238-239)

   c. These cells analyze what characteristic? (239)

4. D-cells serve what function? (239)

   a. Where are they located? (239)

   b. In the perception of motion, what two pieces of information must the visual system have? (239)

   c. There are two types of specialized D-cells. List and describe the function of each. (239-241)

   d. Where are each of these types of specialized D-cells located? (239, 241)

   e. Where does the information from the vestibular and visual senses come together according to Saito (1986)? (242)

5. Where in the parietal lobe is information about the form of the figure, its movements in and its location space with reference to the body brought together? (242)

   a. What are opponent vector cells and where are they found? (242)

   b. According to Motter and Mountcastle (1981), these cells are probably involved in what kind of visual perception? (242-243)

   c. Contraction-type opponent vector cells may have what other important function? (243)

6. What is the major problem with viewing the visual system in terms of pathways? (245-246)

PRE-EXAM QUIZ

Multiple-Choice
Select the choice that best completes the stem in each question and indicate your selection in the appropriate space to the left of the question.

_____ 1. By contracting or relaxing it can change the amount of light that is admitted to the inner chamber of the eye. The structure defined is the
   a. lens
   b. cornea
   c. pupil
   d. iris
   e. none of these

_____ 2. The eyeball is too long, which causes the image to focus in front of the retina. This condition is called
   a. myopia
   b. presbyopia
   c. astigmatism
   d. hyperopia
   e. none of these

_____ 3. The greatest concentration of cones in the eye is found in which of the following?
   a. the optic disc
   b. the front of the retina
   c. the back of the sclera
   d. the outer segment
   e. the fovea

_____ 4. The output cells of the retina are the
   a. amacrine
   b. rods and cones
   c. ganglion cells
   d. bipolar cells
   e. horizontal cells

_____ 5. Visual agnosia results from destruction to the
   a. retina
   b. Brodmann's area
   c. lateral geniculate nucleus
   d. inferotemporal cortex
   e. superior colliculus

6. Viewed from the classic model of vision of the 1960s the lateral geniculate nucleus was seen as
   a. one of several major pathways to the striate cortex
   b. a major analyzer of visual information from the retina
   c. an appendix to the visual projection system
   d. a structure that merely passes the image on to the cortex unchanged
   e. none of the above

7. The role of the pretectal area in vision has to do with
   a. location of objects in space and the visual orienting reflex
   b. processing of form information
   c. controlling the pupillary response to light and focusing of the lens
   d. regulation of diurnal rhythms based on light-dark cycles
   e. more than one of the above

8. In the detection of form, the retinal analyzer needs what kind of stimulus in its receptive field?
   a. a whole object
   b. a complex of lines
   c. at least one angle
   d. a part of an arc
   e. a shift from a light area to a dark area

9. The D cells, or field neurons, usually ignore figure but respond nicely to a background. They are found only in the
   a. inferotemporal cortex
   b. medial superior temporal cortex
   c. lateral geniculate nucleus
   d. V2
   e. medial temporal cortex

10. At what point in the processing of color information does the nervous system abandon the trichromatic representation proposed by the Young-Helmholtz theory?
    a. lateral geniculate nucleus
    b. V1
    c. retina
    d. V2
    e. none of the above

11. A V1 complex cortical neuron demands that if an edge is to be detected it must
    a. end at a particular point
    b. fall in a particular area of the cell's retinal field
    c. be in a particular angle of orientation
    d. more than one of the above
    e. none of the above

12. Desimone et al. (1984) discovered the existence of object-specific neurons in which of the following cortical areas of the macaque monkey?
    a. V3
    b. V1
    c. anterior inferotemporal cortex
    d. posterior inferotemporal cortex
    e. superior temporal sulcus

13. Blob cell output feeds into which of the following?
    a. interstripe cells
    b. interblob cells
    c. end-stopped cells
    d. thick stripes
    e. none of these

_____14. At present, which of the following is probably the best way of thinking about the visual system?
   a. as a single pathway leading from retina to striate cortex
   b. as multiple, parallel pathways
   c. as a network of interconnected analyzers
   d. our current knowledge of the visual system cannot be encompassed by any of the above
   e. none of the above

_____15. The connection between cortical areas 7a and the ventral inferior parietal cortex and the frontal eyefields explains how
   a. depth perception is accomplished
   b. a shift in conscious attention can direct eye movements to a new focus of attention
   c. information from all analyzers comes together to form a visual image
   d. movement in both the object and the retina can be brought together to produce motion perception
   e. none of these

True/False

_____ 1. The fovea is night blind.

_____ 2. A surface that absorbs all lightwaves would be a mirror surface.

_____ 3. The transduction process that occurs in the photoreceptor cell stops a current rather than initiating one.

_____ 4. According to the Young-Helmholtz theory of color vision, color perception is due to the fact that each different absorption pattern yields a different pattern of activity in the three cone types.

_____ 5. Another name for the inferotemporal cortex is the peristriate area.

_____ 6. The task of ambient vision is to maintain a low-level background of the world around the point in space to which you are directing the bulk of your attention.

_____ 7. The X-cells: the retinotectal pathway. The Y-cells: the geniculostriate pathway.

_____ 8. The important thalamic center for both the retinotectal path and the geniculostriate path to the cortex is the lateral geniculate cortex.

_____ 9. Damage to the frontal eye fields would mean that the determination of what objects in space our attention was drawn to would be handled reflexively.

_____10. Edge analyzers first appear in the cortex of the human.

_____11. The receptive field of the complex cortical cell is much smaller than that of the simple cortical cell.

_____12. Delayed match-to-nonsample studies using monkeys as subjects point to the anterior inferotemporal cortex as a visual memory center.

_____13. Stereoscopic depth vision is possible only if the eyes are positioned at the front of the head so that there is almost no overlap of the visual fields.

_____14. There is no stereopsis beyond 30 feet.

_____15. Layer 4 of V1 is the initial "receiving" area for input from the lateral geniculate area and as such does no processing.

6.1 absolute threshold (209)	6.6 ambient vision (218)
6.2 accommodation (201)	6.7 analyzer (210)
6.3 achromatic (209)	6.8 astigmatism (202)
6.4 acuity (208)	6.9 bipolar cells (202)
6.5 amacrine cells (202)	6.10 blob cells (236)

6.6

According to Trevarthan, that type of vision for perceiving "space at large around the body." Type of vision dependent on the retinotectal path.

6.7

A set of synaptic connections between a group of input neurons and a group of output neurons that is arranged to detect a particular feature in a stimulus input; same as processor.

6.8

A condition caused by tiny flat places on the cornea that produce small blurred areas in the image.

6.9

Retinal neurons that connect receptors to ganglion cells.

6.10

These cells are found in dark areas, called blobs, which are arranged in rows that run along the centers of the ocular dominance bands.

6.1

The least amount of a stimulus needed to obtain a response from a cell. It is reciprocally related to sensitivity.

6.2

A process by which the shape of the lens is changed to allow for focusing on near vs. far objects.

6.3

Lacking in color.

6.4

The degree of sharpness or clarity in vision.

6.5

Retinal cells that interconnect bipolar and ganglion cells.

Copyright 1990 by Wadsworth, Inc.

6.11

broad-band cell

(233)

6.12

center-surround receptive field

(211)

6.13

color constancy

(234)

6.14

color perception

(206)

6.15

complex cortical neuron

(224)

6.16

cones

(202)

6.17

contrast

(210)

6.18

convergence

(230)

6.19

cornea

(200)

6.20

cytochrome oxidase

(236)

6.16

Receptor cells located toward the back of the retina. They are the color receptors.

6.11

A type of retinal ganglion cell that responds to a wide range of wavelengths rather than being tuned to a particular region of the spectrum. Such cells are Y-cells.

6.17

The rate of change from one level of illumination to another as you move across the retina.

6.12

A receptive field that is arranged concentrically so that one of the two areas is a circle at the center of the receptive field, and the other is a ring completely surrounding the circle.

6.18

The movement of the eye that results in the eyes being rotated toward one another to keep the fixation.

6.13

The ability to perceive a stimulus as having an unchanging color despite changes in the intensity and wavelength of the stimulating light.

6.19

The transparent anterior portion of the sclera through which lightwaves reflected from the objects in the environment enter the eye. The rounded shape of this structure focuses the rays of the light as they pass through it.

6.14

The ability to discriminate between wavelengths.

6.20

A neuronal enzyme present in greatest abundance when the cell is active; used experimentally as a way of labeling active neurons.

6.15

Cortical cells found by Hubel and Wiesel in area 17 that detect the angle of orientation of the straight line.

Copyright 1990 by Wadsworth, Inc.

6.21

dark adaptation

(209)

6.22

D cell

(239)

6.23

dark current

(204)

6.24

delayed match-to-nonsample task

(225)

6.25

dual visual projection system

(217)

6.26

electromagnetic radiation

(199)

6.27

electromagnetic spectrum

(199)

6.28

end-stopped cell

(238)

6.29

face cell

(228)

6.30

far disparity

(231)

6.26

A form of wave energy.

6.21

A gradual increase in sensitivity produced by lowering the level of illumination.

6.27

An ordered arrangement of all the known forms of electromagnetic radiation, of which light is one small source.

6.22

Directionally selective motion detector neurons probably arranged in columns within MT.

6.28

Cells that are located in large numbers in V2. They have elongated receptive fields with an excitatory area in the middle and inhibitory zones at both ends. They are orientation selective and require that the contour not cross much of the inhibitory area if they are to respond.

6.23

The strong depolarizing current flowing into the outer segment of a receptor cell that is constantly depolarized in the dark.

6.29

Type of neuron in IT cortex that is selective for faces.

6.24

Discrimination learning problem in which the stimulus not previously presented must be chosen for reinforcement to occur.

6.30

Condition in which eyes focus on an object that is nearer, while light reflected from the faraway object falls on noncorresponding points of the retina. This produces a double image of the faraway object.

6.25

Viewpoint that sees the visual system as divided between the geniculostriate path and the retinotectal path.

Copyright 1990 by Wadsworth, Inc.

6.31

field neurons

(241)

6.32

figure

(239)

6.33

figure neurons

(241)

6.34

focal vision

(218)

6.35

fovea

(202)

6.36

frontal eye fields (FEF)

(219)

6.37

ganglion cells

(202)

6.38

geniculostriate path

(217)

6.39

ground

(239)

6.40

hand cell

(228)

6.36

Located in the frontal lobes, they direct eye movements. This allows the higher cognitive functions of the cortex to play a role in choosing the objects at which we direct our gaze.

6.37

Cells located near the front of the retina that receive input from bipolar and horizontal cells of the retina. They are the output neurons of the retina. Their axons gather together from all points in the retina and form the optic nerve.

6.38

That part of the dual visual projection system that extends from the lateral geniculate nucleus of the thalamus to the striate area of the cortex. This projection system according to Trevarthan is specialized for pattern and color vision.

6.39

That part of the image, other than the figure, to which you are not attending.

6.40

Type of neuron in IT cortex that is selective for faces.

6.31

A type of D cell that responds to the motion of the ground instead of the figure. Found in the MST.

6.32

The object on which you are fixating and to which your attention is directed.

6.33

Cells in the MT that respond to the motion of a figure relative to the ground.

6.34

According to Trevarthan, that type of vision that is used to analyze the fine spatial detail in small areas of the visual field. Type of vision that is dependent chiefly on the geniculostriate path.

6.35

A tiny area right at the center of the retina where the network of blood vessels parts. It is the retina area of greatest visual acuity.

Copyright 1990 by Wadsworth, Inc.

6.41

horizontal cells

(202)

6.42

[^{3}H] proline

(235)

6.43

hyperopia

(201)

6.44

ice-cube model

(237)

6.45

inferotemporal (IT) cortex

(214)

6.46

interblobs

(236)

6.47

interstripes

(239)

6.48

iris

(201)

6.49

landmark discrimination

(244)

6.50

lateral geniculate nucleus (LGN)

(214)

6.46

V1 areas within ocular dominance columns but outside of blobs. They contain cells that are selective for particular line orientations but not for color.

6.41

Retinal cells that interconnect rod, cones, and bipolar cells.

6.47

Areas of V2 into which V1 interblob regions project. This area contains most of the V2 end-stopped cells and analyzes for shape.

6.42

Tritiated proline. A radioactive chemical used in anterograde tracing of pathways.

6.48

The ring of muscle that, by contracting or relaxing, can control the size of the pupil and thereby the amount of light that may pass to the inner chamber of the eye.

6.43

Referred to as "far-sightedness," it is a condition in which the eyeball is too short and image blurring occurs because the focal point is behind the receptors.

6.49

A learning task in which a monkey must choose a stimulus closest to a "landmark" object. Tests for spatial vision.

6.44

Hubel and Wiesel's early theory of how the blobs, ocular dominance columns, and layers of V1 are arranged.

6.50

The thalamic nucleus in which the optic tract terminates.

6.45

Lower portion of the temporal lobe that receives input from the prestriate cortex. The posterior inferotemporal cortex has been shown to be important for the ability to discriminate between objects on the basis of some vital dimension such as pattern, shape, size, brightness, and color.

Copyright 1990 by Wadsworth, Inc.

6.51

lens

(201)

6.52

light adaptation

(209)

6.53

line-orientation analyzers

(222)

6.54

local currents

(202)

6.55

magnocellular layers

(219)

6.56

medial superior temporal area (MST)

(239)

6.57

middle temporal area of the cortex (MT)

(239)

6.58

multiple parallel processing pathways

(219)

6.59

myopia

(201)

6.60

nanometer

(206)

6.56

This area contains the analyzers for the visual perception of motion.

6.57

The area of the cortex at the parietal-occipital boundary that contains analyzers for motion.

6.58

The idea that the visual system consists of a collection of pathways from the retina, each leading through a different chain of processors set to detect different features.

6.59

Referred to as "short-sightedness" or "near-sightedness" it is a condition in which the eyeball grows too long and the focus always falls short of the receptors, causing a blurred image.

6.60

Units employed to measure wavelength. Each unit is one-billionth of a meter.

6.51

A transparent crystalline structure that plays a role in the focusing of the light rays.

6.52

A rapid increase in sensitivity produced by increasing the level of illumination.

6.53

Neural connections in V1 that respond selectively to a line oriented at a particular angle.

6.54

Currents similar to EPSPs that are found in receptor cells and retinal bipolars. It is the same as graded potentials.

6.55

The more ventral layers of the lateral geniculate nucleus that contain the large neurons. The Y-cells terminate in these layers.

Copyright 1990 by Wadsworth, Inc.

6.61

near disparity

(231)

6.62

object vision pathway

(221)

6.63

ocular dominance

(228)

6.64

ocular dominance bands

(228)

6.65

opponent processes

(232)

6.66

opponent vector cells

(242)

6.67

opsin

(206)

6.68

optic disc

(202)

6.69

optic nerve

(204)

6.70

orientation columns

(235)

6.66

Motion detectors found in area 7a. The best response for one type of neuron, the expansion type, occurs when contours in the image move outward from the fovea to the periphery; the best response for the other, the contraction type, is the opposite direction of movement.

6.67

The photochemical found in the cones. There are three different types of opsin, and each opsin is sensitive to a different part of the spectrum.

6.68

The point on the retina where the blood vessels of the retina gather together and penetrate the eyeball. This area has no receptors and therefore constitutes a region of blindness called the blind spot.

6.69

Cranial nerve II. It is formed by the axons of the retinal ganglion cells and synapses on the cell bodies of the thalamus and superior colliculi.

6.70

An area of V1 cortex that cuts across the layers from white matter to cortical surface. Each column contains only those simple cortical cells having one particular orientation preference.

Copyright 1990 by Wadsworth, Inc.

6.61

Condition in which the eye focuses on an object that is farther away and light reflected from the nearer object falls on noncorresponding points of the retina. This produces a double image of the nearer object.

6.62

One of Mishkin's two major visual pathways. It leads from the lateral geniculate nucleus through V1, V2, V3, V4, and posterior inferotemporal cortex to anterior inferotemporal cortex. This series of analyzers extracts information about color and form.

6.63

The degree to which a binocular cell is more strongly connected to one or the other eye.

6.64

Alternating bands of cells on the V1 cortex that have been shown to extend from the cortical surface to its depths. The neurons dominated by one eye are arranged in bands that alternate with stripes for the other eye.

6.65

A recording of color information at the retinal ganglion cell level. There are three such processes, each represented by a separate retinal ganglion cell: a red-green cell, a blue-yellow cell, and a broad-band cell.

6.71

outer segment

(204)

6.72

output neurons

(203)

6.73

parvocellular layers

(219)

6.74

peripheral retina

(207)

6.75

peristriate cortex

(214)

6.76

photochemicals

(204)

6.77

photon

(199)

6.78

pigment epithelium

(203)

6.79

polysensory analysis

(242)

6.80

pulvinar

(219)

6.76

Chemicals that react to light.

6.77

The smallest quantity of light possible.

6.78

A layer at the back of the retina next to the sclera that has a very rich blood supply that serves the rods and cones.

6.79

Function carried out by cells that receive input from more than one sense system and act to integrate the two streams of information. One example of this is the posterior parietal region, which receives information about the form of the figure, its movements, and its location in space with reference to the body.

6.80

A key structure in the collicular pathway, this thalamic nucleus receives visual information from the retina and sends visual location information to the frontal eye fields, to the inferotemporal cortex, and to areas 17 and 18.

Copyright 1990 by Wadsworth, Inc.

6.71

That part of the receptor cell that contains the photochemicals.

6.72

The type of neuron in a neural structure such as the retina whose axons carry the processed information to other structures of the nervous system.

6.73

The more dorsal layers of the lateral geniculate nucleus that contain small neurons. The X-cells terminate in these layers.

6.74

The portion of the retina around the edges that receives light from objects around the borders of the visual field.

6.75

Areas 18 and 19.

6.81

pupil

(201)

6.82

receptive field (RF)

(208)

6.83

retina

(202)

6.84

retinal disparity

(231)

6.85

retinotectal path (tectopulvinar)

(217)

6.86

rhodopsin

(204)

6.87

rods

(202)

6.88

sclera

(200)

6.89

sensitivity

(209)

6.90

simple cortical neuron

(223)

6.86

The photochemical found in the rods. It is so sensitive to electromagnetic radiation that a single photon is enough to trigger the release of its energy.

6.87

Receptor cells that are very sensitive to light but do not provide clear, distinct images; not found in the fovea.

6.88

A tough, membranous sac that encloses the eyeball.

6.89

The ability to respond to weak stimuli.

6.90

Cortical cells found by Hubel and Wiesel in area 17 that are analyzers for linear edges in a particular orientation and at particular places within the visual field.

Copyright 1990 by Wadsworth, Inc.

6.81

A hole, formed by a ring of muscles, through which light must pass in order to reach the light-receptive field cells.

6.82

The area of the retina within which light will trigger activity in a neuron is that neuron's receptive field.

6.83

A receptor/processor organ that covers the inside of the eyeball like a cup. Covering the surface of the retina is an extensive network of branching and rebranching blood vessels.

6.84

The difference in the location of the image on the two retinas. The brain uses this disparity to calculate the distance from the eye to the object.

6.85

That part of the dual vision projection system that extends from the retina to the superior colliculus. This projection system, according to Trevarthan, is specialized for locating objects in visual space and orienting the body toward them.

6.91

spatial attention mechanism

(244)

6.92

spatial vision pathway

(221)

6.93

stereo blindness

(232)

6.94

stereopsis

(229)

6.95

tectopulvinar pathway

(219)

6.96

thick stripes

(239)

6.97

thin stripes

(239)

6.98

transduction

(202)

6.99

transposition

(224)

6.100

tuned disparity neuron

(232)

6.96

Area of V2 into which cells from layer 4 of V1 project. These areas contain cells that analyze for orientation, movement, and degrees of retinal disparity.

6.97

Areas of V2 into which blob regions project. Cells in this area analyze for color.

6.98

The process of converting information from one energy form to another.

6.99

The visual capability to recognize a stimulus no matter where it occurs on the retina.

6.100

Visual cortex neuron with connections that enable it to respond selectively to a particular amount of near or far disparity. It is a part of the analyzers for depth.

Copyright 1990 by Wadsworth, Inc.

6.91

The ability to direct visual analyzer activity to focus on one or another part of the visual field.

6.92

One of Mishkin's visual pathway. This pathway ends in the parietal lobe. The route may begin in the superior colliculus through the pulvinar to V2, V3, MT, MST, and 7a. V1 would also provide information for other cortical areas. This set of analyzers extracts information about location in space and stimulus movement in space.

6.93

A visual defect in which persons have an inability to construct a three-dimensional image of their visual world. They are not completely without depth perception, but they do evidence some stereopsis peculiarities.

6.94

A three-dimensional vision. It arises from the fact that the two retinal images are not exactly alike.

6.95

The path from the superior colliculus neurons to the pulvinar.

6.101 V1 (220)

6.102 V2 (220)

6.103 V3 (220)

6.104 V4 (220)

6.105 ventral inferior parietal area (VIP) (242)

6.106 visible spectrum (199)

6.107 visual agnosia (214)

6.108 visual projection system (214)

6.109 X-cells (218)

6.110 Y-cells (218)

6.106

That diminutive section of the electromagnetic spectrum lying between the much larger sections of ultraviolet and infrared. This part of the spectrum contains all the wavelengths from violet to red and constitutes the only fragment of electromagnetic radiation capable of being sensed by the eyes.

6.107

Symptom of brain damage in which objects can be seen but not understood.

6.108

The route that visual information takes from the retina to the visual cortex.

6.109

A type of retinal ganglion cell that has the smaller receptive field and that is found in or near the center of the retina. These cells apparently are sensitive to the fine pattern details of the visual image.

6.110

A type of retinal ganglion cell that has a larger receptive field than that of X-cells; these receptive fields are located away from the center of the retina. These cells are best equipped to sense the larger, broader outlines of form.

Copyright 1990 by Wadsworth, Inc.

6.101

Occipital cortical area in which axons of LGN output cells terminate. It is also called area 17.

6.102

Area 18. It is part of the peristriate visual cortex in the occipital lobe.

6.103

This is part of area 19 in the visual cortex.

6.104

This is part of area 19 in the visual cortex.

6.105

This, together with area 7a makes up the polysensory analyzer area.

6.111

Young-Helmholtz theory

(207)

6.111

Explanation of the role of short-, medium-, and long-wavelength cones in color perception.

Copyright 1990 by Wadsworth, Inc.

CHAPTER SEVEN
AUDITORY AND CHEMICAL SENSES

READ-WRITE-REVIEW

Read pages 254-262 and summary statements 1-5 on page 293, then answer each of the following questions in this section.

---

1. What is meant by the term "audition"? (254)

    a. What is the physical stimulus for hearing? (255)

    Identify each of the components of a sound wave described below.

    b. The molecules of air are packed together to form this area of high pressure. (256)

    c. The physical characteristic most closely associated with the psychological characteristic of loudness. (256-257)

    d. A phase of partial vacuum with only a few molecules of air. (256)

    e. The physical characteristic most closely associated with the psychological characteristic of pitch. (256-257)

2. Identify each of the structures of the human ear described below.

    a. The flexible membrane that serves as the entrance of the inner ear. (257-258)

    b. Funnels the sound waves toward the tympanic membrane. (257)

    c. Contains the receptors for the vestibular system. (257-258)

    d. The middle ear bone that vibrates in response to the vibrations of the tympanic membrane. (257-258)

    e. Contains the hair cells on the organ of Corti. (259-261)

    f. Makeup of fibers that synapse on the hair cells. (257, 259, 261)

    g. An opening in the cochlea that allows the basilar membrane to vibrate. It moves in opposition to (a). (257, 259, 261)

    h. One of the middle ear bones, it is attached to the flexible membrane that serves as an entrance to the inner ear. (257-258, 261)

3. What are the two sources of amplification in the middle ear? (258)

4. Locate the auditory receptor cells in the cochlea. (259)

a. These hair cells synapse with fibers from what major nerve? (259)

   b. Where are the somas of these fibers located? (259)

   c. What are the three "tunnels" that make up the cochlea? (259)

5. Explain what happens when the compression phase reaches the cochlea. (259)

   a. What happens when the rarefaction phase of the sound wave reaches the cochlea? (259)

   b. How are the stereocilia stimulated to generate the electrical current from the sound stimuli? (259-260, 262)

   c. One theory of how this change in the cilia could result in the triggering of a current involves a movement of ions across the membrane of the hair cell. Discuss the particulars of this theory. (262)

Read pages 262-269 and summary statements 6-9 on pages 293-394, then answer each of the following questions in this section.
---

1. According to the frequency theory how is sound wave frequency coded into a pattern of neural activity? (262-263)

   a. According to the frequency theory, how is intensity encoded? (263)

   b. What is the major problem with the frequency theory? (263)

   c. Weaver (1949) attempted to explain the discrepancy between the range of frequencies that could be accounted for by the frequency theory and the evidence that suggests that the cochlear nerve as a whole can follow frequencies at least up to 3000 Hz. What is this explanation called? (263)

   d. What is his explanation for this discrepancy? (263-264)

2. Describe the basic idea behind the place theory. (264)

   a. What phenomenon is used to explain how the basilar membrane is able to change its place of maximal flexion each time the frequency changes? (264-265)

   b. The correlation between frequency and maximum displacement is due to several factors. Which is the most important? (265)

   c. Demonstrate how this works with a high-frequency tone and then with a low-frequency tone. (265)

d. Why is it necessary for the place theory to make an assumption about maximum displacement and the number of hair cells stimulated? (265)

3. Common sense tells us that the traveling wave, of place theory stimulates a great number of neurons as it travels up the cochlea; however, experience tells us that our auditory system allows us to achieve very fine tone discriminations. Research designed to determine the tuning curves of cochlear nerve fibers has also contributed some information. What is a tuning curve? (266)

   a. Based on these studies of traveling waves and tuning curves, where within the range of frequencies does the greatest frequency specificity with respect to place theory occur? (267)

   b. Describe briefly how our hearing system is arranged in terms of frequency and place theory. (267)

4. It appears that the basilar membrane may be able to vibrate itself thus doing something to increase the sharpness of the traveling wave peak. What are the sounds generated by this activity called? (267)

   a. This process depends on what structures? (267-268)

   b. What is the hypothesized activity of these structures? (267-268)

Read pages 269-274 and summary statements 10-14 on page 294, then answer each of the following questions in this section.
---

1. Identify the branch of the cranial nerve and the name and number of the cranial nerve that carries frequency and intensity information of auditory stimuli from the receptor cells to the brain. (269)

2. Identify each of the components of the auditory projection system described below.

   a. Uses both interaural time and intensity differences to help localize sounds in space. (269-271)

   b. Collects the auditory frequency and localization information from the nuclei below, combines it, and provides a spatial map that gives each frequency in the sound stimulus a spatial location. (270, 272)

   c. Carries the auditory information from the cochlear nucleus to the inferior colliculus. (270)

   d. This group of cell bodies is responsible for unleashing the whole-body reaction called the auditory startle reflex. (270-272)

3. Identify the two parts of the superior olivary complex. (269)

   a. Suppose a low-frequency, auditory stimulus is presented on your left side, 45 degrees from midline. What would be heard at the right and left ear? (270)

139

b. What is the difference between what is heard at the right and left ear called? (270)

c. Which part of the olivary complex responds to this type of difference? (270)

d. What is the limitation of this phase difference cue in sound localization? (270)

e. What other feature of auditory stimuli can the system use to localize sound in space? (271)

f. What is sound shadow? (271)

g. Sound intensity differences input is received by which part of the superior olivary nucleus? (271)

h. How does this part of the superior nuclei respond to a stimulus presented to the left side? At the midline? On the right side? (271)

4. You are sitting on the front porch of your girlfriend's house engaged in some heavy kissing, etc., when out of the darkness of the night you hear the deep wheezing cough of her father. Trace the pathway taken by the neural impulses from cranial nerve VIII to the point where you leap to your feet and begin running. (272)

5. Although the results of lesioning studies have been somewhat disappointing, microelectrode studies have given us some insight into the role of the inferior colliculus. According to these findings what is that role? (272)

a. Output of the inferior colliculus goes where? (272)

b. What is the role of the superior colliculi in regard to orientation to sound? (272)

6. To what specific nucleus of the thalamus do the brain-stem auditory pathways project? (273)

a. Describe the connection between this nucleus and the cortical projection center. (273)

b. Besides serving as a simple relay station for the auditory system, this nucleus probably serves a second function. What is it? (273)

7. In which lobe of the cortex do we find the highest levels of auditory analysis? (273)

a. Within this lobe you'll find AI. What is AI and where exactly is it located? (273)

b. Where is AII and from where does it receive its input? (273)

c. In addition to AI and AII there are other auditory zones. Where are these zones located and from where do they receive their input? (273)

d. What role do these cortical structures play in the analysis of pitch or loudness? (273)

e. Lesioning of the AI cortex in the cat and lesioning of the AI cortex in the human produce far different results. What is the significance of this finding? (273)

Read pages 274-279 and summary statements 15-16 on page 294, then answer each of the following questions in this section.
---

1. What are the two general types of hearing impairment? (275)

    a. Conductive loss is a defect of what part in the auditory system? (275)

    b. In middle age a common source of conductive loss is what? (275)

    c. What causes this condition? (275)

    d. If loss is due to damage in the cochlea or nervous system, what is it called? (275)

    e. Since you were 16 you have wanted a very fine, very expensive high-fidelity sound system but until your 55th birthday you simply could not afford it. Why would I be right in telling you that it is too late in your life to buy your dream set? (275)

    f. What is the apparent function of the tensor tympani and where is it located? (277)

    g. What is tinnitus? (277)

2. What is an audiometer used for? (277)

    a. Briefly explain how this instrument is employed. (277)

    b. In testing for hearing loss as a result of damage to the auditory projection system what is generally used and why? (277)

    c. More recently audiology has been successful in borrowing what technique from electrophysiological research? (277)

    d. In using this procedure an EEG electrode is attached to the skull just over the temporal cortex, and a click is played into the subject's ear. The large wave that is recorded just after the click is presented represents what? (277)

e. What is this wave called? (277)

f. Why do we not see any further waves unless the averaging procedure is used? (277)

3. For what kind or kinds of hearing loss does the hearing aid offer some relief? (278)

   a. What are some of the limitations of this device? (279)

   b. For what reason is the hearing prosthesis being developed? (279)

Read pages 279-286 and summary statements 17-20 on pages 294-295, then answer each of the following questions in this section.
---

1. What are the two major chemical senses? (279)

   a. At what point in evolution did these chemical senses differentiate? (280)

   b. In fish, why were the chemical receptors scattered over the skin not well suited for detecting airborne particles? (280)

2. Where are most taste receptors found? (280)

   a. Describe precisely how these taste receptors are organized. (280)

   b. What is necessary for a molecule to stimulate one of these receptors? (280)

   c. What is the average life span of a taste receptor? (281)

   d. What is the effect of age on the sense of taste? (281)

   e. Describe the structure of the taste receptor cell. (281)

   f. These taste receptors are contacted by fibers from what three cranial nerves (name and number)? (281)

   g. Fibers from those cranial nerves finally synapse where? (281)

   h. This nucleus is found where in the brain stem? (281)

   i. This nucleus receives information from where else in the body? (281)

   j. The response of neurons in this nucleus to taste stimuli is affected by what two factors? (281)

   k. The output of this nucleus is sent to the _____ or to the _____ via the _____. (281)

   l. Other output of this nucleus goes to the _____, which is part of the _____. It is probably here that the decision of whether to approach or avoid a tasted substance is made. (281)

142

3. According to Henning (1916) there are four primary taste qualities. Name them. (281)

   a. Which of the primary taste qualities seems to be linked to acids? (281)

   b. Which of the taste qualities seems to be produced by alkalines? (281)

   c. Which of the primary taste qualities is associated with compounds that ionize but do not produce hydrogen or hydroxyl molecules? (281)

4. What is proposed by the lateral-line theory of taste coding? (283)

5. What is proposed by the across-fiber pattern theory? (283)

   a. Studies measuring electrical activity of nerve fibers carrying information from taste receptors to the brain have made use of what branch of what cranial nerve? (283)

   b. Why was this branch used? (283)

   c. The results of such studies tend to support which of the theories of taste coding? (283)

   d. The fact that the tongue varies in its sensitivities to the primaries as you move the stimulus across it supports which of the theories of taste coding? (283)

   e. Recordings of electrical activity in the nucleus solitarius offer problems for which of the theories of taste coding? Why? (285)

   f. A taste suppressant such as potassium gymnemate suppresses a single primary taste rather than a whole group of tastes. Such a finding offers difficulty for which taste-coding theory? (285)

6. Keverne (1978) has offered a third possible explanation for taste coding. Describe his approach to the problem. (285)

   a. What is this theory called? (285)

   b. Specifically, what are some of the problems with which Keverne's theory has yet to deal? (286)

Read pages 286-293 and summary statements 21-26 on page 295, then answer each of the following questions in this section.

---

1. To be an olfactory stimulus a substance must meet what two conditions? (286)

   a. What is a flavor? (286)

b. Why are the smell and taste of food so often confused? (286)

2. Where are the olfactory receptor cells located? (286)

   a. What other kinds of cells are also located here and why are they necessary to olfaction? (286)

   b. How do the impulses set up by the activity of the olfactory cells get to the brain? (286-287)

   c. Where in the brain do the fibers of this nerve (from 8b) finally synapse? (287)

   d. One plausible explanation of olfactory transduction is called the lock-and-key theory. Using this theory, explain how chemical information can be transformed into nerve impulse patterns. (288)

   e. Amoore and colleagues (1964) employing a variation of the lock-and-key theory, proposed that there are only a handful of different receptor site types and that each molecule fits best in only one type of site. What conclusions concerning odors did this theory lead to? (289)

   f. What problems are there concerning a labeled-line theory of olfaction? (289)

3. What area is probably the olfactory cortex? (289)

   a. Why? (289)

   b. In terms of evolution, the olfactory system shows a unique progression from lower vertebrates to primates. What is it? (289)

   c. What is the function of the accessory olfactory system? (290)

4. What are pheromones? (290)

   a. What is an attractant? (290)

   b. What is a primer? (290-291)

   c. Describe the mechanism called pregnancy block. (291)

   d. What is the purpose of the pregnancy block? (291)

   e. What is copulin and what is its proposed function? (292)

PRE-EXAM QUIZ

Multiple-Choice
Select the choice that best completes the stem in each question and indicate your selection in the appropriate space to the left of the question.

_____ 1. At what point in evolution did animals develop two separate chemical senses?
a. with the development of the worm
b. when animals began to spend much of their time in the air
c. when animals moved out of the water and onto the land
d. with the development of human beings
e. none of the above

_____ 2. The response of neurons in the nucleus of tractus solitarius to taste stimuli is influenced by which of the following?
a. the level of the somatotrophic hormone in the blood
b. the blood sugar level
c. the basal metabolic level
d. how full the stomach is
e. more than one of the above

_____ 3. What is the brain-stem structure that puts together incoming information on the frequency and intensity and time differences of an auditory stimulus to provide the organism with the ability to locate the source of sound that is heard?
a. superior olivary complex   d. inferior colliculi
b. superior colliculus   e. thalamus
c. hypothalamus

_____ 4. A common middle-age hearing loss brought about by the calcification of the oval window with complete elimination of stirrup movement is
a. osteophoresis   d. tinnitus
b. otosclerosis   e. none of the above
c. otoporesis

_____ 5. To determine what pitch will be heard, place detection and frequency following work together within which of the following frequency ranges?
a. 20 Hz - 100 Hz   d. 10,000 Hz - 20,000 Hz
b. 100 Hz - 4000 Hz   e. none of the above
c. 4000 Hz - 10,000 Hz

_____ 6. Whether a tasted substance should be avoided as dangerous or sought after as "good tasting" is decided by which of the following?
a. gustatory cortex   d. amygdala
b. thalamus   e. taste buds
c. nucleus of tractus solitarius

_____ 7. Anatomically, taste receptors most closely resemble
a. skin cells   d. visual receptor cells
b. muscle cells   e. none of the above
c. olfactory receptor cells

_____ 8. The psychological correlate of the physical dimension of frequency of a sound wave is
a. intensity   d. loudness
b. timbre   e. none of these
c. pitch

_____ 9. This theory of gustatory coding proposes the existence of four primary tastes, each with its own type of receptor cells and cranial nerve fiber. It is the
    a. dual-processing theory
    b. lock-and-key theory
    c. labeled-line theory
    d. across-fiber pattern theory
    e. place theory

_____ 10. The round window moves in and out in opposition to movements of the
    a. basilar membrane
    b. Reissner's membrane
    c. tympanic membrane
    d. organ of Corti
    e. round window

_____ 11. The actual conversion of sound waves to electric current takes place in the hair cells, which are located on the
    a. basilar membrane
    b. organ of Corti
    c. vestibular membrane
    d. tectorial membrane
    e. cochlear membrane

_____ 12. The ventriloquist relies on which of the following findings concerning sensory processing to make the act work?
    a. the basilar membrane is a self-tuning mechanism
    b. interaural phase difference information dominates over interaural time difference information in the processing of sound localization cues
    c. sound localization is processed solely at a subcortical level
    d. the visual system, because of its greater proficiency for localizing stimuli in space, tends to overwhelm data from other senses
    e. none of the above

_____ 13. Which of the following is a problem for those who argue for the labeled-line theory of gustatory coding?
    a. taste suppressant substances seem to eliminate a single primary taste rather than affecting a whole group of tastes
    b. the sensitivity variation across the surface of the tongue is sizable only for the sweet and the bitter
    c. a rat without appropriate gustatory neocortex cannot remember previously learned taste aversions
    d. cells of the solitary nucleus are not very specific to a single primary taste quality
    e. more than one of the above

_____ 14. Compounds that ionize but do not produce hydrogen or hydroxyl ions taste
    a. salty
    b. spicy
    c. sour
    d. bitter
    e. sweet

_____ 15. The stereocilia are attached at their tips to the
    a. organ of Corti
    b. tectorial membrane
    c. basilar membrane
    d. Reissner's membrane
    e. tympanic membrane

True/False

_____ 1. Despite the fact that there are only a limited number of taste receptor cells and that each receptor cell has a life span of only 10 days, research has demonstrated that age has little or no effect on gustatory sensitivity.

_____ 2. The fact that some acids taste sweet and thousands of organic compounds taste anything but sweet has made it clear to some researchers that primary taste qualities will not be very useful in attempting to understand the sense of taste.

_____ 3. The middle ear is an air-filled cavity.

_____ 4. The lateral line is a system of receptors that sense chemical stimuli in the environment of the fish.

_____ 5. Among the several functions of the middle ear, perhaps the most important is that of amplifying the sound wave.

_____ 6. All auditory fibers leaving the inferior colliculus travel directly to the thalamus where they synapse on cell bodies in the medial geniculate nucleus.

_____ 7. None of the auditory cortical analyzers seems to have anything to do with pitch or loudness perception.

_____ 8. Contrary to what is commonly believed, the type of temporary hearing loss experienced by many hard-rock musicians does not have the potential to produce any permanent sensorineural loss.

_____ 9. Interaural intensity differences are used in the localization of low-frequency sounds, whereas interaural time differences are used in the localization of high-frequency sounds.

_____10. Primer pheromones are usually secreted by the female for the purpose of luring and guiding the mate.

_____11. Conscious experience of taste is probably dependent on the gustatory cortex.

_____12. The hammer is the middle ear bone that is connected to the oval window of the inner ear.

_____13. Tinnitus is an inflammation of the vestibulocochlear nerve.

_____14. The four primary taste qualities are sweet, sour, salty, and spicy.

_____15. The loudness of an auditory stimulus is coded in terms of the number of fibers that fire in response to the stimulus.

7.1 accessory olfactory bulb (289-290)	7.6 area AII (273)
7.2 across-fiber theory (283)	7.7 attractant (290)
7.3 amplitude (256)	7.8 audiometer (277)
7.4 amygdala (289)	7.9 audition (254)
7.5 anvil (258)	7.10 auditory projection system (269)

7.6

A secondary auditory zone found on the lip of the lateral fissure. It receives auditory information from a portion of the medial geniculate body that differs from the portion that projects to AI.

7.7

A pheromone that is usually secreted by the female for the purpose of luring and guiding the male.

7.8

An instrument employed to assess middle-ear and cochlear impairment by presenting pure tones at graded intensities up and down the frequency scale.

7.9

The sense of hearing.

7.10

The entire hierarchy of sound system analyzers from the cochlea to cortex.

7.1

Part of the sub-primate olfactory system, it receives input from the vomeronasal organ which projects to the rest of the brain through the accessory olfactory system.

7.2

Gustatory coding theory that contends that there are no primary taste qualities and that each separate chemical stimulus is coded into a different pattern of active fibers.

7.3

The amount of pressure change between the point of greatest compression and the point of greatest rarefaction. Graphically shown by the height of the wave.

7.4

Part of the olfactory system, it receives fibers from the olfactory tract and in turn sends fibers to the hypothalamus.

7.5

The middle of the three tiny bones of the middle ear. It is set in vibration by the hammer and in turn it sets the stirrup in vibration.

Copyright 1990 by Wadsworth, Inc.

7.11

auditory startle reflex

(272)

7.12

auricle

(257)

7.13

basilar membrane

(259)

7.14

chorda tympani

(283)

7.15

cochlea

(258)

7.16

cochlear duct

(259)

7.17

cochlear emissions

(267)

7.18

cochlear nuclei

(269)

7.19

compression phase

(255)

7.20

conductive loss

(275)

7.16

The middle canal that runs through the cochlea. It contains the auditory receptor cells.

7.17

Tiny sounds thought to be generated by the same process that allows the basilar membrane to sharpen the traveling waves.

7.18

Nuclei in the medulla that receives auditory information from the cochlear nerve.

7.19

The high-pressure phase of a sound wave in which the air molecules have been compressed.

7.20

Auditory sensitivity loss that can be traced to middle-ear damage.

7.11

The whole-body reaction to a novel, intense, or unexpected auditory stimulus.

7.12

Part of the outer ear that is built to collect the sound waves.

7.13

The piece of elastic tissue that forms the base of the cochlear duct and on which is located the organ of Corti.

7.14

One branch of cranial nerve VII that runs across the face of the tympanic membrane thus making it relatively easy to position electrodes.

7.15

That part of the inner ear that in form resembles a snail shell. It contains the receptors for audition.

Copyright 1990 by Wadsworth, Inc.

7.21 cranial nerve VIII (269)	7.26 flavor (286)
7.22 cycle (256)	7.27 frequency (256)
7.23 decibel (257)	7.28 frequency following (263)
7.24 dual-processing theory (285)	7.29 frequency theory (262-263)
7.25 evoked potential (277)	7.30 gustatory cortex (281)

7.26

A compound stimulus consisting of both tastes and odors.

7.27

The number of waves generated per second. It is measured in units called hertz.

7.28

The case where the number of times a neuron fires per second (frequency) follows the frequency of the sound wave.

7.29

Auditory theory that contends that nerve cells carry the sound-wave frequency information through the nervous system in the form of nerve-impulse frequency.

7.30

A part of the face of the parietal somatosensory cortex that forms the "ceiling" of the lateral fissure. It is probably necessary for your conscious experience of tastes.

Copyright 1990 by Wadsworth, Inc.

7.21

Also called the vestibulocochlear nerve, it carries the raw frequency and intensity information generated by the cochlea to the brain.

7.22

Part of a sound wave that begins at the point where the air pressure first increases above normal and then dips below normal.

7.23

The measurement unit of amplitude.

7.24

A gustatory coding theory that suggests that the subcortical areas of pons, hypothalamus, and amygdala use the input as labeled lines, the neocortex as a across-fiber patterns.

7.25

A large wave occurring in an EEG record when EEG electrodes are placed on the skull over the auditory cortex and a click is presented to the ear. This wave represents the voltage changes occurring in the cortex as the burst of impulses enters it from the medial geniculate nucleus of the thalamus.

7.31

hair cells

(259)

7.32

hammer

(258)

7.33

hearing prosthesis

(279)

7.34

helicotrema

(259)

7.35

hertz (Hz)

(256)

7.36

Heschl's gyrus (A1)

(273)

7.37

incentive

(291)

7.38

inferior colliculus

(272)

7.39

inner ear

(258)

7.40

intensity

(256)

7.36

The anterior portion of the floor of the lateral fissure. It is the primary cortical area that receives auditory information from the thalamus. It is also referred to as A1.

7.37

Stimulus which has acquired positive motivational properties.

7.38

A midbrain structure that combines the frequency information from the cochlear nuclei and the time and intensity difference information from the superior olives to produce a spatial map that gives each frequency in the sound stimulus a spatial location.

7.39

A complex of chambers and tunnels through the bone of the skull. It contains the vestibular organs and the cochlea.

7.40

Often substituted for amplitude when discussing sound waves as psychological stimuli.

Copyright 1990 by Wadsworth, Inc.

7.31

Receptor cells located on the organ of Corti. The actual conversion of sound waves to electrical currents takes place in these cells.

7.32

The first of three tiny bones in the middle ear, it is set in vibration by the movement of the tympanic membrane.

7.33

An artificial part which replaces a lost organ or its function for patients with complete hearing loss due to cochlear damage. Such parts are currently in the research phase of development.

7.34

A small opening at the tip of the cochlea where the vestibular canal and tympanic canal join together.

7.35

Units of measurement for frequency of sound waves.

7.41

interaural intensity differences

(271)

7.42

interaural time differences

(269-270)

7.43

labeled-line theory

(283)

7.44

lock-and-key theory

(288)

7.45

loudness

(257)

7.46

medial geniculate body

(273)

7.47

middle ear

(258)

7.48

nucleus of tractus solitarius

(281)

7.49

odorant

(286)

7.50

olfactory bulb

(287)

7.46

The thalamic nucleus that is part of the auditory projection system. It relays auditory information to the appropriate cortical center.

7.47

Air filled cavity which begins with the tympanic membrane and contains three tiny bones; the hammer, anvil, and stirrup. Its major function is to amplify sound.

7.48

Cluster of cell bodies found in the medulla and pons where all three cranial nerves (VII, IX and X) synapse. It also receives input from the liver and digestive tract.

7.49

Any substance that serves as an olfactory stimulus.

7.50

Part of the olfactory projection system located near the bottom of the skull. The fibers of the olfactory nerve synapse here.

7.41

A cue used by the auditory system to locate a sound stimulus source. It is employed with higher sound frequencies. It results from the effects of distance and the sound shadow of the ear opposite the source on the intensity of the sound wave when it reaches the two ears.

7.42

A cue used by the auditory system to locate a sound stimulus source. It is a phase difference that arises because the waves take a little longer to get to the far ear.

7.43

Theory of gustatory coding that proposes that there are four primary tastes, each with its own type of receptor taste cell and cranial nerve fiber.

7.44

A theory of olfactory transduction that holds that the odorant molecule stimulates the cillium of a receptor cell by fitting into an olfactory receptor site. This triggers reactions in the cell that open ion channel gates and initiate an EPSP.

7.45

The psychological sensation that is best correlated with the physical dimension of sound wave amplitude.

Copyright 1990 by Wadsworth, Inc.

7.51 olfactory epithelium	7.56 otosclerosis
(286)	(275)
7.52 olfactory nerve	7.57 outer ear
(286)	(257)
7.53 olfactory transduction	7.58 outer hair cells
(288)	(267-268)
7.54 orbitofrontal cortex	7.59 oval window
(289)	(258)
7.55 organ of Corti	7.60 papillae
(259)	(280)

7.56

A middle-age condition that results in a conductive hearing loss due to a calcification of the oval window with complete elimination of stirrup movement.

7.57

That division of ear that includes the auricle and the external auditory canal.

7.58

Hair cells of the organ of Corti that synapse on the efferent fibers of the auditory nerve. It is suggested that the information entering the auditory nerve from these hair cells has to do with the state of the organ of Corti. This might allow the brain to adjust the tension of the basilar membrane to bias it in favor of different frequencies at different times.

7.59

The flexible membrane that is the entrance to the inner ear. Its connection with the stirrup of the middle ear allows the introduction of sound vibrations into the inner ear.

7.60

Wartlike bumps covering the tongue. Their vertical sides are lined by taste buds.

7.51

A patch of specialized skin in the back of the olfactory cavity that contains both receptor cells and mucous cells.

7.52

Cranial nerve I. It is extremely short and spread out and is made up of the axons of olfactory receptor cells that find their way through holes in the bottom of the skull and then synapse in the olfactory bulb.

7.53

The conversion of chemical information into nerve impulse patterns.

7.54

That part of the cortex that may be the area best designated as the auditory cortex because both the olfactory bulb--amygdala--hypothalamus and the olfactory bulb--pyriform cortex--thalamus paths terminate here.

7.55

This structure is found on the basilar membrane of the cochlear duct and contains the auditory hair cells.

Copyright 1990 by Wadsworth, Inc.

7.61 pheromone	7.66 primers
(290)	(290)
7.62 pitch	7.67 pyriform cortex
(257)	(289)
7.63 place theory	7.68 rarefaction phase
(264)	(255-256)
7.64 pregnancy block	7.69 Reissner's membrane
(291)	(259)
7.65 primary taste qualities	7.70 round window
(281)	(259)

7.66

Pheromones that produce changes in the recipient animal's endocrine gland system. These changes can profoundly affect the functioning of the animal's body.

7.67

Part of the olfactory system, it receives fibers of the olfactory tract and projects fibers through the thalamus to the orbitofrontal cortex.

7.68

The low pressure, partial vacuum zone of a sound wave immediately behind the compression zone.

7.69

The wall of the cochlear duct.

7.70

An opening in the cochlea that allows the basilar membrane to vibrate. During the compression phase, fluid in the tympanic canal is shoved down toward the round window that bulges into the middle ear. During rarefaction the process reverses.

Copyright 1990 by Wadsworth, Inc.

7.61

Chemical secreted by organisms for the purpose of communication with other members of the species. There are two types of pheromones: attractants and primers.

7.62

The psychological dimension that best correlates with frequency.

7.63

Auditory theory that contends that each frequency of sound wave is represented in the nervous system by the firing of a different set of neurons as each sound wave frequency flexes the basilar membrane maximally at a different place along its length.

7.64

Occurs when an impregnated female rat is exposed to a new male rat of a different strain. The pheromones from the male act on her hypothalamus to prevent implantation of the fertilized egg in her womb.

7.65

Henning's theory that sweet, salty, sour, and bitter were the primary tastes and that all other tastes were some combination of these.

7.71 sensorineural loss (275)

7.72 shearing action (260)

7.73 sound (255)

7.74 sound shadow (271)

7.75 sound wave (255)

7.76 stereocilia (259)

7.77 stirrup (258)

7.78 superior olivary complex (269)

7.79 taste buds (280)

7.80 taste cell (280)

7.76

The hair-like protuberance on the top of the hair cells. These protuberances trigger the electrical activity.

7.77

Of the three tiny bones of the middle ear, it is the innermost and is attached to the oval window. When it is set in vibration by the anvil, it sets the oval window in vibration.

7.78

A cluster of cell bodies located at the medulla-pontine border consisting of the medial superior olive and the lateral superior olive. It receives input from the cochlear nuclei on the opposite side of the brain stem. It is the primary step in the mechanism for detecting the location of a sound in space.

7.79

Small clusters of taste cells that line the vertical sides of the papillae.

7.80

Taste receptor cells organized in small clusters called taste buds. They are located primarily on the tongue.

7.71

Hearing deficit due to disease or overstimulation by intense sounds that result in damage to the cochlea.

7.72

Action that causes the stereocilia to be bent in response to a sound wave. When a sound wave depresses Reissner's membrane and the organ of Corti, receptor cells are carried both downward and slightly to the side. During this sideways movement, the tectorial membrane and the organ of Corti move in opposite directions and the stereocilia attached to both are bent.

7.73

The event within the nervous system of the listener; the psychological sensation of audition.

7.74

The shadow produced by the head on the ear on the opposite side of the head from the sound's source. The head blocks direct reception of sound waves arriving from the side of the head opposite to the ear. This produces a difference in intensity of sound at the two ears.

7.75

The physical stimulus for audition.

Copyright 1990 by Wadsworth, Inc.

7.81 tectorial membrane (260)

7.82 temporary threshold shift (277)

7.83 tinnitus (277)

7.84 traveling wave (264)

7.85 tuning curve (266)

7.86 tympanic canal (259)

7.87 tympanic membrane (258)

7.88 vestibular canal (259)

7.89 vestibular organs (258)

7.90 volatile (286)

7.86

One of the two cochlear canals that join together through the opening at the tip of the cochlea called the helicotrema.

7.87

The eardrum. It separates the outer from the middle ear and is set into vibration by the sound waves.

7.88

One of the two cochlear canals that join together through the opening at the tip of the cochlea called the helicotrema.

7.89

The chambers that connect with the semicircular canals and contain the receptors for the vestibular senses.

7.90

The ability of a substance to release some of its surface molecules into the air.

Copyright 1990 by Wadsworth, Inc.

7.81

A membrane that is anchored to the wall of the cochlea at the narrow side of the cochlear duct. Many of the cilia are attached at their top to this membrane.

7.82

A type of sensorineural loss suffered by people exposed to periods of loud noise. This condition usually lasts for a brief time; however, there may be some unnoticeable permanent loss.

7.83

A hearing impairment that is characterized by a ringing in the ears.

7.84

According to von Bekesy, a wave that is created by the stirrups as it pushes the oval window in and out travels up the basilar membrane growing taller and taller until it reaches its maximum height at some point along the way.

7.85

A graphic representation of the sensitivity of an auditory cell or fiber to a range of frequencies at varying intensity levels. Allows identification of both the frequencies for which the cell's or fiber's threshold is lowest and the range of frequencies to which it will respond.

7.91

volley principle

(263)

7.92

vomeronasal organ

(289)

7.91

Principle that suggests that not all the cochlear nerve fibers must fire in response to sound waves; some can recover while others fire. This principle meant that the cochlear nerve could follow frequencies up to 3000 Hz.

7.92

It is an olfactory epithelium found in snakes similar to but separate from the main olfactory epithelium, which makes it possible to find its mate or food.

CHAPTER EIGHT
THE SOMATIC SENSES

READ-WRITE-REVIEW

Read pages 300-309 and summary statements 1-4 on page 336, then answer each of the following questions in this section.
---

1. List the three sense modalities discussed in this chapter that make up the somatic senses. (300)

   a. What kinds of information are provided by these senses? (300)

   b. What is the other sense modality that is also a somatic sense? (300)

   c. Distinguish between deep somatic receptors and somatic skin receptors. (301)

2. List the three layers of skin in order from surface to depth and describe each. (302)

   a. What are hair follicles and what have they to do with mechanoreception? (302)

   b. What are free nerve endings? (302)

   c. List two specialized receptor cells in the skin. (302)

   d. Contrast pattern theory and specificity theory of somatic sense receptors. (303)

   e. All this time, evidence supports what theory of somatic sense receptors? (303)

3. Nerve fibers that respond to mechanical stimuli fall into two categories. List these two categories and show how they differ in their response. (303)

   a. List and describe the two categories formed on the basis of receptive field size. (304)

   b. Combining these two dimensions we have four distinct types of primary afferent mechanoreceptive fibers. Identify the four resultant fibers and the specialized receptor associated with each. (304)

4. The sensitivity of the somatic senses is probably due to what two specialized receptors? (305)

169

a. What is shape recognition? (307)

b. What kind of receptor cell is probably best suited for localizing stimuli? (307)

c. What is spatial acuity and what specialized receptor cell is best suited to serve this function? (307)

d. What is two-point threshold and where is the smallest two-point threshold found? (307)

e. What is meant by frequency matching? (308-309)

f. What part of somatic perception uses frequency matching? (309)

g. What types of fibers are probably most responsible for this kind of somatic perception? (309)

h. The detection of vibrations is accomplished by what type of cell? (309)

i. How does the structure of this cell type make the cell a good candidate for the task of detecting vibrations? (309)

j. Grip control depends on the somatic skin cells being able to detect what? (309)

k. What type of cell is best equipped to sense this? (309)

Read pages 309-318 and summary statements 5-8 on page 336, then answer each of the following questions in this section.
---

1. Trace the route of the primary afferent neuron of the somatosensory system until it synapses. (309-310)

   a. What is a T-cell? (310)

   b. Trace the pathway of the T-cell to the point of synapse. (310)

   c. Where do these T-cells synapse in the thalamus? (310)

2. What are the two somatic projection areas called? (310)

   a. Input from the left side of the body goes where? From the body's right side? (310)

   b. Locate S1. (310)

   c. Damage to S1 will produce what changes in somatosensory perception? (311)

   d. What is stereognosis and what causes it? (311-312)

3. Describe the location of S2. (312)

4. From the Woolsey and Ven der Loos (1970) studies of rodents, we know that S1 neurons are organized in what type of arrangement? (313)

   a. This arrangement should remind you of what other cortical area? (313)

   b. What are the vibrissae and what is their function? (313)

   c. What are the barrels and where are they located? (313)

   d. This columnar arrangement has been found in what other species? (315)

5. Describe how the map of the body is laid down within the tracts of the somatosensory system. (315)

   a. Until this decade it was pretty much agreed that the cortical body maps were determined and inexorably fixed for the life of the organism by the genetically controlled growth process that created the nervous system during embryonic development. How did Merzenich and Kaas and the three fingers of the right hand of an owl monkey help to change our position? (315-317)

   b. What happens to somatosensory cortical neurons when they are deprived of their normal input? (317)

   c. How do Merzenich and Kaas explain their findings? (317-318)

   d. What may be the effect of the addition of extra cortical neurons on the function of the cortical areas for the remaining fingers? (318)

Read pages 318-322 and summary statement 9 on pages 336-337, then answer each of the following questions in this section.
---

1. What is the mechanism of thermal summation? (318)

   a. Identify three problems which became apparent when sensitivity spots were first discovered. (319)

   b. What is the phenomenon of paradoxical cold? (319)

   c. What have researchers been able to do with microelectrode recording that they were not able to do using other techniques? (319)

2. Describe adaptation in the thermoreceptor. (320)

   a. What is psychological zero and what has it to do with adaptation of these receptors? (320)

   b. What is the relationship between adapted skin temperature and stimulus threshold? (320-322)

Read pages 322-328 and summary statements 10-11 on page 337, then answer each of the following questions in this section.
---

1. What is conversion reaction and what does it have to do with pain? (322)

a. What are some of the stimuli for pain? (323)

b. What do we mean when we say "pain is a sensation"? (323)

c. What is phantom limb pain? (323)

b. What is a placebo and what does it have to do with pain? (323)

2. There are two nociceptive projection systems. Beginning with the T-cells in the spinal cord, trace each route through the nervous system. (323)

   a. Casey (1978) has suggested that pain has two aspects. List these and relate them to the appropriate nociceptive route. (324)

   b. How might the finding from behavioral data that anxiety increases pain help you to answer the questions "Is neurotic pain real?" and "If a placebo can relieve pain, does that mean that the pain wasn't real?" (325)

3. What is chronic pain? (326)

   a. Describe the new treatment alternative for chronic pain which involves neither surgery nor drugs. (326)

   b. What are its limitations? (326-327)

4. List and describe briefly the basic opiates. (327)

   a. What are the two major effects of opiates? (328)

Read pages 328-336 and summary statements 12-15 on page 337, then answer each of the following questions in this section.

---

1. Below is a diagram of the brain stem and spinal cord and a primary afferent neuron. Using this outline, draw in the descending pain-suppression pathway and label all parts. (327-328)

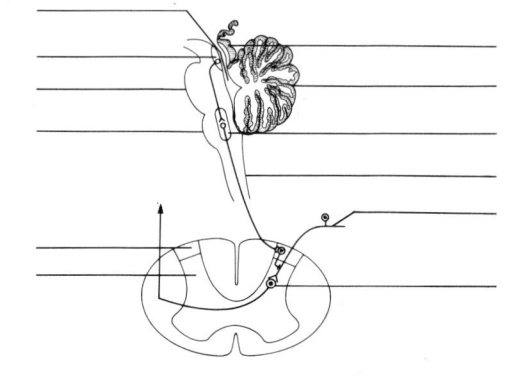

172

a. Because pain information is so vital to survival, why would a pain-suppression system develop? (328)

b. What is the relationship between somatosensory fibers other than pain and the pain-suppression system? (328-329)

c. Describe the role of the presynaptic inhibition in the descending pain-suppression system. (329)

2. What is an opiate antagonist? (329)

a. Give an example of an opiate antagonist. (329)

b. What led researchers to search for "natural opiates" in the nervous system? (329)

c. What are the two major categories of endogenous opioids? (330)

3. What does the technique of acupuncture analgesia involve? (330)

a. What reason can you give for believing that acupuncture produces something more than anxiety relief? (330-331)

b. What evidence can you give for concluding that acupuncture produces analgesia by way of the pain-suppression pathway? (331)

c. What is hypoalgesia? (331)

4. What conclusions can be reached from research to determine whether pain can reduce pain and if so, how? (332)

5. What is the phenomenon of learned helplessness? (333)

a. The comparison between animals who develop hypoalgesia through learned helplessness and animals who develop hypoalgesia after two or three shocks suggests what? (333)

b. Research suggests the existence of three types of hypoalgesia based on duration of stimulus and whether the stimulus is escapable or nonescapable. Summarize these findings. (333)

6. What is the Bolles and Fanselow (1982) theory? (335)

a. Hunt et al. (1988) tested the Bolles and Fanselow theory in a clinical setting using systematic desensitization and naloxone. What were the results? (335)

b. What two restrictions on pain suppression exist according to this theory? (335)

c. How does the restriction that fear is required to produce hypoalgesia fit with the anatomy of the pain-control system? (335)

d. Stressful situations can produce hypoalgesia. How can the functioning of the pituitary gland be used to explain this pain suppression? (336)

PRE-EXAM QUIZ

Multiple-Choice
Select the choice that best completes the stem in each question and indicate your selection in the appropriate space to the left of the question.

_____ 1. Which receptors provide the brain with part of the information needed to create pain sensations?
    a. nociceptors
    b. kinesthetic receptors
    c. thermoreceptors
    d. mechanoreceptors
    e. more than one of the above

_____ 2. Which of the following types of nerve fibers is best suited to carry information concerning vibration?
    a. SAII
    b. SAI
    c. FRI
    d. FRII
    e. two of the above

_____ 3. The smallest two-point thresholds are found where?
    a. the inside forearm
    b. the back
    c. the forehead
    d. the thigh
    e. none of the above

_____ 4. Which of the following mechanoreceptors consists of many layers of tissue arranged like an onion around the end of its neural fiber?
    a. Ruffini endings
    b. Pacinian corpuscles
    c. Merkel endings
    d. Meissner's corpuscles
    e. free nerve endings

_____ 5. Of the four body maps found in S1 it is proposed that the map in area _____ is concerned with the function of tactile discrimination.
    a. 3a
    b. 3b
    c. 1
    d. 2
    e. more than one of the above

_____ 6. Of the six layers in the S1 cortex that receives input from the ventroposterior thalamus is
    a. VI
    b. V
    c. IV
    d. III
    e. none of these

_____ 7. Which of the following best explains what happens when cortical neurons of S1 are deprived of their proper input?
    a. they slowly degenerate and are "eaten" by glial cells
    b. they remain healthy neurons but have no neural function
    c. the cortical map is simply readjusted so that these neurons become responsive to adjacent normal input
    d. they continue to discharge in a random manner, thereby providing us with such phenomena as the phantom limb
    e. none of the above

_____ 8. The function of the S2 cortex is
   a. pain perception
   b. kinesthetic awareness
   c. thermal sensitivity
   d. stereognosis
   e. unknown

_____ 9. The site in the nervous system that is most strongly associated with the conscious experience of pain is the
   a. thalamus
   b. hypothalamus
   c. limbic system
   d. midbrain
   e. S2 cortex

_____ 10. There is fairly good evidence that the localization of the pain-producing stimulus depends on which of the following pathways?
   a. posterior thalamus--S2 cortex
   b. posterioventral thalamus--S1 cortex
   c. medial and intralaminar thalamic nuclei--limbic system--hypothalamus
   d. medial and intralaminar thalamic nuclei--limbic system--S2 cortex
   e. posterioventral thalamus--reticular system--S2 cortex

_____ 11. The active ingredient in opium is
   a. enkephalin
   b. heroin
   c. endorphin
   d. morphine
   e. cocaine

_____ 12. In the descending pain-control system the cells in the nucleus raphe magnus
   a. synapse on and excite cells in the substantia gelatinosa
   b. synapse on and inhibit cells in the substantia gelatinosa
   c. synapse on and excite T-cells of the dorsal horn
   d. synapse on and inhibit T-cells of the dorsal horn
   e. none of the above

_____ 13. Which of the following findings led to the frenzied race in research to become the first to discover the brain's own "natural opiate"?
   a. the development of a chemically altered version of morphine
   b. the discovery of a pain-suppression pathway
   c. the finding that pain was not the only somatosensory modality that was affected by the administration of an opiate
   d. the discovery that naloxone accomplished its effects by binding to the receptor sites in the postsynaptic membranes
   e. none of the above

_____ 14. Research suggests that an animal receiving 100 shocks in a no-escape condition is experiencing which of the following kinds of hypoalgesia?
   a. opioid neural
   b. nonopioid
   c. hormonal
   d. attentional
   e. opioid neural with hormonal amplification

_____ 15. Suppose a painful stimulus is presented to a subject and he rates it as a very painful 8, on a 10-point scale. The subject is given acupuncture, and after allowing it to reach maximum analgesia the painful stimulus is once again presented and the subject rates it as a 2 on the 10-point scale. Finally, naloxone is given to the subject before the painful stimulus is presented for the third time. This time the subject rates the pain experienced as an 8 or 9. The result suggests that
   a. naloxone is an endogenous opioid
   b. acupuncture works through suggestion
   c. acupuncture works by way of the pain-suppression pathway
   d. naloxone is an opiate antagonist
   e. the hypoalgesic effect of acupuncture is due to the fact that it is a pain stimulus

True/False

_____ 1. A sensation is more likely to result from a change in energy rather than from energy presented at a continuous level.

_____ 2. Research strongly suggests that Meissner's corpuscles, Merkel's endings, Ruffin's endings, and Pacinian corpuscles are solely mechanoreceptors.

_____ 3. Fast-adapting nerve fibers react to a mechanical stimulus initially by firing very rapidly and then continuing to fire, although at a slower and slower rate as the stimulus pressure is continued.

_____ 4. Frequency matching is the way in which roughness information is carried in the somatic system.

_____ 5. T-cells are primarily afferent neurons of the somatosensory system that enter the cord via the dorsal root and after crossing over to the opposite side, ascend to the point of first synapse in the thalamus.

_____ 6. Destruction of S1 in the postcentral gyrus produces complete anesthesia.

_____ 7. Research suggests that instead of one there may be as many as six maps of the body's surface on S1.

_____ 8. To date, research data strongly suggest that the columns of the S1 cortex are arranged topographically so that the receptive field centers of the cells in the columns move across the skin as one moves from column to column in a line across the cortex.

_____ 9. Unfortunately, although the skin can be mapped into a mosaic of spots in which warmth or cold or both are perceivable, these spots do not appear to represent single receptor endings.

_____ 10. Thermoreceptors are capable of adaptation only within physiological zero.

_____ 11. Pain is a stimulus, not a sensation.

_____ 12. The threshold point at which a stimulus will be felt as warm or cool changes as a function of the adapted skin temperature.

_____ 13. The connecting point between the informational and motivational pain systems is probably the pretectal area.

_____14. One of the newer techniques used in the treatment of chronic pain is the permanent implantation of electrodes placed in an area of the midbrain and pons called the periaqueductal gray.

_____15. The inhibitory regulation of incoming sensory information occurs at the terminals of the primary afferent rather than on the dendrites of the T-cells.

8.1 acupuncture

(330)

8.2 adaptation

(303)

8.3 analgesia

(328)

8.4 analgesics

(326)

8.5 antagonist (blocker)

(329)

8.6 barrels

(313)

8.7 Bolles-Fanselow theory

(335)

8.8 Braille system

(307-308)

8.9 chronic pain

(326)

8.10 conversion reaction

(322)

8.6

Found in layer IV of S1 they are rings of neurons that send their dendrites into a central "core" area in layer IV where they collect inputs from telodendria arriving from the ventroposterior thalamus.

8.7

This theory posits that shock elicits fear, which turns on the pain-suppression system.

8.8

A system for the blind whereby they can read using their fingertips, which have the smallest two-point threshold. Each letter is represented by a different pattern of one to six dots arranged close together in three columns with each dot raised by only 1mm and separated from its neighbors by as little as 2.3mm.

8.9

Pain that persists over a long period of time, months or years, often without any identifiable cause. It does not respond well to mild analgesics or in some cases strong ones.

8.10

The conversion of emotional problems into a physical problem.

Copyright 1990 by Wadsworth, Inc.

8.1

A pain-suppression technique that involves the insertion of needles into the skin and then twirling them for 20 to 30 seconds.

8.2

The loss of response from a receptor, despite continuing stimulation.

8.3

Relief from pain.

8.4

Pain-killing drugs.

8.5

A molecule that fits into a receptor site in such a way that it prevents the intended transmitter from binding but not in such a way as to open the ion channels.

8.11 cutaneous receptors	8.16 euphoria
(301)	(328)
8.12 deep somatic receptors	8.17 fast adapters
(301)	(304)
8.13 dorsal horn	8.18 free nerve endings
(310)	(302)
8.14 dorsal root	8.19 frequency matching
(309)	(309)
8.15 endogenous opioids	8.20 heroin
(330)	(327)

8.16

An emotional state in which one feels especially good, relaxed, happy, and carefree. It is one of the major effects of opiates.

8.11

Receptors found in the skin such as Merkel endings, Meissner's corpuscles, and Pacinian corpuscles.

8.17

Fiber that responds to mechanical stimuli. Such fibers fire very rapidly when the stimulus is first applied and then stop firing after the stimulus pressure is continued for a few moments.

8.12

Somatic receptors that are found inside the body such as those in the blood vessels and sheets of connective tissue that support the intestines.

8.18

Tree-like set of branches into which most sensory neurons in the skin terminate.

8.13

Dorsal gray matter of the spinal cord. It is here that the primary afferent either ends by synapsing or they turn upward and ascend in the spinal cord.

8.19

The way in which roughness information is carried in the somatic system. The frequency of microvariations in the surface is matched by the frequency of firing in the afferent fiber.

8.14

The root of a spinal nerve that contains all of the afferent fibers from that spinal nerve.

8.20

An opiate, it is a chemically altered version of morphine that works faster than morphine because it is able to cross the blood-brain barrier more readily.

8.15

Substances that resemble an opiate and are produced by the body. There are two major categories of endogenous opioids and enkephalins. Both types apparently have receptor sites prepared for them on various neurons within the CNS. Morphine molecules are shaped to fit these receptor sites.

Copyright 1990 by Wadsworth, Inc.

8.21 hypoalgesia (331)

8.22 learned helplessness (333)

8.23 mechanoreceptive threshold (305)

8.24 mechanoreceptors (300)

8.25 medial thalamic nucleus (323)

8.26 Meissner's corpuscles (302, 304)

8.27 Merkel endings (302, 304)

8.28 morphine (327)

8.29 naloxone (321)

8.30 Nociceptors (300)

8.26

A specialized cutaneous receptor ending found in the dermis. FA I primary afferent, mechanoreceptive fibers apparently end here.

8.21

Partial suppression of pain.

8.27

A specialized cutaneous receptor which is found at the base of the epidermis. SA I primary afferent, mechanoreceptive fibers apparently end here.

8.22

Condition that arises when an animal repeatedly experiences an unavoidable shock. The animal appears to "give up" and fails to learn an avoidance when the opportunity is later presented.

8.28

An opiate, it is the active ingredient in opium.

8.23

A threshold is the smallest amount of energy necessary to produce a conscious sensation. Thus a mechanoreceptive threshold is the smallest amount of mechanical stimulation that produces a conscious sensation.

8.29

An opiate antagonist.

8.24

Receptor cells that translate mechanical forms of energy like pressure, twisting, bending, and pulling into patterns of nerve impulses that the brain will combine and interpret as sensations of touch and pressure, and sometimes vibration.

8.30

Receptor cells that react to thermal (temperature) changes and give us our sense of warmth and cold.

8.25

One of the thalamic nuclei involved in nociception. It may be here, together with the intralaminar thalamic nucleus, that the connecting point between the informational and motivational pain systems exists.

Copyright 1990 by Wadsworth, Inc.

8.31

nucleus raphe magnus

(328)

8.32

opiate antagonist (opiate blocker)

(329)

8.33

opium

(327)

8.34

Pacinian corpuscles

(302, 304)

8.35

paradoxical cold

(319)

8.36

periaqueductal gray (PAG)

(326)

8.37

phantom limb

(323)

8.38

physiological zero

(320)

8.39

placebo

(323)

8.40

presynaptic inhibition

(329)

8.36

An area of the midbrain and the pons. Electrical stimulation of this area has been successful in controlling chronic pain. Axons from this area synapse on the cells in the nucleus raphe magnus. Part of the descending pain-control system.

8.37

Sensations in a limb that has just been amputated.

8.38

The 30-36 degree range in which you can obtain complete adaptation. It is the normal range for skin temperatures.

8.39

A pretended, rather than real, treatment.

8.40

Inhibition in which the primary afferent is under continual inhibitory control from some source so that nerve impulses in this fiber suddenly lose strength just as they reach the terminals resulting in the release of less transmitter substance.

Copyright 1990 by Wadsworth, Inc.

8.31

Cluster of cell bodies located in the medulla that receives input from the periaqueductal gray. Its axons descend into the spinal cord to make synapses on neurons in the substantia gelatinosa. Part of the descending pain-control system.

8.32

A substance that can stop the effects of opiates by finding and occupying the neuron receptor sites into which the opiate molecules fit. Naloxone is an example of an opiate antagonist.

8.33

An opiate, it is the active ingredient in opium.

8.34

A specialized cutaneous receptor which is found in the dermis. FA II primary afferent, mechanoreceptive fibers apparently end here.

8.35

A phenomenon where a tip heated to a temperature a little below that required to elicit pain produces a sensation of cold when applied to a previously mapped cold spot.

8.41 projection areas (310)	8.46 shape recognition (307)
8.42 Ruffini endings (302, 304)	8.47 slow adapters (304)
8.43 S1 cortex area (310-311)	8.48 spatial acuity (307)
8.44 S2 cortex area (312-313)	8.49 stereognosis (311)
8.45 sensation (300)	8.50 stimulus (300)

8.46

The ability to perceive the form of an object held in the hand.

8.47

Fiber that responds to mechanical stimuli. Such fibers respond when the stimulus is first applied and keep on firing throughout the stimulus contact time, but the firing rate grows steadily slower.

8.48

The ability that enables you to feel various parts of the stimulus object as separate and distinct even when they are very close to one another on the surface of the skin.

8.49

The ability to perceive the shapes of solid objects with your hands.

8.50

An energy change outside the nervous system that brings about a sensation.

8.41

Regions of the cortex that receive afferent projections from the thalamus.

8.42

A specialized cutaneous receptor which is found in the dermis. SA II primary afferent, mechanoreceptive fibers apparently end here.

8.43

The larger of the two areas of the somatosensory cortex. It takes up most of the postcentral gyrus and appears to be composed of a mosaic of columns, each with a collection of cells having receptive fields that center on one small area of the skin.

8.44

The smaller of the two areas of the somatosensory cortex. It lies farther down the postcentral gyrus and is for the most part hidden from view inside the lateral fissure.

8.45

The pattern of activity within the nervous system and its accompanying conscious experience which is the result of some stimulus.

Copyright 1990 by Wadsworth, Inc.

8.51 substantia gelatinosa (328)

8.52 tail-flick latency (331)

8.53 thermal summation (318)

8.54 thermoreceptors (300)

8.55 transmission cells (T-cells) (310)

8.56 two-point threshold (307)

8.57 ventral root (309)

8.58 ventroposterior nucleus (310)

8.59 vibrissae (313)

8.60 viscerosomatic reflex (330-331)

8.56

The least amount of distance between two points of the stimulator that can still be sensed as two points rather than just one.

8.57

The root of a spinal nerve which contains all of the efferent fibers of that spinal nerve.

8.58

One of the two thalamic nuclei where all of the transmission cells' axons synapse.

8.59

Set of specialized hairs on the snouts of rats and mice. These hairs are much longer and thicker than any in the rest of the animal's fur. They serve to extend the area around the animal's head in which tactile sensing can warn of contacts with other objects.

8.60

The sudden contraction of the abdominal wall to a painful stimulus in the abdominal region.

8.51

Neurons located in the outer column of the dorsal horn. These cells are stimulated by the cells of the nucleus raphe magnus, and in turn they inhibit the T-cells of the dorsal horn, thereby canceling out some of the excitation of these cells by the primary afferent pain fibers. Part of the descending pain-control system.

8.52

The amount of time that passes between the application of a painful stimulus and the rat or mouse flicking its tail in response. Presumably this measure reflects the amount of pain felt.

8.53

The larger the area stimulated by a warm stimulus, the warmer the stimulus appears to be. Thus if a large enough stimulus is used, then areas in the "insensitive" skin can be found in which the stimulus does produce a sensation of warmth.

8.54

Receptor cells that react to thermal (temperature) changes and give us our sense of warmth and cold.

8.55

Secondary afferent cells of the somatosensory projection system whose axons cross the midline of the spinal cord and run upward on the opposite side of the nervous system.

Copyright 1990 by Wadsworth, Inc.

CHAPTER NINE
THE PRODUCTION AND SENSING OF MOVEMENT

READ-WRITE-REVIEW

Read pages 342-347 and summary statements 1-3 on page 393, then answer each of the following questions in this section.

---

1. Distinguish between striate and smooth muscles with respect to:

    a. appearance: (342)

    b. location: (342)

    c. center of control: (342)

    d. degree of control exerted by the individual: (342)

    e. function: (342-343)

2. What is peristalsis and what function does it serve? (343)

3. Within a skeletal muscle there are a number of _____, which, in turn, are made up of _____. (343)

4. What are the components of a motor unit? (343)

    a. What neurotransmitter substances are found in neuromyal junctions? (343)

    b. In terms of the motor units of the involved skeletal muscle, what is the difference between picking up a single book from your desk and picking up your briefcase? (345)

    c. How does the activity of the motor units serve to prevent muscle fatigue? (345)

    d. Suppose I pick up my briefcase and hold it out to you. Has muscle contraction ceased? (345)

    e. In the example above, what is happening at the motor unit level? (345)

5. Identify and describe three kinds of reflex arcs. (345)

    a. Which of the reflex arcs is considered to be the least common? (345)

    b. Describe how rest periods in motor neuron activity and thus in muscle fibers can be produced. Begin with the incoming sensory neuron. (345-346)

    c. Describe two ways in which the rest periods might be shortened so that a muscle can contract more intensely. (346-347)

6. Distinguish between isotonic and isometric contractions. (347)

   a. Which type of contraction is involved in the production of posture? (347)

Read pages 347-354 and summary statements 4-6 on pages 393-394, then answer each of the following questions in this section.
---

1. What is kinesthesis? (347)

   a. Where are the receptors found? (347)

   b. Conscious sensations of body position and movement are produced by a blending of the kinesthetic and _____ input and represented where in the cortex? (347)

   c. What are muscle spindles and what information do they provide? (348)

   d. Where are Golgi tendon organs found, and what specific piece of information do they provide? (348)

   e. Which type of kinesthetic receptor(s) contribute(s) more to our conscious knowledge of body position? (348)

2. What is a stretch reflex? (349-350)

   a. Locate the afferent for a stretch reflex. (350)

   b. When a heavy load is placed in your hand what happens to the hand? What happens to the biceps? (350)

   c. What occurs next to bring about a contraction of the biceps? (350)

   d. Why isn't this level of contraction in the biceps maintained? (350)

   e. What has to happen before the original level of contraction in the biceps returns? (350)

   f. What is the difference between a flexor muscle and an extensor muscle? (350)

   g. It is your physical exam and the doctor strikes your patellar tendon with his little rubber hammer. This produces an out and up swing of the lower leg. Explain precisely what happens at the cellular level to produce this response. (350)

3. How does the stretch reflex fit the definition of a servomechanism? (352)

   a. What is the variable set point for the stretch reflex? (352)

   b. Where is its soma? (352)

   c. Where does it terminate? (352)

d. How does this variable set point mechanism function? (352-353)

e. What is muscle tone? (353-354)

f. Anxiety and relaxation states produce changes in muscle tone, which leads one to suspect that higher brain centers may be involved. Indicate two brain centers that are possible candidates for this role. (354)

Read pages 354-359 and summary statements 7-8 on page 394, then answer each of the following questions in this section.
---

1. List the three sensory capabilities included in the vestibular sense. (354)

    a. Where can the patches of vestibular receptor cells be found? (354)

    b. Describe the structure of the specific vestibular receptors. (354)

    c. Describe how the neural currents are initiated and changed in these receptors. (354)

    d. What allows the macula to sense linear acceleration? (354)

    e. Describe what happens at the receptor level to enable you to sense both linear acceleration and deceleration. (354-357)

2. What is rotary acceleration? (357)

    a. Where are the receptor cells that sense rotary acceleration? (357)

    b. How are the cupula and the macula alike? (358)

    c. When the hair cells are bent they trigger impulses that are then carried by what nerve to the brain stem? (358)

    d. These impulses arrive in the brain stem at a structure called the _____. (358)

    e. This brain-stem structure makes connections with a large variety of _____ and to tracts leading to _____ and _____. (358)

    f. Explain why after a carnival ride in which you have been spun in the same direction for several minutes, you step out of your seat and immediately notice that the leg on the same side as the direction in which you were spun is stiff and sore. (358)

    g. Also explain why, when you get off the ride, you are dizzy and you have to fight a strong tendency to fall over in the direction in which you were spun. (358-359)

Read pages 359-370 and summary statements 9-12 on page 394, then answer each of the following questions in this section.
---

1. Locate the cerebellum and describe its makeup. (359)

    a. Damage to this structure can result in ataxia and/or decomposition of movement. Describe each of these symptoms. (360)

    b. List and identify two other common symptoms of cerebellar damage. (361)

2. Coordination of movements appears to be a major function of the cerebellum. One promising hypothesis concerning how the cerebellum goes about its task revolves around the coordination of agonist and antagonist muscles. Describe and give an example of each of these muscle types. (361)

    a. I am tired and decide to take off my glasses. Trace the impulses from their beginnings in the motor cortex to the point at which my arm begins to come up and in toward my face. (361)

    b. At about this same time what is happening that will facilitate this movement? (361)

    c. What purpose does the afferent feed from the muscle spindle of the flexor serve and how? (361-362)

    d. The arrangements of the two muscles involved in this movement is an example of what? (363)

    e. Because the muscles involved in this movement are arranged in this fashion, how is the decision made as to which of the muscles will contract and which will be inhibited? (362)

    f. What is the role of the cerebellum here and how does it accomplish this role? (362-363)

    g. Describe what we might expect to see in a patient with intention tremor? (363)

    h. What role does cerebellar damage play in intention tremor? (363)

    i. What will finally produce termination of the overshoot in intention tremor? (363)

    j. Explain why tremor occurs once overshoot terminates. (363)

3. What are the extensor thrust and stepping reflexes? (364)

    a. Explain in detail how these two reflexes operate in the newborn. (364)

b. When the infant learns to walk, what is it that he or she is actually learning? (364)

c. If we accept the idea that learning to walk is simply a matter of learning to organize reflexes into a sequence, we find it difficult to deal with either the treadmill studies that employ decortate cats or the treadmill studies that employ deafferented cats and electromyogram data. Explain why results from these two types of studies are so difficult to interpret using only the organization of reflexes hypothesis. (364-365)

d. Based on these findings what else did researchers conclude was necessary to postulate and identify? (365)

4. What is a central pattern generator? (365)

a. Why is most of the research on the central pattern generators carried out on very simple nervous systems like insects and crayfish? (365)

b. From such studies we have developed some fairly secure notions of central pattern generators in mammals. What do we believe is true regarding:

(1) what they actually are? (366)

(2) where they are probably located? (366)

(3) what they must be able to influence? (366)

c. Where do such findings leave the reflex explanation of locomotion? (368)

d. If we liken the stepping behavior to a computer program, then where do the central pattern generators fit? (370)

5. We know that central pattern generators are probably switched on and off by what? (370)

a. What is the probable role of the cerebellum in motor behavior if we accept the notion of central pattern generators? (370)

b. What area of the brain stem also probably plays an important role in influencing central pattern generators? (370)

c. List two major structures above the level of the brain stem that probably influence movement through their connections with cord central pattern generators. (370)

Read pages 370-380 and summary statements 13-17 on pages 394-395, then answer each of the following questions in this section.
---

1. Locate the corpus striatum. (370)

a. List the major components of the corpus striatum and locate each of these structures. (370)

b. What is the internal capsule and of what is it composed, in part? (371)

c. Locate the substantia nigra. (371)

2. Much of the current theorizing about the function of the structures that compose the corpus striatum is based on what? (371)

   a. Identify and describe the central symptom of Huntington's disease. (371)

   b. What specifically causes the symptoms we see in Huntington's disease? (373)

   c. The specific cells that are lost in Huntington's disease use what neurotransmitter and what do they normally do? (373)

   d. What two reasons can you give for suspecting that the neurotransmitter dopamine may also be involved in Huntington's disease? (373)

   e. Using the connections between the striatum and the substantia nigra explain how the choreic movements are produced. (373)

   f. What hypothesis exists concerning the cause of Huntington's disease? (374)

3. List and describe the three chief symptoms of Parkinson's disease. (375)

   a. What is the cause of the parkinsonian symptoms? (376)

   b. What makes it especially difficult for researchers to find the ultimate cause in any single case of Parkinson's disease? (376)

   c. What is the single most effective treatment yet devised for the symptoms of Parkinson's disease? (376)

   d. How is this treatment carried out? (376)

   e. What happens to the effectiveness of such therapy over several years and why? (376)

4. What do we mean when we describe the motor system of vertebrates as a hierarchical motor system? (377)

   a. What are species-typical behaviors and how are they related to central pattern generators? (377)

   b. What appears to be the relationship between the more recently evolved corpus striatum and the central pattern generators? (377)

   c. What reason can you give for concluding that the corpus striatum is responsible only for subconscious motor routines? (379)

5. According to Penny and Young (1983) it is the _____ that starts and maintains a response, while the _____ initiates an interrupt signal that works through the _____ when the response is complete. (379)

   a. According to this theory what happens if the corpus striatum has been damaged? (379-380)

b. Penny and Young are able to explain bradykinesia in Parkinson's disease but only if what condition is met? (380)

c. How do these theories explain bradykinesia? (380)

d. Provide any support you can for Penny and Young's explanation for bradykinesia. (380)

Read pages 380-393 and summary statements 17-21 on page 395, then answer each of the following questions in this section.
---

1. Beginning with the precentral gyrus and moving forward, identify the three cortical areas that compose the motor cortex. (380-383)

    a. Trace the axons of cells in the premotor cortex. (381)

    b. What is the function of the prefrontal cortical areas? (382)

    c. Trace the axons of cells located in the primary motor cortex. (383)

2. One of the symptoms commonly seen in cases where there is damage to the primary motor cortex is flaccid paralysis. Describe this condition. (383)

    a. If the damage to M1 is restricted to the left hemisphere, then the loss of motor ability will appear where? Why? What is this condition called? (383)

    b. Describe how the loss of muscle control actually observed when M1 is destroyed differs from the loss that would have been predicted on the basis of the original view of that area. (383)

    c. What is paresis? (383)

3. The corticospinal tract is made up of axons of the cells located where? (384)

    a. Using electrical stimulation what did Woosley find that led many researchers to label the precentral and postcentral gyri called the sensory-motor complex? (384)

    b. The results of studies on deafferented monkeys, like Woosley's, and the study of a human patient with a left hemisphere S1 lesion suggest what? (385)

4. According to the motor system hierarchy theory what prediction could we make about the role of M1? (385-386)

    a. From an anatomical point of view what would be the problem with such a prediction? (386)

    b. What is the concept of fractionation? (387)

c. How is fractionalism used to explain the role of M1 in the control of motor behavior? (387)

5. Locate M2 and identify the two major projection routes taken by the axons of the cells in this part of the cortex. (387)

   a. Compare M1 and M2 on the following:

      (1) From where does each part get its sensory input? (387)

      (2) What are the response cues for each? (387)

   b. Bilateral damage to M2 will produce what kinds of symptoms? (387)

   c. What is the vertex readiness potential and from where is it recorded? (387-388)

   d. Describe the detailed procedure of the study carried out by Tanji and Kurata (1985) in which they identified two sets of M2 neurons. (388)

   e. Describe the results of the Tanji and Kurata (1985) study. (388)

   f. What is a preparatory set and how can the establishment of such a set be explained by the Tanji and Kurata results? (388)

   g. What basis can you provide for the following statement: "Akinesia is not a form of paralysis but rather a loss of ability to get ready to move at a particular time." (389-390)

   h. What other function may be ascribed to M2? (390)

   i. How did the Brinkman (1984) study using monkeys with unilateral lesions of M2 provide evidence for this function? (390)

6. Locate the premotor cortex and identify the three major hypotheses concerning premotor cortex function that have been proposed. (390)

   a. What anatomical evidence is there for suggesting that visual and auditory information might play a role in fine movements? (390)

   b. Early experimental observations of monkeys with premotor damage led to what conclusion? (391)

   c. How did this conclusion change as a function of further observations? (391)

   d. Which of the hypothesized functions for the premotor cortex appears to be shared with M2? (391)

   e. Reviewing the symptoms produced by unilateral damage to the premotor area and comparing them to similar damage in M2, what did Freund (1984) conclude? (391)

   f. What anatomical finding supports Freund's conclusion? (391)

PRE-EXAM QUIZ

Multiple-Choice
Select the choice that best completes the stem in each question and indicate your selection in the appropriate space to the left of the question.

_____ 1. The motor neuron synapses on
   a. a striate muscle
   b. a muscle fascicle
   c. a bone
   d. a muscle fiber
   e. more than one of the above

_____ 2. The Renshaw cell is an interneuron that synapses on
   a. an afferent neuron
   b. another interneuron
   c. a motor neuron
   d. a recurrent collateral
   e. a muscle fiber

_____ 3. Conscious sensations of body position and movement are represented where?
   a. corpus striatum
   b. postcentral gyrus of the parietal lobe
   c. precentral gyrus of the frontal lobe
   d. premotor cortex
   e. none of the above

_____ 4. Which of the following is not true of the stretch reflex?
   a. the stretch reflex causes the responding muscle to stretch
   b. the stretching of the muscle spindle causes the afferent to fire
   c. the efferent in this reflex connects back to the muscle that was stretched
   d. the stretch reflex is a basic part of the isometric contraction that creates a posture
   e. all of the above are true

_____ 5. Steady isometric contraction is called
   a. posture
   b. load
   c. inertia
   d. dysmetria
   e. tone

_____ 6. The gamma efferent
   a. has its cell body in the peripheral nervous system
   b. terminates on the muscle spindle
   c. synapses on a muscle fascicle
   d. when it fires, causes the muscle spindle to relax, and this means that it will take less stretch to trigger the spindle afferent
   e. none of the above

_____ 7. Which of the following does not belong?
   a. rotary acceleration
   b. pressure
   c. linear acceleration
   d. gravity
   e. all of these belong to the same category

_____ 8. The two hemispheres of the cerebellum are connected by the
   a. corpus callosum
   b. corpora quadrigemenia
   c. pons
   d. vestibular nuclei
   e. none of the above

_____ 9. The breaking of a movement is not accomplished at the right moment because of cerebellar damage. This produces an overshoot of the movement and
   a. reciprocal inhibition
   b. ataxia
   c. dysmetria
   d. decomposition of movement
   e. intention tremor

_____ 10. The reflex explanation of locomotion
   a. fails to explain how the simple simultaneous backward motion of all paws of the decortate cat on the treadmill could stimulate the right-left sequence of walking
   b. is not wrong, it is just an oversimplified early version of our current understanding
   c. explains how a newborn infant can walk with help
   d. excludes higher level neural control of such behavior
   e. more than one of the above

_____ 11. Which of the following constitutes the striatum?
   a. globus pallidus and caudate nucleus
   b. caudate nucleus and putamen
   c. caudate nucleus and substantia nigra
   d. internal capsule and putamen
   e. putamen and globus pallidus

_____ 12. L-DOPA rather than dopamine is used to increase the availability of dopamine in the treatment of Parkinson's disease because
   a. synthetic dopamine cannot be produced in sufficient quantity to make such treatment readily available
   b. dopamine would produce serious side effects including liver damage, nausea, dizziness, and occasional hallucinations
   c. dopamine would only serve as a temporary solution, with symptoms returning in three or four years
   d. dopamine cannot cross the blood-brain barrier
   e. none of the above

_____ 13. A malfunction of an interrupt signal that originates in the _____ may be the cause of the choreiform movements seen in Huntington's disease and is due to cell deaths throughout the brain but most specifically in the _____.
   a. substantia nigra; substantia nigra
   b. corpus striatum; substantia nigra
   c. substantia nigra; corpus striatum
   d. corpus striatum; corpus striatum
   e. none of the above

_____ 14. Research studies suggest that which of the following is a function of M2?
   a. preparation of the brain for movement to be made on the arrival of some event in the environment
   b. the integration of movement into some sequence
   c. fractionation
   d. division of labor between the two sides of the body
   e. more than one of the above

_____ 15. Which of the following has strong interhemisphere connections and works closely with its mate on the other hemisphere?
   a. M2
   b. PM
   c. M1
   d. SMA
   e. all of the above

True/False

_____ 1. The cardiac muscle is actually a striate muscle.

_____ 2. The way in which you are able to exert additional muscle force is to simultaneously excite more motor units.

_____ 3. It is the isometric contractions of the skeletal muscles that move our body parts.

_____ 4. Orthopedic patients who have had a joint surgically removed and replaced by a metal prosthesis can still feel where the limbs are in relation to the rest of the body.

_____ 5. Flexor and extensor muscles work in opposition to each other.

_____ 6. Alpha motor neurons serve the role of variable set point for the stretch reflex.

_____ 7. It is the principle of inertia that allows one to sense where the body parts are in relation to one another.

_____ 8. It is impossible for the macula to sense constant motion.

_____ 9. The aftereffects of prolonged rotation may last well past the point that the motion of the fluid in the ampulla has ceased because the vestibular system had adapted to the rotation and must now re-adapt to the lack of it.

_____10. The role of the afferent feed from an agonist muscle back to the spinal cord is to counteract the antagonist muscle's stretch reflex.

_____11. The cerebellum has direct control over all muscle pairs in a reciprocal inhibition arrangement.

_____12. The corpus callosum probably is responsible for subconscious motor routines and in constructing such sequences of motor behavior from past experience.

_____13. Bradykinesia, a symptom observed in Parkinson's disease, can be explained by the Penny and Young (1983) theory only if bradykinesia is viewed as a difficulty in response termination.

_____14. The motor system hierarchy theory and the projections from M1 would both lead one to conclude that the function of this part of the cortex is to oversee the entire motor system by telling the corpus striatum what behaviors should be elicited from the brain stem and spinal cord.

_____15. Akinesia is a loss of ability to get ready to move at a particular time and is produced by damage to M2.

9.1 acetylcholine (Ach) (343)	9.6 antagonists (361)
9.2 agonists (361)	9.7 ataxia (360)
9.3 akinesia (387)	9.8 autoimmune disease (374)
9.4 alpha motor neuron (352)	9.9 biceps (361)
9.5 ampulla (357)	9.10 bradykinesia (375)

9.6

Muscles that pull the body part in the direction opposite that of the intended movement.

9.7

Disturbance of gait that involves walking in an unsteady manner, requiring the patient's concentration on every step. May be a result of cerebellar damage.

9.8

A disease condition in which the body may begin mistakenly forming antibodies against a particular protein that is fairly specific to striatal neurons, thus bringing about its own destruction.

9.9

Muscle that is located between your shoulder and elbow above the long bone and whose job it is to pull the forearm out and away from the body. It is an extensor.

9.10

Slowness and deliberateness of movement.

9.1

A neurotransmitter released from the presynaptic vesicles of the motor neuron. It diffuses across the gap to the receptor sites in the muscle fiber, which responds by generating an action potential that travels down its whole length and produces a contraction as it goes.

9.2

Muscle whose contractions propel the body part in the direction of the intended movement.

9.3

A severe difficulty in the initiation of movements of any kind. Occurs when the M2 areas in both hemispheres are lost or heavily damaged.

9.4

Regular motor neurons with the cell bodies in the ventral horn and axons that run out the ventral root and terminate on muscle fibers.

9.5

The swelling at the base of each semicircular canal in which the actual receptor cells for rotary acceleration are located.

Copyright 1990 by Wadsworth, Inc.

9.11

caudate nucleus

(371)

9.12

central pattern generators (CPG)

(365)

9.13

cerebellum

(359)

9.14

chorea

(371)

9.15

coordination

(361)

9.16

corpus striatum

(370-371)

9.17

corticoreticulospinal tract

(391)

9.18

corticospinal tract

(383)

9.19

cupula

(357-358)

9.20

deafferentation

(365)

9.16

Located between the cortex and thalamus, it consists of the caudate, the putamen, and the globus pallidus. Most believe that this is strictly a motor structure. Others hold that it has a cognitive function because of its strong connections with sensory and planning areas of the cortex.

9.17

Carries projection from the premotor cortex cells down to the reticular and then into the spinal cord. However the premotor cortex cells reach no farther than the brain-stem.

9.18

A tract formed by axons of cells found in the precentral gyrus. It terminates in the ventral horns of the spinal cord.

9.19

The gelatinous mass that fills the ampulla so that there can be little flow of fluid past it. The stereocilia have their hairs embedded in the cupula.

9.20

Spinal cord surgical procedure in which the dorsal roots serving a limb are cut, thus severing only the sensory fibers because the motor fibers are almost all in the ventral root.

9.11

The largest nucleus of the corpus striatum with the head lying beneath the cortex of the frontal lobe and a tail that extends posteriorly toward the occipital lobe and and then swings down and forward into the temporal lobe. The head forms a wall with the anterior end of the lateral ventricle.

9.12

Networks of interconnected neurons that collectively control a set of muscles needed to produce a movement or sequence of movements. The pattern of contractions can be generated from within the nervous system itself without need of sensory input.

9.13

Brain structure located halfway up the brain stem on its dorsal side. Like the cerebrum, it consists of a cortex wrapped and folded around a set of deep-lying nuclei. It also possesses two hemispheres that are connected by the pons.

9.14

The central symptom of Huntington's disease. It is the presence of continual, involuntary jerky movements of the face, the tongue, the extremities and occasionally, the trunk and respiratory muscles. The twitches and jerks are especially apparent when the patient is trying to hold a posture or make a voluntary movement.

9.15

The adjustments made involving the altering of the timing of contractions in the various muscles that produce the movement in such a way that they do not conflict with one another.

Copyright 1990 by Wadsworth, Inc.

9.21 decomposition of movements

(360)

9.22 disynaptic arc

(345)

9.23 dysmetria

(361)

9.24 electromyogram (EMG)

(365)

9.25 extensor muscle

(350)

9.26 extensor thrust reflex

(364)

9.27 flaccid paralysis

(383)

9.28 flexor muscle

(350)

9.29 fractionation

(387)

9.30 globus pallidus

(371)

9.26

One of the genetically determined motor circuits that provide the building blocks from which behaviors like walking will be constructed as the organism matures.

9.27

Symptom that follows damage to the primary cortex. In this condition the muscles remain limp.

9.28

Any muscle that by contracting draws the limb back into the body. The semitendinosus muscle of the lower leg is an example.

9.29

Used to describe the type of direct control over the smallest units of motor organization by bypassing the established motor hierarchy and going straight to the cord itself. Even here the central pattern generators of the cord may have to be circumvented. The idea is that M1 deals with fractions of central pattern generators.

9.30

Light-colored gray matter lying just medial to the putamen. It is one of three major components of the corpus striatum.

9.21

Breakdown of movement into the various individual muscle contractions of which the movement is composed.

9.22

A reflex arc in which the afferent enters the spinal cord and synapses with an interneuron, which will then synapse with a motor neuron in the ventral horn.

9.23

One of the two common symptoms of cerebellar damage, it involves the wobbly, jerky path of the arm's trajectory.

9.24

A recording of the electrical potentials produced by muscles as they contract and relax.

9.25

Any muscle that moves a limb out and away from the body. The quadriceps muscle of the lower leg is an example.

Copyright 1990 by Wadsworth, Inc.

9.31 gamma efferent (352)

9.32 Golgi tendon organ (348)

9.33 gravitational sense (354)

9.34 hemiplegia (383)

9.35 hierarchical motor system (377)

9.36 inertia (354)

9.37 intention tremor (363)

9.38 internal capsule (371)

9.39 interrupt signal (379)

9.40 isometric contraction (347)

9.36

The idea that all objects tend to continue in their present state. If the object is at rest it will resist being moved; if the object is moving it will resist being stopped.

9.37

A kind of tremor commonly seen in cerebellar trauma or in disease patients when the patient is nearing the termination of a movement. It is especially evident when the body part must arrive at a fairly precise location.

9.38

A band of white matter that separates the caudate nucleus from the putamen. Many of the axons that make up this portion of the internal capsule come from the cell bodies that make up these two structures and also the overlying cortex.

9.39

Signal from a command structure that interrupts an ongoing behavior.

9.40

The balanced condition of contraction without movement. There is a contraction of the muscle without any shortening in this condition. It is this kind of contraction that produces posture.

Copyright 1990 by Wadsworth, Inc.

9.31

The key element in the variable set point of a stretch reflex that increases or decreases the amount of stretch needed to trigger the reflex. It is a motor neuron with a cell body also in the ventral horn. Its axon travels to the ventral root, to the same muscle as its neighbors, and synapses with a muscle spindle fiber.

9.32

A sensory ending attached to each tendon. It responds to the tension on the tendon.

9.33

Sensory capacity basic to our ability to orient ourselves in our physical world and to be able to maintain our balance while moving about. It is one of the vestibular capabilities.

9.34

Paralysis of muscles on only one side of the body.

9.35

A motor system arranged by units such that those at each level command the units at lower levels and are commanded by those at higher levels. This term describes the motor system of vertebrates.

9.41 isotonic contractions (347)	9.46 macula (354)
9.42 kinesthesis (347)	9.47 mesencephalic locomotor region (370)
9.43 linear acceleration (354)	9.48 monosynaptic arc (345)
9.44 load (350)	9.49 motor unit (343)
9.45 L-DOPA (376)	9.50 multisynaptic arcs (345)

9.46

The patch of receptor cells found in the saccule and utricle of the vestibular organs.

9.47

The pontine-midbrain border where an area of the reticular formation exerts considerable influence over central program generators.

9.48

A reflex arc in which the afferent enters the spinal cord and synapses directly with a motor neuron in the ventral horn.

9.49

The motor neuron together with the muscle fibers with which it connects. This is a permanent combination that works together for the life of the organism.

9.50

A reflex arc having more than one interneuron.

Copyright 1990 by Wadsworth, Inc.

9.41

These are contractions that actually move the body parts.

9.42

The sense modality that tells you where your body parts are in relation to one another and tells where they are moving, at what speed, and with what force. Its receptors are found in muscles, joints, skin, and tendons.

9.43

Speeding up or slowing down while traveling in a straight line.

9.44

The amount of force acting against the muscle.

9.45

The precursor for dopamine, it is a molecule that has little trouble passing out of the bloodstream and into nerve tissue. Because of this, L-DOPA has a therapeutic use in the treatment of parkinsonian symptoms.

9.51

muscle fibers

(343)

9.52

muscle spindles

(348)

9.53

muscle tone

(353-354)

9.54

mutism

(387)

9.55

M1 (primary motor cortex)

(380)

9.56

neuromyal junction

(343)

9.57

nigrostriatal pathway

(376)

9.58

otoliths

(354)

9.59

paresis

(383)

9.60

patella

(350)

9.56

The point at which a motor neuron of the peripheral nervous system makes contact with the muscle fiber forming the synapse or junction.

9.57

Composed of neurons that have their cell bodies located in the substantia nigra and extend their axons forward through the hypothalamus and up into the corpus striatum where they synapse. They use dopamine as their neurotransmitter and their death causes parkinsonian symptoms.

9.58

Tiny bone fragments that cap the jelly-like mass into which the stereocilia of the vestibular sense protrude. These tiny fragments play a role in the bending of the stereocilia.

9.59

A reported weakness in the affected muscles rather than a total paralysis.

9.60

A small circular piece of bone that forms your "kneecap."

9.51

The elements that make up the fascicles of a striate muscle.

9.52

Special fibers found in every muscle that contribute nothing to the contraction of that muscle but rather act as receptors that tell the nervous system whether the muscle is contracting or relaxing.

9.53

Also called muscle tension, it is a steady isometric contraction and varies from one situation to another.

9.54

The absence of speech brought about when the M2 areas in both hemispheres are lost or heavily damaged.

9.55

Primary motor cortex, which lies in the precentral gyrus and whose output neurons send their axons down into the cord to synapse with the motor neurons.

Copyright 1990 by Wadsworth, Inc.

9.61

patellar tendon reflex

(350)

9.62

peristalsis

(343)

9.63

posture

(347)

9.64

precentral gyrus

(380)

9.65

precursor

(376)

9.66

premotor cortex (PM)

(381)

9.67

preparatory set

(388)

9.68

program

(369)

9.69

putamen

(371)

9.70

reciprocal inhibition

(362)

9.66

Lies just forward to the primary motor cortex and contains the cells that send their axons across into the primary motor cortex and also down to the reticular formation of the brain stem.

9.67

A readiness for making a particular response to a particular stimulus.

9.68

The sequence of steps needed to bring about some specific result.

9.69

One of the nuclei of the corpus striatum that is split off from the caudate by the band of white matter called the internal capsule. Because they do seem to share some common functions, the caudate and putamen are frequently spoken of as a unit and called the striatum.

9.70

A muscle arrangement in which a pair of muscles work together in a two-way system, with each muscle being capable of inhibiting the other through its stretch reflexes.

Copyright 1990 by Wadsworth, Inc.

9.61

The reflex that results in the lower leg swinging up and out when the tendon from the patella to a bone in the lower leg is struck by a rubber hammer. It is actually a disguised quadriceps stretch reflex.

9.62

Continuous rippling contractions that begin at the upper end of an intestinal segment and slowly migrate to the other end, moving the intestinal contents along as they go.

9.63

The maintenance of body parts in a certain relatively fixed position.

9.64

Cortical landmark that lies just anterior to the central fissure.

9.65

A substance from which the chemical of interest is made. One of the precursors of dopamine is L-DOPA.

9.71 recurrent collateral (345)

9.72 Renshaw cell (345)

9.73 reticulospinal tract (381)

9.74 rigidity (375)

9.75 rotary acceleration (357)

9.76 saccule (354)

9.77 semicircular canals (357)

9.78 servomechanisms (352)

9.79 set point (352)

9.80 smooth muscles (342)

9.76

One of the two largest globular cavities in the bone of the skull. It contains a patch of vestibular receptor cells.

9.77

The vestibular organs for rotary acceleration. There is one canal in each middle ear for each of the three dimensions: up-down, front-back, and right-left.

9.78

Devices that respond to environmental changes by making adjustments designed to counteract some unwanted system change. The house thermostat is an example of this.

9.79

The target point for a servomechanism; the desired state that is set to maintain.

9.80

These muscles appear whitish with no striations and are found in the esophagus, stomach, intestines, bladder, heart, and blood vessel walls. Most contractions are involuntary or reflexive and controlled through the autonomic nervous system.

Copyright 1990 by Wadsworth, Inc.

9.71

An axon branch of the motor neuron that provides input into a Renshaw cell.

9.72

A type of interneuron whose function is to produce a rest period for the muscles. The axon of this cell leads back to the original motor neuron where it makes an inhibitory synapse, and the IPSPs produced counteract to some extent the EPSPs triggered by the sensory neuron.

9.73

The connection between the reticular cells and the ventral horn cells.

9.74

Stiff limbs and postures with little spontaneous movement.

9.75

The change of speed of rotation. The sense of rotary acceleration comes into play most often when you turn your head.

9.81 species-typical behaviors (377)

9.82 stepping reflex (364)

9.83 stereocilia (354)

9.84 stretch reflex (349)

9.85 striate muscles (342)

9.86 striatum (371)

9.87 subroutine (370)

9.88 substantia nigra (371)

9.89 supplementary motor cortex (SMC) (383)

9.90 synergists (366)

9.86

Name given to the caudate nucleus and putamen when they are spoken of as a unit.

9.81

Large motor patterns that probably organize whole sequences of central pattern generators. They exist in the reticular formation of the midbrain, specifically the periaqueductal gray area.

9.87

A standard sequence that fits as a unit into a great number of larger programs. Central pattern generators are examples of a subroutine.

9.82

One of the genetically determined motor circuits that provide the building blocks from which behaviors like walking will be constructed as the nervous system matures. It is the flexion counterpart of the extensor thrust.

9.88

Located near the top of the brain stem in the midbrain region. It is a darkly colored nucleus, and although it is not part of the corpus striatum, it works in very close relationship with it.

9.83

The hairs on the hair cells that are the receptor cells of the vestibular organs. They protrude out of their top surface into a mass of jelly-like substance.

9.89

A motor cortex area found on the medial surface of the frontal lobe that may be a part of the premotor area but that has characteristics that give it somewhat different functions.

9.84

The automatic contraction of a muscle that is either lengthening when it shouldn't be or not contracting fast enough. It is responsible for making many of the automatic muscle adjustments that produce posture.

9.90

Muscles whose contractions aid the agonist muscle by pulling a body part in the same direction.

9.85

Also called striped or skeletal muscles, they are attached to bones and move the parts of our bodies around or hold them in fixed positions (postures). Because they are controlled by the central nervous system, we have voluntary control over them in most situations.

Copyright 1990 by Wadsworth, Inc.

9.91

S+

(388)

9.92

S−

(388)

9.93

tendon

(348)

9.94

triceps

(361)

9.95

tremor

(361)

9.96

tremor at rest

(375)

9.97

utricle

(354)

9.98

vertex readiness potential

(387-388)

9.99

vestibular nuclei

(358)

9.96

Trembling of hands that diminishes during voluntary hand movement.

9.91

A stimulus that signals that a particular response will now be reinforced.

9.97

One of the two largest globular cavities in the bone of the skull. It contains a patch of vestibular receptor cells.

9.92

A stimulus that signals that no reinforcement will follow the response.

9.98

An EEG wave recorded from electrodes placed on the top of the skull at the midline, a point called the vertex. This wave always occurs just before a movement and seems to be associated with the intention to move or a readiness to make the response rather than the response itself.

9.93

Found at the end of each muscle, it consists of fibers that join together and fuse into a band of exceptionally tough connective tissue, which connects muscle to bone.

9.99

Nuclei located in the brain stem that receive impulses from the vestibular receptors. Connections are made from these nuclei to a wide variety of reflex arcs and to tracts leading up to the thalamus and cortex.

9.94

Muscle that is located between your shoulder and elbow below the long bone and whose job it is to pull the forearm out and away from the body. It is an extensor.

9.95

One of the two common symptoms of cerebellar damage, it involves the tiny back-and-forth oscillations of the finger at the end of each movement.

Copyright 1990 by Wadsworth, Inc.

CHAPTER TEN
SLEEP AND ATTENTION

READ-WRITE-REVIEW

Read pages 400-408 and summary statements 1-4 on page 434, then answer each of the following questions in this section.

---

1. What is the one kind of data that is absolutely necessary if we are to see objectively an individual's arousal level? (401)

    a. What is meant by the term "synchrony" and what kinds of brain-wave patterns are produced by synchrony? (401)

    b. What is meant by the term "desynchrony" and what kinds of brain-wave patterns are produced by desynchrony? (401)

    c. Complete the table below. (401-402)

Waveform	Degree of Synchrony	Amplitude	Frequency
Alpha Waves			
Beta Waves			
Delta Waves			

2. What is "alpha blocking" and under what conditions does it occur? (402)

3. Under what conditions does the orienting reaction occur? (402-403)

    a. What is the purpose of the orienting reaction? (403)

    b. A number of components make up the orienting reaction. List several of these components including any brain-wave activity. (403)

4. What are the three major aspects of arousal? (403)

    a. What part of the brain is responsible for arousal? (403)

b. What is unusual about the projection of the pontine reticular cells? (403)

c. What does the projection of these cells suggest about their function? (403)

d. To where do the cells of the midbrain reticular formation project? (403)

e. Explain why the input to the midbrain reticular formation is described as nonspecific (There are two reasons). (404-405)

f. Locate the reticular and intralaminar nuclei. (406)

g. These nuclei are also considered to be a part of the reticular system. Functionally, how do these nuclei differ from the midbrain reticular system? (406)

5. What is the basic learning process by which a stimulus loses its ability to evoke the orienting response? (408)

   a. Suppose you were teaching this class and wanted to demonstrate the phenomenon of generalization of habituation. Describe exactly how you would do this. (408)

   b. What kinds of stimuli do not habituate? (408)

   c. One possible explanation of the habituation phenomenon is fatigue. Provide one bit of evidence against the fatigue theory. (408)

   d. What is the probable brain site where habituation occurs? (408)

Read pages 408-417 and summary statements 5-8 on pages 434-435, then answer each of the following questions in this section.
---

1. Describe the characteristic EEG pattern in initial stage 1 sleep. (409)

   a. Compare the EEG record during the drowsy presleep period with that of initial stage 1 sleep. (410)

   b. Subsequent stage 1 sleep periods are called what (two terms)? (410)

   c. What distinguishes emergent stage 1 sleep from other stage 1 sleep stages? (410-411)

   d. What is characteristic of the EEG record during stage 2 sleep? (409-410)

e. Stages 3 and 4 sleep EEG patterns are characterized by what? (410)

2. Trace the typical sleep cycle beginning with the drowsy condition. (410-413)

   a. Minimally, a typical night's sleep will include how many sleep cycles? (413)

   b. What is the duration of a typical sleep cycle? (413)

   c. Describe the difference in the mentation that takes place during REM and NREM sleep. (413)

3. Usually EEG recordings from a number of brain structures are supplemented by recordings from what two other sites? (413)

   a. Cortical EEG evidences what change as the brain of the animal shifts from NREM to REM sleep? (413)

   b. What change in neck muscle EMG is seen as the animal moves from NREM into REM sleep? (414)

   c. What is sleep atonia? (414)

   d. In REM sleep what happens to the stretch reflex of the striate muscle system? (414)

   e. Describe the observations Jouvet (1967) made when he produced lesions in the dorsomedial part of the pontine brain stem of the cat. (414)

   f. What do the findings by Jouvet (1967) and by Morrison (1979) suggest about the function of the neurons of the dorsomedial pons? (414)

4. Describe the appearance of a PGO wave. (416)

   a. From where in the brain can PGO waves be recorded? (416)

   b. Where in the brain do PGO waves originate? (416)

   c. What do these areas have in common? (416)

   d. Although it is clear that PGO waves have something to do with one of the sense modalities, it is probable that they also have something to do with what other kind of behavior during REM sleep? (416)

   e. Explain how PGO waves bring about this behavior. (416)

   f. Both PCPA and reserpine have been used experimentally to produce what? (416)

   g. These drugs produce this effect by acting on what brain site? (416)

   h. What do these drugs do to produce this effect? (416)

Read pages 417-423 and summary statements 9-10 on page 435, then answer each of the following questions in this section.
---

1. Several studies (Bremer, 1937; Batini et al. 1958; Morruzzi and Magoun, 1949; and Steriade et al. 1980) point to what specific brain area as being the waking or arousal mechanism? (418)

2. Jouvet (1967) was the first to propose a theory of REM-NREM cycling. What two brain centers were discussed in this theory and what were the proposed functions of each? (418-419)

   a. According to Jouvet's theory how did these two brain-stem areas operate in concert to bring about the cycling of REM-NREM sleep? (419)

   b. Cite three pieces of research evidence that refute predictions made on the basis of Jouvet's theory. (419)

   c. What part of Jouvet's theory seems to have outlasted the theory itself? (419)

3. According to the Hobson-McCarley reciprocal interaction model, what two specific brain areas are involved in the control of the sleep cycle? (419)

   a. Describe the interaction between these two centers during the waking state. (419)

   b. Describe the interaction between these centers during NREM. (419)

   c. Describe the interaction between these centers during early REM. (419)

   d. What changes in the interaction between these centers occur during late REM? (419)

   e. What more recent findings concerning gigantocellular tegmental field neurons have caused some problems for the reciprocal interaction model of sleep cycle control? (420-421)

4. In giving up attempts to find those "executive" cells that initiate REM sleep, researchers have turned their attention to what? (421)

   a. What two specific brain-stem areas appear to be especially important in the generating of PGO waves? (422)

   b. According to Jouvet, cells in what areas of the brain stem function to initiate postural atonia? (422)

c. What brain center or centers act as generators of the desynchrony found in REM? (422)

5. Many studies that have reported finding a sleep center above the brain stem must be "taken with a grain of salt." Why? (422-423)

   a. Locate the pre-optic area. (423)

   b. What findings suggest that the pre-optic area may play a role in sleep? (423)

   c. These findings suggest what role for the pre-optic area? (423)

Read pages 423-429 and summary statements 11-13 on page 435, then answer each of the following questions in this section.
---

1. According to everything you have read up to this point there are two kinds of sleep. List these two kinds of sleep. (423)

   a. Identify the stage or stages involved in each of these kinds of sleep. (423)

   b. List three distinctions that can be made between these two kinds of sleep. (423)

   c. At what point in evolution do we first see a division of sleep into REM and NREM? (424)

2. The notion that waking activity puts some sort of wear on the body that sleep repairs forms the basis for what theory of sleep? (424)

   a. If we eliminate the effects of exercise-induced arousal, what is the effect of exercise on NREM onset and duration? (424)

   b. According to Webb (1981) what might serve just as well as sleep in providing for body recuperation? (424)

   c. In contrast to Webb's (1979) position, Moruzzi believes that sleep is essential for recuperation. In what other way does Moruzzi's position differ? (424)

   d. Sleep deprivation studies have resulted in what kind of behavioral deficit? (424-425)

   e. How does Oswald (1966) explain the lapses in attention demonstrated by sleep-deprived subjects? (425)

   f. What was unusual about their sleep once Oswald's (1966) subjects were allowed to fall asleep? (425)

g. How does this finding fit with the restorative theory? (425)

h. Describe the syndrome fibrositis and explain what it has to do with sleep. (425)

i. How is depression related to sleep and what do these findings say about antidepressant drug effects? (425)

3. Boredom, such as a student might experience while sitting through yet another of those lectures by Professor Stifling, seems to be another term for what simple learning process? (426)

   a. Sokolov (1963) observed that habituation of the OR occurred in several stages. Discuss what happens at both the cortical level and the brain-stem level during each of these stages. (426)

   b. What follows the last stage of habituation? (426)

4. Cycles that are approximately 24 hours in length are called what? (427)

   a. List three body functions other than sleeping and waking that operate on such a 24 hour cycle. (427)

   b. What rhythm intrinsic to individual cells might be related to sleep? (427)

   c. A major function of a cell is to synthesize new protein for enzymes continually and to replace worn out structure. Describe the rhythm of this protein synthesis. (427)

   d. This rhythm of the cell in producing protein comes from where? (427)

   e. Explain the theory of negative feedback as an explanation of protein synthesis in the cell. (427)

   f. What is entrainment and where is it controlled in the rat brain? (428)

Read pages 429-434 and summary statements 14-16 on page 435, then answer each of the following questions in this section.
---

1. Short-term memory is a very brief, temporary storage mechanism. The only way to save a memory is to transfer it to long-term memory. This transfer is called what? (429)

   a. The extent to which this process is carried out depends on what? (429)

b. What reason can you give for hypothesizing the existence of a second temporary storage memory? (429)

c. What findings could be explained if a second temporary storage memory is posited? (429)

d. Provide one explanation as to how REM sleep aids consolidation. (429-430)

2. If we accept the notion that consolidation involves the construction of new tissue in the brain then what would be a crucial part of the learning process and why? (430)

   a. Amino acid levels in the blood have a circadian rhythm. Demonstrate this fact using the amino acid tyrosine. (430)

   b. Half the sleep time of infants is spent in REM sleep, whereas only 15% of the adult sleep time is REM. How might this discrepancy be explained? (430)

   c. Protein synthesis is under the control of what hormone? (430)

   d. During what part of the 24-hour period is most of this hormone secreted? (430)

   e. Demonstrate logically how it might be possible for this hormone to trigger the onset of REM sleep. (430)

3. Interestingly, when persons complain that they suffer from insomnia they probably are not complaining about the actual number of hours spent in sleep as measured objectively by EEG records. On what are they basing the complaint? (431)

   a. Of the two types of insomnia which is the more common and which is more likely to be symptomatic of neurochemical problems? (431-432)

   b. What is affective disorder? (432)

   c. Describe the two major types of sleep patterns found in individuals with mood disorder. (432)

   d. Of the two major drugs employed in drug therapy of insomnia, the one of choice for the past decade is sold under the trade name of Dalmane. What is the chemical name of this drug and to what class of drugs does it belong? (432)

   e. What is the other class of drugs that is commonly used in the treatment of insomnia? (432)

   f. The drugs used in the treatment of insomnia produce many negative side effects. What are some of these? (432-433)

g. Given that the cost/benefit is so poor, what prompts the medical profession to continue the use of drugs in the treatment of insomnia? (433)

4. What major symptom do we find associated with narcolepsy? (433)

   a. List and define three additional symptoms that make up this syndrome. (433-434)

   b. What do these symptoms suggest concerning the dynamics of narcolepsy? (434)

PRE-EXAM QUIZ

<u>Multiple-Choice</u>
Select the choice that best completes the stem in each question and indicate your selection in the appropriate space to the left of the question.

_____ 1. They are high-amplitude and very "low" frequency (about 1-4/second) EEG waves.
   a. alpha waves
   b. alpha blocking
   c. beta waves
   d. delta waves
   e. none of the above

_____ 2. Which of the following is now accepted as the standard way of assessing a subject's state of arousal and attention?
   a. alpha
   b. cortical synchrony
   c. cortical desynchrony
   d. delta
   e. none of the above

_____ 3. Peculiar bursts of eye movement beneath closed lids occur during _____ sleep.
   a. initial stage 1
   b. stage 3
   c. stage 4
   d. stage 2
   e. emergent stage 1

_____ 4. Which of the following contains neurons that desynchronize the cortical EEG record during arousal?
   a. preoptic area
   b. inferior colliculus
   c. midbrain reticular formation
   d. locus coeruleus
   e. gigantocellular tegmental field

_____ 5. In which of the following stages do you <u>first</u> find sleep spindles?
   a. initial stage 1
   b. stage 2
   c. stage 3
   d. stage 4
   e. emergent stage 1

_____ 6. Which of the following is <u>not</u> true of PGO waves?
   a. it is quite possible that the body twitches characteristic of REM sleep originate in the firing of the pontine reticular formation during the PGO waves
   b. PGO waves indicate a chain of activity beginning in the pontine reticular formation and sweeping up through the midbrain reticular formation, the lateral geniculate, and finally the visual areas of the cortex
   c. PGO waves trigger the eye movements characteristic of emergent REM sleep
   d. it is possible to produce PGO waves during the waking state by altering brain-stem functions with a drug
   e. more than one of the above is not true of PGO waves

_____ 7. Which of the following research findings would not be predicted from Jouvet's (1979) theory of REM/NREM cycling?
   a. REM sleep does not occur when the locus coeruleus has been destroyed
   b. recordings from single cells in the dorsal raphe nucleus should show that they are more active during the waking than during the NREM sleep
   c. dorsal raphe cells are found to have higher firing rates in an active waking condition than in quiet waking
   d. lesioning of the locus coeruleus does not alter sleep cycling
   e. more than one of the above research findings would not be predicted from Jouvet's theory

_____ 8. The medullary neurons that actually produce the REM sleep atonia form the
   a. locus coeruleus-α
   b. raphe nucleus
   c. X area
   d. nucleus reticularis magnocellularis
   e. more than one of the above

_____ 9. From the evolutionary standpoint, the first two animals to show a division of sleep into REM and NREM are
   a. fish and amphibians
   b. birds and mammals
   c. amphibians and reptiles
   d. reptiles and birds
   e. none of the above

_____ 10. If we could completely eliminate the effect of exercise-induced arousal, then we could expect exercise to _____ NREM onset and _____ NREM duration.
   a. increase; increase
   b. increase; decrease
   c. decrease; increase
   d. decrease; decrease
   e. none of the above

_____ 11. Prolonged sleep deprivation in previously normal subjects will result in
   a. memory lapses
   b. hallucinations
   c. delusions
   d. inability to perform on simple motor learning tasks
   e. none of the above

_____ 12. Which of the following appears to be the entrainment center for the rat brain?
   a. preoptic area
   b. locus coeruleus-α
   c. visual cortex
   d. suprachiasmatic nucleus
   e. X area

_____ 13. Most of the growth hormone secreted by the _____ is produced during _____.
   a. anterior pituitary; REM sleep
   b. posterior pituitary; NREM sleep
   c. anterior pituitary; waking
   d. posterior pituitary; REM sleep
   e. anterior pituitary; NREM sleep

_____ 14. Which of the following is not one of the symptoms found in narcolepsy?
   a. automatic behavior
   b. cataplexy
   c. waking nightmares
   d. depression
   e. sleep attacks

_____ 15. James Sheepcounter recently paid his family physician a visit because he was not sleeping well at night. He had made his own self-diagnosis of insomnia and after some discussion with Doc Neveright, he was given a prescription for an anti-insomnia drug. More than likely the drug was a member of which of the following drug families?
   a. narcotic
   b. benzodiazepine
   c. enkephalin
   d. barbiturate
   e. two of the above

True/False

_____ 1. Delta waves only occur when a person is unconscious.

_____ 2. The size of an EEG wave is a reflection of the number of active neurons near an electrode.

_____ 3. The normal route to REM sleep is through the waking state.

_____ 4. Localized areas of cortical activation occur when neurons of the midbrain reticular formation are activated.

_____ 5. All stimuli will eventually habituate.

_____ 6. Stage 4 sleep is characterized by both sleep spindles and delta wave activity.

_____ 7. In adults the normal route to REM sleep is via NREM sleep.

_____ 8. In normal individuals the only mentation that occurs during sleep is dreaming.

_____ 9. The electrical muscle activity from the forehead is used to supplement the EEG readings from a number of brain sites during sleep research.

_____10. The degree of muscle tone is regulated by higher brain centers facilitating or inhibiting the motor neuron in the reflex arc.

_____11. The firing rate of the gigantocellular tegmental field cells during NREM sleep diminishes until the onset of REM sleep, at which time these cells completely shut down.

_____12. The rebound effect of sleep deprivation gives priority to REM over NREM when sleep is being made up.

_____13. Antidepressant drugs have their effects by decreasing the proportion of time spent in REM sleep.

_____14. Once total habituation to his environment has occurred sleep is almost inevitable since the reticular system does not seem capable of arousing itself.

_____15. The major reason that physicians continue to prescribe and patients suffering from insomnia continue to take the anti-insomnia drugs has to do with the effective advertising campaigns put on by the various pharmaceutical companies.

10.1

alpha blocking

(402)

10.2

alpha waves

(401)

10.3

arousal

(403)

10.4

automatic behavior episodes

(434)

10.5

barbiturates

(432)

10.6

benzodiazepines

(432)

10.7

beta waves

(401)

10.8

cataplexy

(433)

10.9

circadian rhythms

(427)

10.10

consolidation

(429)

10.6

A class of drugs. These drugs are sometimes called the "minor tranquilizers." It include Valium, Librium, and Dalmane.

10.7

Brain waves that are quite small and the variations are very rapid, about 30-45 Hz. They are best correlated with thinking, perceiving, and decision making.

10.8

A sudden attack of atonia that frequently strikes the neck muscles, which results in a sudden drop of the chin onto the chest but can appear in any muscle group or even involve the entire body. It often seems to be triggered by an emotion like surprise, anger, sadness, excitement, or laughter.

10.9

One type of daily cycle found in living tissues. This type of cycle is approximately 24 hours in length. Human body physiology operates on circadian rhythms.

10.10

The process whereby information is transferred from short-term memory to long-term memory.

10.1

The sudden replacement of alpha rhythm with beta rhythm, which is an indication that the cortex has stopped "idling" and begun processing input.

10.2

Brain waves that are moderately synchronous and occur at a rate of about 8-12 per second. They are generated by the thalamus and seem to represent an "idling rhythm" that occurs when the visual parts of the cortex are not particularly busy.

10.3

An altering of consciousness in the direction of becoming more alert, with increased concentration on selected stimuli.

10.4

A symptom of narcolepsy that begins with the individual experiencing drowsiness, which he or she attempts to fight off with increased stimulation but to no avail. Gradually awareness of both self and environment is lost and only automatic behavior remains. Only simple, unskilled behaviors are performed adequately, and the patient is always amnesic for the events that transpired.

10.5

A class of drugs. These drugs were the original "sleeping pills."

Copyright 1990 by Wadsworth, Inc.

10.11 delta waves

(401-402)

10.12 desynchrony

(401)

10.13 electromyogram (EMG)

(413)

10.14 electro-oculogram (EOG)

(413)

10.15 emergent stage 1

(410)

10.16 entrainment

(428)

10.17 fibrositis

(425)

10.18 flower-pot technique

(429)

10.19 flurazepam

(432)

10.20 generalization of habituation

(408)

10.16

The brain's exact matching of the protein-synthesis cycles to the day-night cycle by speeding or slowing the synthesis.

10.17

A syndrome in which the patient complains of chronic fatigue, stiffness, muscle pain, and irritability.

10.18

A research technique in which the rat is placed on an upside-down flower pot in a large pool of water for some time. The rat cannot escape from the pool by swimming and so must crouch on the flower pot with its tail sticking over one edge and its nose over the other.

10.19

One of the benzodiazepines, it is better known by its trade name, Dalmane. It is currently the drug of choice against insomnia.

10.20

The amount of time required for a stimulus to habituate diminishes as the stimulus becomes more like the initially habituated stimulus.

Copyright 1990 by Wadsworth, Inc.

10.11

Brain waves having a high amplitude and very low frequency, about 1-4 per second.

10.12

The condition in which electrical events are spread out randomly in time. It produces small, high-frequency waves.

10.13

A record of the electrical activity of a muscle. In sleep research the EMG is typically recorded from neck muscles.

10.14

A display of voltage shifts generated by the eyes as they move. This display is a straight line that can move away from center in either direction according to the direction of the eye movement.

10.15

The type of stage 1 that is entered from stage 2. In this stage the eyes show peculiar bursts of movement beneath the closed lids. For this reason this sleep state is often called the rapid eye movement sleep.

10.21 gigantocellular tegmental field (FTG) (419)

10.22 growth hormone (GH) (430)

10.23 habituation (408)

10.24 initial stage 1 (410)

10.25 insomnia (431)

10.26 K-complex (410)

10.27 locus coeruleus (419)

10.28 locus coeruleus-α (LC-α) (422)

10.29 mentation (413)

10.30 midbrain reticular formation (MBRF) (403)

10.26

The pattern of brain waves that is a combination of a few high-voltage slow waves followed by about 1 second of 14 Hz waves. Along with sleep spindles they represent the dominant waveforms in stage 2 sleep.

10.27

A small cluster of cells in the dorsal brain stem at the pontine-midbrain border. The cells use norepinephrine as a neurotransmitter, and the axons of these cells spread throughout the nervous system. Jouvet held that as activity built up in this structure it could reach a point where it inhibited the activity of the raphe nucleus and trigger REM sleep.

10.28

A subdivision of the reticular formation. It consists of a group of cells just ventral and lateral to the locus coeruleus. The cells contain cholinergic neurons and receive input from both the dorsal raphe nucleus and locus coeruleus. Probably involved in producing sleep atonia.

10.29

Mental activity. Dreaming is a form of mentation.

10.30

The part of the reticular formation just above the pontine level. The high levels of arousal that characterize the waking state are heavily dependent on this part of the reticular formation.

Copyright 1990 by Wadsworth, Inc.

10.21

An area of the pontine reticular formation. Cells in this area are active during REM sleep but not during the waking or NREM states.

10.22

A hormone released by the anterior pituitary on command from the hypothalamus. It helps amino acids enter cells and apparently also aids protein synthesis.

10.23

A very basic form of learning; it refers to the loss of a stimulus's ability to evoke the orienting response.

10.24

The type of stage 1 that is entered from the drowsy condition. There is no rapid eye movement.

10.25

Usually understood to mean a failure to obtain enough sleep; however, the condition apparently has more to do with the degree of emotional comfort or discomfort that the person feels during the sleep period and/or during the next day. Insomnia patients usually complain of feeling tired, uninterested, and washed out the next day.

10.31

narcolepsy

(433)

10.32

NREM sleep

(411)

10.33

nucleus reticularis magnocellularis (NRMC)

(422)

10.34

orienting reaction

(403)

10.35

PGO waves

(416)

10.36

preoptic area (POA)

(423)

10.37

raphe nuclei

(416)

10.38

rapid eye movement sleep (REM sleep)

(411)

10.39

reciprocal interaction model

(419)

10.40

reticular formation

(403)

10.36

Area of the hypothalamus located just above and forward of the optic chiasm. Stimulation of this area produces cortical synchrony typical of NREM sleep. Neurons in this area that do fire during NREM sleep do not fire during waking or REM sleep.

10.37

A group of midline brain-stem cell clusters that are the only cells in the nervous system that use serotonin as their transmitter. Once the raphe looses its control over the pontine reticular formation that area is allowed to produce PGO waves.

10.38

Emergent stage 1 sleep in which the eyes show peculiar bursts of movement beneath the closed lids.

10.39

A model of sleep-cycle control proposed by Hobson and McCarley. It states that in the waking state FTG cells are inhibited by LC cells, which are very active at that time. In NREM sleep some LC cell activity is diminished and this allows a low level of activity in FTG. The rate of FTG cell firing increases in NREM until it overwhelms the inhibition from locus coeruleus and REM sleep begins.

10.40

A long column of gray matter that starts at the bottom end of the spinal cord and runs up through the brain stem into the thalamus. It is the brain-stem portion that is mostly intimately connected with arousal.

Copyright 1990 by Wadsworth, Inc.

10.31

A disorder in which the dominant symptom is an overwhelming desire to sleep. These episodes last only 2-5 minutes and usually occur in a fairly monotonous environment. Three additional symptoms make up this syndrome: cataplexy, waking nightmares, and automatic behavior episodes.

10.32

Sleep stages 2, 3, 4 and initial stage 1.

10.33

A part of the reticular formation in the medulla that actually produces the sleep atonia. The axons of these cells run down into the spinal cord to make inhibitory synapses with the motor neurons there.

10.34

A response that involves a whole list of components. It is a reflex-like response pattern, involving the entire body and brain, that would completely interrupt ongoing behavior in favor of immediately collecting all possible information about a novel stimulus to be classified.

10.35

High-voltage, spiked waves that begin at the end of a NREM episode as the shift to REM begins and continue throughout the REM episode. They indicate a chain of activity that begins in the pontine reticular formation and sweeps up through the midbrain reticular formation, the lateral geniculate, and finally the visual cortex.

10.41

serotonergic neurons

(418)

10.42

sleep spindle

(410)

10.43

stretch reflex

(414)

10.44

suprachiasmatic nucleus (SCN)

(428)

10.45

synchrony

(401)

10.46

waking nightmares

(434)

10.47

X area

(422)

10.46

A symptom of narcolepsy in which the individual experiences vivid, frightening sensory images, especially just before sleep or just after waking. These "hallucinations" are probably dreams emerging into the waking state.

10.47

A subdivision of the reticular formation that consists of a group of cholinergic cells just anterior to locus coeruleus. It receives input from both the dorsal raphe nucleus and that locus coeruleus and is probably involved in producing sleep atonia.

10.41

Nerve cells that employ the neurotransmitter serotonin.

10.42

Alpha-like, synchronized waves of about 10-16 Hz that first increase in amplitude and then decrease, which gives them a spindle shape.

10.43

The mechanism that is responsible for producing muscle tone. Receptors for this reflex are found in the muscles, and they respond to the stretching of the muscle. As soon as the muscle relaxes it stretches out and the receptors fire impulses back to motor neurons in the spinal cord, which respond by recontracting the muscle, thus maintaining muscle tone.

10.44

An area of the hypothalamus that is believed to be the entrainment center for the rat's brain.

10.45

The clustering of electrical events. It produces large, slow waves.

Copyright 1990 by Wadsworth, Inc.

CHAPTER ELEVEN
THE CONTROL OF INGESTION

READ-WRITE-REVIEW

Read pages 440-445 and summary statements 1-3 on page 476, then answer each of the following questions in this section.
---

1. What is the state of homeostasis and how is it maintained? (440)

2. Consider the diagram of the digestive system below:

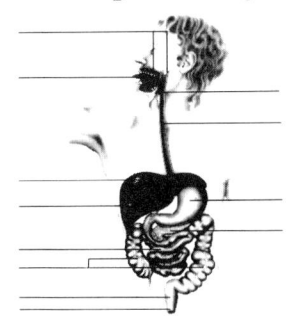

   Below is a series of statements that identify the various parts of the digestive system. Your task is to decide which of the structures is being identified and then label that structure with both the letter of the statement and the correct name.

   a. Reacts to the shift from absorptive phase to fasting phase by secreting glucagon. (443)

   b. Absorption of food into the blood vessels that line its walls is its major task. (441)

   c. Mixes food with hydrochloric acid and digestive enzymes to break it down. (441)

   d. Contains receptors that are sensitive to the presence of sugars, fats, and proteins. Most of the digestion takes place here. (441)

   e. It is the passageway from throat to stomach. (441)

   f. A ring of muscles that closes the outlet to the stomach. (441)

3. When does the absorptive phase of the eating cycle begin? (441)

   a. During the absorptive phase, starches and carbohydrates are broken down into what? (441)

   b. What are proteins broken down into during this phase? (441)

c. During the absorptive phase fats are broken down into what? (441)

d. What is an enzyme? (441)

e. Normally, neurons burn only what to provide energy? (441)

f. Of what importance are ketones? Where and from what are they manufactured? (441, 443)

g. Excess glucose can be stored in different forms. Where can it be stored and in what form must it be? (441, 443)

h. For what does the body use amino acids? (443)

i. What does the body do with excess amino acids? Where does this take place? (443)

4. When does the fasting phase of the eating cycle begin? (443)

a. When the shift from absorptive to fasting phase occurs the pancreas secretes what hormone? What is its function? (443)

b. During this phase what can happen to the triglycerides stored in the lipocytes? (443)

c. What happens to the protein in muscles when muscle cells run out of glycogen during the fasting phase? (443)

5. Describe how Carlson (1916) attempted to explain hunger in terms of a glucostatic theory. (444)

a. Show how a study in which rats were injected with insulin might provide support for a glucostatic theory. (444)

b. What problem did the disease diabetes mellitus cause for the glucostatic theory? (444)

c. How did Mayer (1952) attempt to solve the problem posed by the condition diabetes mellitus? (444-445)

d. Based on available research findings what is the current status of the glucostatic hypothesis? (445)

6. What is postulated by the aminostatic hypothesis? (445)

a. Available research findings support the existence of brain receptors that monitor the amino acid balance of the blood passing through it. Current thinking suggests what purpose for this monitoring? (445)

7. What is proposed by the lipostatic theory? (445)

a. Research, such as that of Carpenter and Grossman (1982), suggests that the presence of what substance in the blood might serve as a signal to the brain concerning the amount of stored lipids? (445)

Read pages 445-453 and summary statements 4-5 on page 476, then answer each of the following questions in this section.
---

1. Define the term "satiety." (445)

    a. "When glucose and lipid levels have been restored to normal, hunger stops." What is wrong with this satiety hypothesis? (445-446)

    b. What is "dumping"? (447)

    c. How is it anatomically possible that stomach distention could serve as a satiety cue? (447)

    d. What findings suggest that there may be more than a single satiety signal sent to the brain from the stomach? (447)

2. What is the bloodborne chemical most often suggested as a satiety signal? (447)

    a. What cells secrete this substance? (447)

    b. Where and under what conditions is this substance secreted? (447)

    c. What findings suggest that this substance has its effect entirely within the gastrointestinal tract? (447)

    d. This substance can be found in the brain and its target may be what specific area? (448)

    e. Suggest two ways in which this substance may come to be in the brain. (448)

3. Stellar (1954) proposed the existence of two brain centers, one excitatory and the other inhibitory, to control hunger. What prompted researchers to focus their activity on the hypothalamus? (448)

4. Brobeck (1943) bilaterally lesioned the ventromedial hypothalamus of a group of rats. What effect did this surgical manipulation have on the eating behavior of these rats? (448)

    a. What did Brobeck call this behavior? (448)

    b. How were Brobeck's findings interpreted? (449)

5. Studies such as that by Anand and Brobeck (1951) suggested that the excitatory hunger center is located where in the hypothalamus? (449)

    a. What is aphagia? (449)

6. Teitlebaum and Epstein (1962) bilaterally lesioned the lateral hypothalamus of rats and obtained results that could not be handled by the hypothalamic theory of hunger. What were these findings, and what problem did they pose for the hypothalamic theory? (451)

a. Anatomical findings also suggested some problems for the hypothalamic theory of hunger. What did the anatomists find, and what problem did this pose for the hypothalamic theory of hunger? (451)

7. The nigrostriatal tract and the mesolimbic system are part of a large collection of axons collectively called what? (451)

   a. What are the points of origin and termination of the nigrostriatal tract? (451)

   b. Explain why some researchers ascribed all of lateral hypothalamus aphagia to motor problems with eating. (451)

   c. Where are the origin and termination of the mesolimbic system? (451)

   d. The mesolimbic system is a central portion of what behavioral system of the brain? (451)

   e. Explain how lesions in the lateral hypothalamus might result in food and eating-related stimuli losing their reinforcing qualities. (451-452)

8. What kinds of research show that the lateral hypothalamus does seem to have a role in the initiation of hunger? (452)

   a. What is unique about kainic acid? (452)

   b. What role in hunger does the lateral hypothalamus play, as suggested by the intimate connections between the mesolimbic system and the lateral hypothalamus? (453)

   c. A second possible role proposed for the lateral hypothalamus is that of coordinating the secretion of insulin with glucose levels. What neural circuitry might make this function possible? (453)

   d. What evidence suggests that the lateral hypothalamus may play the role of glucostat? (453)

Read pages 453-461 and summary statements 6-7 on pages 476-477, then answer each of the following questions in this section.
---

1. According to the Brobeck et al. (1943) study there are two distinct phases of hyperphagia. List and describe these two phases. (454-455)

   a. What results were obtained by Hoebal and Teitlebaum (1966) when they lesioned the ventromedial hypothalamus of obese rats? (455)

   b. How would the appetite of a ventromedial hypothalamic rat best be described? (455)

2. Describe the basic components of the set-point theory of body weight regulation. (455)

   a. How might the behavior of the ventromedial hypothalamic lesioned rat be explained if one ascribes to the set-point theory of body weight regulation? (455)

   b. Identify three major flaws facing advocates of the set-point theory of body weight regulation. (455-456)

   c. Describe the parabiotic-twins technique. (456)

   d. Studies that have employed this technique obtain findings that support what theory of hunger? (457)

   e. Describe the insulin hypothesis of hunger. (457)

   f. How might the function of the ventromedial hypothalamic lesioned rat be explained by the insulin hypothesis? (457)

3. Selafani (1971), using small, discrete knife cuts just outside the boundary of the VMH, and Gold (1973), comparing the effects of such cuts to the effects of very carefully placed electrical lesions of the VMH that remained within the VMH boundaries, came to what conclusion? (458)

   a. Based on the findings of Selafani (1971) and Gold (1973), what bundle of fibers appears to be involved in the production of hyperphagia when it is damaged? (458)

   b. From where does this tract receive its major input and where is its major point of termination in the hypothalamus? (458)

   c. List several lines of evidence that suggest that despite Selafani's (1971) and Gold's (1973) findings, the VMH does play a role in satiety. (458)

   d. What alternative explanation can be offered to explain the hyperphagia that follows the destruction of the paraventricular nucleus or its input? (458-459)

   e. What two unrelated functions does the paraventricular nucleus have? (459-460)

   f. Studies show that both the lateral hypothalamus and the paraventricular nucleus are involved in the regulation of insulin levels. What is the reason for having two hypothalamic nuclei regulating insulin levels? (460-461)

Read pages 461-466 and summary statement 8 on page 477, then answer each of the following questions in this section.

---

1. What are the three main types of obesity? (462)

   a. What two explanations have been offered to account for genetic obesity? (462)

b. Discuss each of these explanations. (462)

   c. What two medical problems are likely to produce pathological obesity? (462)

   d. At present it would appear that functional obesity is due to what? (462)

2. List three extreme measures people take as a means of weight control and identify the one most commonly used. (463)

   a. What is usually found in appetite-suppressant drugs, and how does it function to control body weight? (463)

   b. What is involved in intestinal bypass surgery, and how does it function to control body weight? (463)

   c. Fasting usually produces measurable weight loss in just a day or two; however to what is this weight loss usually due? (463)

   d. Why is it that in fasting you not only lose fat, you also lose muscle? (463)

   e. What is the "pinch" test? (464)

   f. According to Woods and colleagues (1974) there are three circumstances that could lead to the oversecretion of insulin. List these. (464)

   g. Using the principles of classical conditioning show how it would be possible to gain weight by "eating" a diet drink for lunch. (464)

   h. In light of what you now know about functional obesity and weight loss what recommendations would you give a functionally obese person who wants to lose weight? (466)

Read pages 466-471 and summary statements 9-12 on page 477, then answer each of the following questions in this section.

---

1. The body water can be divided into two compartments. What are they? (466)

   a. The extracellular space can be divided into two parts. List and identify both parts. (466)

   b. Suppose that you have a large beaker of water that is divided into equal-sized right and left compartments by a membrane that will allow water and certain ions such as sodium and chloride to pass through it. Now also suppose that you dump a spoonful of table salt into the right compartment. Describe what will happen next and why. (466-467)

c. What would have happened in the example above had the holes in the membrane been so small that sodium and chloride ions could not pass through it? (467)

2. Describe what happens in the collecting sacs of the kidney and explain why this happens. (468)

   a. The blood that leaves the kidneys has a normal concentration and contains most of the glucose and sodium it originally had. What goes on in the renal tubules to account for this? (469)

   b. It is one of those "dog-days" of summer. The temperature is in the 90s and the humidity is almost as high. It seems to you that about the only thing you can do well is sweat. On such a day, what is the stimulus that specifically triggers the release of renin? (469)

   c. What secretes renin? (469)

   d. Renin is altered when it enters the bloodstream. What does it become? What are the target cells of this altered substance? What do these target cells secrete? What is the function of this hormone? (469)

   e. Locate the nucleus circularis. What is thought to exist in the nucleus circularis? (470)

   f. How would the cells located in the nucleus circularis bring about the release of adrenocorticotrophic hormone, and what specific effect would this hormone have on water balance? (470)

   g. What happens in the illness diabetes insipidus? (471)

3. What is probably the most immediate problem that arises when the body loses water? At a cellular level why is this such a problem? (471)

   a. What are baroreceptors and where are they located? (471)

   b. How do the messages from these baroreceptors reach the supraoptic nucleus? (471)

   c. How does antidiuretic hormone affect blood pressure? (471)

   d. Why do physicians put their hypertensive patients on a low-salt diet? (471)

Read pages 471-476 and summary statements 13-14 on page 477, then answer each of the following questions in this section.
---

1. Where are the drinking circuits that are associated with osmotic thirst located? (472)

   a. Where are the osmoreceptors that are associated with osmotic thirst located? (472)

   b. What is adipsia and how might you surgically produce it? (473)

c. Distinguish between osmotic and hypovolemic thirst. (475)

   d. What is the function of the subfornical organ in hypovolemic thirst? (475)

2. Why is it necessary that there be some inhibitory mechanism that cuts off drinking behavior before the body is rehydrated? (475)

   a. What neural structure would be a good candidate for such an inhibitory center and why? (475)

   b. What is water intoxication? (475)

PRE-EXAM QUIZ

Multiple-Choice
Select the choice that best completes the stem in each question and indicate your selection in the appropriate space to the left of the question.

_____1. John has just finished eating a 2-inch thick sirloin steak and a half-dozen eggs for breakfast along with toast and coffee. What will probably happen to all this protein?
   a. it will be broken down into glycerol and free fatty acids and stored in the muscles and liver
   b. it will be broken down into amino acids to be used by body cells for cellular structure, and the excess amino acids will be converted to glucose by the liver and then to fats by the lipocytes
   c. it will be broken down into amino acids by the liver, and the excess will be stored as ketones
   d. it will be broken down into glycogen by the liver and stored both there and in the muscle while the excess will be eliminated from the system in the form of a waste product
   e. none of the above

_____2. Insulin is a hormone secreted by the _____, which enables _____ to enter the body cells where it can be used.
   a. liver; glycogen
   b. pancreas; triglyceride
   c. liver; amino acids
   d. duodenum; glycerol
   e. pancreas; glucose

_____3. Cholecystokinin is secreted by the cells in the _____ and its target organ is probably the _____.
   a. liver; medial areas of the hypothalamus
   b. pancreas; mesolimbic system
   c. stomach; supraoptic nucleus in the hypothalamus
   d. small intestine; medial areas of the hypothalamus
   e. liver; medial forebrain bundle

_____4. The fact that the _____ and _____ are interrupted by lateral hypothalamus lesions led researchers to question the role of the lateral hypothalamus as a hunger center.
   a. ventral noradrenergic bundle; ventrotegmental tract
   b. mesolimbic system; nigrostriatal tract
   c. ventrotegmental tract; nigrostriatal tract
   d. rubrospinal tract; mesolimbic system
   e. ventral noradrenergic bundle; ventrotegmental tract

_____5. Which of the following is probably not one of the roles played by the lateral hypothalamus?
   a. acts as a glucostat to initiate hunger
   b. provides associative connections between food-related stimuli and the reinforcement mechanism
   c. acts as the excitatory hunger center of the brain
   d. coordinates insulin secretion with glucose levels
   e. none of the above (i.e., all of the above are roles played by the lateral hypothalamus)

_____6. In the parabiotic-twins technique two rats are surgically joined together so that they share the same
   a. nervous system   d. circulatory system
   b. digestive system   e. none of the above
   c. hormonal system

_____7. The negative-feedback mechanism known as receptor down regulation explains
   a. the dynamic phase of hyperphagia following VMH lesioning
   b. the finickiness of VMH-lesioned animals
   c. the recovery period following LH lesioning
   d. the static phase of hyperphagia following VMH lesioning
   e. the role of the paraventricular nucleus in satiety

_____8. One of the major problems with using fasting as a means of weight control is that
   a. our bodies have all sorts of automatic reactions to food shortages that tend to protect reserve nutrient supplies in our fat tissues
   b. it will lead to serious eating disturbances such as anorexia
   c. it has serious side effects such as chronic diarrhea, mineral imbalance, abdominal bloating, and liver changes
   d. weight loss is so slow that the faster receives little if any reinforcement
   e. more than one of the above

_____9. As dieters it is clear that we should not eat two or three large meals and we should avoid high amounts of carbohydrates. Why?
   a. both conditions produce increased amounts of cholecystokinin
   b. both conditions produce increased neural activity in the hypothalamus, which leads to overeating
   c. both conditions produce increased insulin secretion
   d. both conditions lead to increased activity in the medial forebrain bundle, which reinforces further eating behavior
   e. none of the above

_____10. Renin is secreted by the cells in the
   a. nuclei circularis   d. adrenal medulla
   b. liver   e. kidney
   c. adrenal cortex

_____11. Antidiuretic hormone is released in response to which of the following situations?
   a. too much fluid in the cells   d. loss of extracellular fluid
   b. too much glucose in the cells   e. none of the above
   c. too much water in the blood

_____12. In the illness diabetes insipidus
   a. too little water is retained   d. all of the above are true
   b. extreme thirst is experienced   e. none of the above are true
   c. too little antidiuretic hormone is released

_____13. Baroreceptors, located in the _____, can trigger the secretion of antidiuretic hormone in response to a drop in blood pressure.
   a. kidneys
   b. adrenal cortex
   c. heart
   d. supraoptic nucleus
   e. adrenal medulla

_____14. Which of the following best describes the route for osmotic thirst?
   a. osmoreceptors in the nucleus circularis--supraoptic nucleus--posterior pituitary--drinking
   b. osmoreceptors in the medial preoptic area--mesencephalic locomotor area--drinking
   c. kidney--adrenal cortex--drinking
   d. kidney--subfornical organ--drinking
   e. none of the above

_____15. Which of these neural centers is a prime candidate for the title "inhibitor of drinking behavior"?
   a. subfornical organ
   b. medial preoptic area
   c. septal nucleus
   d. lateral preoptic area
   e. supraoptic nucleus

True/False

_____1. Because the body requires calcium, a homeostatic mechanism will become active when blood calcium levels drop below normal and cause the individual to feel that lack or have a desire to find and ingest sources of this mineral.

_____2. Normally, neurons burn only glucose, but during starvation, when glucose is not available, the neurons fall back on amino acids for their source of energy.

_____3. Rats injected with insulin evidence lowered blood sugar levels and eat less than noninjected rats.

_____4. Rats maintained for a period of time on a diet containing 50% protein and then offered a choice between diets containing 50% or 25% protein will select the 25% protein diet.

_____5. Research findings suggest that satiety in the human is dependent on the restoration of normal levels of glucose, amino acids, and lipids.

_____6. It is possible that cholecystokinin mediates the closing of the pyloric sphincter as food enters the duodenum.

_____7. Recent studies have demonstrated that all of the aphagia seen after electrode lesions of the lateral hypothalamus can be traced to disturbances in the functions of the motor and reinforcement systems.

_____8. A VMH-lesioned animal will work extremely hard for food.

_____9. Results of paraventricular nucleus studies have ruled out any possible role for the ventromedial nucleus in the production of satiety.

_____10. Research data clearly demonstrate that excessive eating creates more lipocytes than are called for by the genes.

_____11. Osmoreceptors are probably located in the nucleus circularis, which connects directly to the posterior pituitary, where antidiuretic hormone is manufactured.

_____12. It is in the collecting sacs of the kidney that water, along with glucose and sodium, is osmosed back into the bloodstream.

_____13. The stimuli for thirst are intracellular dehydration and hypotension.

_____14. Confusion, poor motor control, and even seizures are possible symptoms of water intoxication.

_____15. Studies in which the septal nucleus has been bilaterally lesioned in rats report adipsia as the major effect.

11.1 absorptive phase (441)	11.6 antidiuretic hormone (470)
11.2 adipsia (473)	11.7 aphagia (449)
11.3 aldosterone (468-469)	11.8 baroreceptors (471)
11.4 amphetamines (463)	11.9 capillaries (467-468)
11.5 angiotensin (469)	11.10 cholecystokinin (447)

11.6

A hormone produced by cells in the suraoptic nucleus of the hypothalamus and stored in and released from the posterior pituitary. It acts on the renal tubules of the kidneys to increase their reabsorption of water from the urine.

11.7

Complete lack of interest in eating.

11.8

Blood pressure level detectors located in the heart. They send impulses via the vagus nerve to nucleus tractus solitarius and then to the supraoptic nucleus where antidiuretic hormone is manufactured.

11.9

Very fine, hair-like blood vessels that form a network between small arteries and veins.

11.10

Chemical secreted by intestinal cells when food enters the duodenum and appears to play a role in stimulating the secretion of digestive enzymes from the pancreas. Research findings suggest that it may serve as a bloodborne satiety signal.

Copyright 1990 by Wadsworth, Inc.

11.1

The phase of the eating cycle entered into just after a meal when the concentrations of nutrients are high.

11.2

Cessation of the drinking behavior.

11.3

Hormone secreted by the adrenal cortex that reaches the kidneys by way of the blood and increases the rate of sodium reabsorption.

11.4

A class of drugs. These drugs act as central nervous system stimulants. They increase "nervous energy" and decrease appetite. For this reason one or more of these drugs are found in some amount in appetite-suppressant drugs.

11.5

A substance formed in the blood from renin. It is capable of stimulating the cells in the adrenal cortex.

11.11

corticotropin-releasing factor

(460)

11.12

diabetes insipidus

(471)

11.13

diabetes mellitus

(444)

11.14

duodenum

(441)

11.15

dynamic phase

(454-455)

11.16

enzymes

(441)

11.17

extracellular space

(466)

11.18

fasting

(463)

11.19

fasting phase

(441)

11.20

genetic obesity

(462)

11.16

Chemicals that assemble molecules out of smaller parts or break down molecules into their constituents.

11.17

One of the body's two major water compartments; it is the area between the cells and includes both the space between cells and the volume within the blood vessels.

11.18

A technique of weight control that involves taking absolutely no food of any form for days or weeks at a time.

11.19

The phase of the eating cycle during which the concentrations of nutrients have fallen below set point. It follows the absorptive phase.

11.20

Obesity that occurs when the individual's genes program an excessive number of lipocytes in relation to the number of muscle cells.

Copyright 1990 by Wadsworth, Inc.

11.11

A hormone secreted by certain cells within the paraventricular nucleus of the hypothalamus that stimulates the anterior pituitary to secrete adrenocorticotrophic hormone.

11.12

An illness in which insufficient amounts of antidiuretic hormone are secreted, which results in abnormally low water retention, substantially increased frequency of urination, and considerable thirst.

11.13

A disorder characterized by the inadequate production of insulin. In diabetes body cells slowly starve for glucose while plentiful supplies of blood glucose flow past them in the blood vessels, unable to cross the cell-membrane barrier.

11.14

The initial 12-inch length of small intestine in which most of the digestion by enzymes occurs. It also contains receptors that can detect the presence of sugars, fats, and proteins.

11.15

Initial phase of hyperphagia in which the animal eats voraciously and gains weight very rapidly.

11.21

globus pallidus

(451)

11.22

glucagon

(443)

11.23

glucocorticoids

(460)

11.24

glucose

(441)

11.25

glycerol

(441)

11.26

glycogen

(441)

11.27

homeostasis

(440)

11.28

hyperdipsia

(475)

11.29

hypertension

(471)

11.30

hypodipsia

(471)

11.26

Found in muscles and liver, it is the stored form of excess glucose. Glycogen stores are a short-term energy supply and are used up in minutes.

11.27

The body's attempt to maintain the concentrations of many chemicals at nearly the same level from moment to moment by employing neural circuits and hormonal secretions called homeostatic mechanisms.

11.28

Excessive drinking behavior.

11.29

High blood pressure.

11.30

Inadequate water intake.

11.21

One of the nuclei in the corpus striatum.

11.22

Hormone secreted by the pancreas that enables the liver and muscles to convert glycogen to glucose.

11.23

A class of adrenal hormones secreted by the adrenal cortex in response to stimulation by the adrenocorticotrophic hormone. These hormones have a variety of effects on tissues throughout the body, which are all related to stress resistance.

11.24

A simple sugar that is one of the breakdown products of starch and other carbohydrates.

11.25

One of the breakdown products of fats.

Copyright 1990 by Wadsworth, Inc.

11.31

hypothalamic hyperphagia

(448)

11.32

insulin

(444)

11.33

intestinal bypass

(436)

11.34

intracellular space

(466)

11.35

ketones

(441)

11.36

lipocytes

(441)

11.37

lipoprotein lipase

(462)

11.38

medial preoptic area

(472)

11.39

mesencephalic locomotor area

(472-473)

11.40

mesolimbic system

(451)

11.36

Fat cells.

11.31

An unnatural overeating as a result of lesioning the ventromedial hypothalamus.

11.37

The most important enzyme for converting circulatory fats into stored triglycerides. The more lipoprotein lipase an individual possesses, the more readily the fats are stored rather than burned.

11.32

A hormone secreted by the pancreas that enables glucose to enter the body cells where it can be used.

11.38

A zone of the hypothalamus found at the anterior tip of the third ventricle. This area is believed to contain osmoreceptors.

11.33

Technically called jejunileal bypass, this surgical technique involves the making of a short connection that routes food past most of the small intestine.

11.39

Contains the neural circuitry that controls the drinking response.

11.34

One of the body's two major water compartments; it is the area inside the cells.

11.40

Tract originating in the midbrain nucleus called the ventrotegmental area and terminating in the limbic areas. It is a central portion of the hypothesized reinforcement system of the brain.

11.35

Chemicals that are manufactured from fats by the liver. They can be used by neurons for fuel when glucose is unavailable as in the case of starvation.

Copyright 1990 by Wadsworth, Inc.

11.41

nigrostriatal tract

(451)

11.42

nucleus of tractus solitarius

(453)

11.43

osmoreceptors

(470)

11.44

osmotic pressure

(466)

11.45

pancreas

(443)

11.46

parabiotic-twins technique

(456)

11.47

pathological obesity

(462)

11.48

pyloric sphincter

(441)

11.49

receptor down regulation

(457)

11.50

renal tubules

(468)

11.46

Research technique in which two rats are surgically joined together like "Siamese" twins so that they share the same circulation.

11.41

Part of the medial forebrain bundle; this tract begins in the substantia nigra of the midbrain and terminates in the corpus striatum. Damage to this tract makes it difficult for the individual to start and stop movements.

11.47

Type of obesity that includes patients suffering from endocrine gland disorders and ventromedial hypothalamic tumors. Such obesity is very rare.

11.42

Nucleus of the medulla that receives input from taste receptors and lateral hypothalamic nucleus.

11.48

The ring of muscles that closes the outlet from the stomach into the duodenum.

11.43

Specialized hypothalamic cells that were sensitive to stretch. Thus, according to Verney, such cells would fire when dehydrated but stop firing as they swelled up with water and the receptor elements attached to the membrane were stretched.

11.49

A negative feedback mechanism that senses that there is too much insulin activity and slows the creation of insulin receptor sites on cell membranes.

11.44

The force that moves ions across a semi-permeable membrane from a compartment of higher concentration to one of lower concentration according to the natural tendency of these ions to distribute themselves evenly throughout any space.

11.50

Small tubes located in the kidney that provide a large area of contact with the capillaries, along which the water in the tubules can osmose from the thinly concentrated urine to the more concentrated blood.

11.45

Small organ located near the base of the stomach and beginning of the small intestine. It reacts to the shift from the absorptive to the fasting phase by secreting the hormone glucagon.

11.51 renin (469)

11.52 satiety (445)

11.53 septal nucleus (475)

11.54 set-point (440)

11.55 set-point theory (455)

11.56 static phase (455)

11.57 triglyceride (441, 443)

11.58 vascular space (466)

11.59 ventromedial hypothalamus (448)

11.56

Second phase of hyperphagia in which just enough is eaten to maintain the new body weight.

11.51

A chemical secreted by the kidney in response to signals from low blood volume detectors located in the blood vessels of the kidneys.

11.57

A type of fat found in lipocytes. It is a stored form of excess glucose.

11.52

The state of being "full" and no longer hungry.

11.58

One of two major subdivisions of the extracellular water compartment of the body. It includes the volume within the blood vessels, heart, and lymph ducts.

11.53

A midline structure lying immediately in front of the anterior hypothalamus. It has strong connections with both the anterior hypothalamus and the brain stem and is thought to function as an inhibitor of drinking.

11.59

One of the hypothalamus nuclei classically thought to be the satiety center for hunger.

11.54

The desired level of a needed chemical that is maintained by homeostatic mechanisms.

11.55

Proposes that body weight is regulated homeostatically and therefore must have a set point toward which the system strives.

Copyright 1990 by Wadsworth, Inc.

CHAPTER TWELVE
SEXUALITY AND REPRODUCTION

READ-WRITE-REVIEW

Read pages 482-488 and the summary statements 1-3 on page 509, then answer each of the following questions in this section.
---

1. What constitutes a male, genetically? (483)

    a. What constitutes a female, genetically? (483)

    b. At what time during the organism's development do gonads first form? (483)

    c. Describe these gonads. (483)

    d. By the sixth week the gonads differentiate into ovaries and testes. Research has not yet been able to determine the precise process by which this occurs, but what is known is that the _____ influence it. (483)

    e. From this point on in prenatal development sexual differentiation is under _____ influence. (483)

2. What is the relationship between testosterone and the estrogens? (483)

3. What are the two temporary structures found in each embryo called? (485)

    a. If the embryo has developed testes, which of these systems will continue its development and what structures will develop? (485)

    b. What will happen to the other structure? (485)

    c. Describe how this is accomplished. (485)

    d. If the embryo had developed ovaries, into what would the other temporary structure have developed? (485)

    e. When in the development of the organism do the external genitalia begin to differentiate? (485)

    f. What is meant by the statement, "When in doubt, nature makes a female"? (485)

4. At what point does the final burst of physical development occur? (485)

    a. What controls the secretion of the gonadotropic hormones and from where do they come? (485)

b. The two gonadotropic hormones that are secreted are ____ and ____. Specifically, what endocrine gland secretes these hormones? (485)

   c. The result of these two hormones will be the awakening of the gonads and the tremendous increase in the secretion of testosterone and estrogen. This sudden increase in gonadal hormones results in what two things? (487)

5. The gonadotropic hormones continue to play a vital role throughout the reproductive life of the individual. Explain the role of the follicle-stimulating hormone in the menstrual cycle. (488)

   a. What role does luteinizing hormone play in the menstrual cycle? (488)

   b. Once the ruptured follicle releases its ovum it becomes an endocrine gland and is called what? (488)

   c. What hormone is produced by this gland and what are the effects of this hormone? (488-489)

Read pages 489-493 and the summary statements 4-5 on pages 509-510, then answer each of the following questions in this section.
---

1. What is the difference between gender identity and gender assignment? (489-490)

2. In the case of androgen insensitivity syndrome, what chromosomal combination does the individual have? (490)

   a. Why does the Wolffian duct not develop? (490)

   b. Why doesn't the Mullerian duct develop? (490)

   c. What is the usual gender assignment in such a case? (490)

   d. At what stage in development does this initial gender assignment become a problem? (490)

   e. Why? (490)

   f. In the case of an individual, when conflicts arise between the factors determining gender identity, the individual is labeled what? (491)

3. List any two female hermaphrodism syndromes. (491-492)

   a. Describe the specific cause in each condition. (491-492)

   b. Describe the internal and external genitalia that are developed in each case. (491-492)

   c. In each condition how is the child normally raised? (491-492)

4. What is the function of the enzyme 5-alpha reductase? (492)

   a. What effect does the lack of this enzyme have on the development of the external genitalia? (492)

5. List and briefly identify the six determinants of gender. (493)

Read pages 493-501 and the summary statements 6-8 on page 510, then answer each of the following questions in this section.
---

1. The developmental process that leads to sex-specific brain circuits is called what? (493)

2. Phoenix et al. (1959) described the hormonal influences on the brain's circuitry in terms of two very distinct effects. What are these effects called and when do they occur? (494)

   a. In the male neonatal finch how is masculinization of the brain accomplished? (494-495)

   b. Why is alpha fetoprotein necessary in the neonatal female? (494)

   c. How does this protein work? (494)

   d. Nottebaum's (1981) study of masculinization of brain circuits focused on the song nucleus of the male finch. To what did he attribute the larger-sized neurons he found in this nucleus? (495)

   e. How did Nottebaum (1981) explain the greater number of neurons found in this song nucleus? (495)

3. The spinal nucleus of the bulbocavernosus of the male rat is easily distinguishable from that found in the female rat. What characteristics can be used to distinguish between these two structures? (497)

4. Penile erection is a reflexive response. Briefly describe how this reflex operates. (497-498)

   a. Provide a possible biological explanation for secondary impotence. (498)

5. There are a number of brain areas that appear to play some role in the sexual behavior of the adult. Below is a sagittal view of the rat brain and immediately below the diagram is a series of six statements that describe some of these areas. Read each of these statements and identify the structure by name in the space provided. Then locate the structure on the diagram and label it using the identifying letter of the statement.

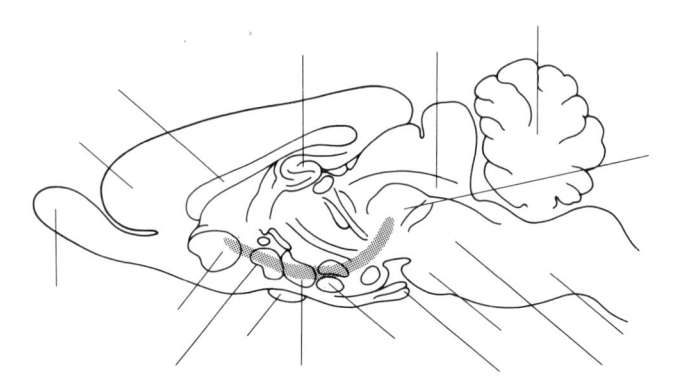

   a. Destruction of this area results in a permanent loss of the male's ability to copulate. (498)

   b. The secretions of this greatly influence the circulating testosterone levels. (499)

   c. This is a major bundle of fibers connecting segments of the limbic system with the midbrain. (499)

   d. This is part of a larger area that probably makes it possible for sexual thoughts to elicit penile erections. (498)

   e. Together with c it is a major component of the reinforcement system and probably links sex and pleasure. (498)

   f. The receptive behaviors of females are under the control of this area. (498)

6. What explanation can you give for the fact that whereas the male sexual behavior is controlled by the rather complex set of structures described in the preceding section, female sexual behavior appears to be controlled by a hypothalamic nucleus that also plays a role in the control of food intake? (498)

   a. What reason can you give for maternal behavior being controlled by the same brain circuitry as male sexual behavior? (498)

7. A male rat is castrated shortly after it is born. When the rat is an adult he is given an injection of estrogen. What behavior would you expect from this rat when put with another rat? (500)

   a. Why would you expect to see such behavior? (500)

Read pages 501-510 and the summary statements 9-12 on page 510, then answer each of the following questions in this section.
---

1. Concerning sexual motivation, what kinds of effects can you expect to see in animals that have been castrated as adults? (502-503)

    a. What effects would you expect to see from the post-pubertal castration of human males? (503)

    b. What is the important determinant of female sexual motivation according to the findings of the Chambers and Phoenix (1987) study, which used ovariectomized, adult female rhesus monkeys? (503-504)

    c. As one moves up the phylogenetic scale what happens to the role played by hormones in the determination of behavior? (503)

2. Studies of rats and lower primates suggest that the role played by androgen levels on certain kinds of aggression can best be described as _____. (504)

3. What has caused some people to view homosexuality as the result of a biological error early in life? (505)

4. Explain briefly the Ellis and Ames (1987) biological theory of sexual orientation. (505)

    a. It has been demonstrated that male rats castrated at birth demonstrate little interest in females but may seek out other males and allow them to mount and then display lordosis. Sexual inversion may be one interpretation. What other possible interpretation has been offered? (505-506)

    b. Stressing a pregnant female rat produces what kind of behavior in the male offspring? (506)

5. In addition to the animal evidence, Ellis and Ames also offer three lines of human evidence, the first of which focuses on the LH surge. What is the LH surge? (506)

    a. How do Ellis and Ames use this phenomenon as supportive evidence for their theory? (506-507)

    b. What are the objections to this interpretation that have been raised by the critics of this theory? (507)

6. According to Ellis and Ames the Dominican Republic study findings also provide support for their theory. Describe briefly this study. (507)

   a. How do Ellis and Ames explain the fact that the subjects of this study were raised as females for more than a decade, were taught to think of themselves as girls, but at puberty expressed a male sexual orientation? (507)

   b. What alternative explanations of these findings have been offered? (507-508)

7. Identical twin studies constitute the third line of evidence offered by Ellis and Ames. What are the results of these studies? (508-509)

   a. What might be inherited that would produce sexual inversion? (509)

8. Which of the lines of evidence seem to offer the greatest promise for the Ellis and Ames theory? (509)

PRE-EXAM QUIZ

Multiple-Choice
Select the choice that best completes the stem in each question and indicate your selection in the appropriate space to the left of the question.

_____ 1. The role of Sertoli cells is to
   a. serve as a part of the neural circuitry involved in the pleasure derived from reproductive behavior
   b. produce the gonadotropin-releasing hormone factors
   c. provide protection for maturing the ovum while in the ovary
   d. provide the neural circuitry involved in song production in the canary
   e. none of these

_____ 2. Follicle-stimulating hormone
   a. has an inhibitory effect on the female receptivity
   b. brings about the release of the ovum from the follicle in the ovary
   c. encourages the maturation of the ova
   d. prepares the uterus for implantation of the ovum
   e. more than one of the above

_____ 3. The lack of enzyme 21-hydroxylase produced by the inheritance of two recessive genes results in
   a. an inability to maintain a proper salt balance
   b. an inability to produce dihydrotestosterone
   c. androgen insensitivity syndrome
   d. a female hermaphrodism syndrome
   e. more than one of the above

_____ 4. If we injected a neonatal female finch with estrogen it will result in
   a. feminization of the brain
   b. masculinization of the brain
   c. inhibition of the Mullerian ducts
   d. inhibition of the Wolffian ducts
   e. more than one of the above

_____ 5. Lesioning of the medial preoptic area of the hypothalamus of the female rat results in
   a. disruption of female sexual receptivity
   b. masculinization of the brain
   c. interruption of the estrous cycle
   d. disruption of maternal behaviors
   e. none of the above

_____ 6. The fact that Joe Cool experiences an erection while thinking about the date he has tonight can probably be explained by the activity of
   a. testosterone
   b. limbic system
   c. sympathetic nervous system
   d. ventromedial nucleus
   e. medial preoptic area of the hypothalamus

_____ 7. The fact that sexual behavior is pleasurable (at least for the male rat) can best be explained in terms of
   a. the limbic-posterior hypothalamic connection
   b. comparative circulating levels of testosterone and estrogen
   c. the medial preoptic hypothalamic area-ventrotegmental area connection
   d. the ventromedial hypothalamic nucleus
   e. none of the above

_____ 8. Relative to rats and lower primates, the role of androgens in aggressive behavior can best be described as
   a. having an activational effect on the brain
   b. causing sex differences in aggressive play
   c. having an organizational effect on the brain
   d. having both an organizational and activational effect on the brain
   e. having no effect at all

_____ 9. Progesterone is a hormone secreted by the
   a. anterior pituitary
   b. uterus
   c. corpus luteum
   d. preoptic hypothalamic area
   e. posterior pituitary

_____10. Testosterone is but one of a family of chemicals that are derived from
   a. estrogen
   b. steroids
   c. phosphorated proteins
   d. diphosphates
   e. cholesterol

_____11. Alpha fetoprotein accomplishes its task by
   a. instructing the gonads to produce androgens or estrogen, thus initiating the activational phase of development
   b. converting some progesterone to cortisol to aid in the resistance of stress
   c. binding the circulating estrogen in the female finch neonate so that it cannot cross the blood-brain barrier
   d. converting testosterone to estrogen
   e. none of the above

_____12. The female receptive behavior called lordosis is probably a result of activity of neural circuits in the
   a. preoptic area of the hypothalamus
   b. ventromedial hypothalamus
   c. limbic system
   d. medial forebrain bundle
   e. none of the above

_____13. Castration of a postpuberty human male
   a. will show a sharp decline in sexual motivation unless there has been a history of frequent copulatory behavior
   b. will initially produce a decrease in sexual motivation and an inability to maintain an erection
   c. will initially result in an inability to ejaculate
   d. appears to have little effect on sexual behavior
   e. none of the above

_____14. Development of the male external genitalia is encouraged directly by which of the following?
   a. estrogen   d. testosterone
   b. 5-alpha reductase   e. none of the above
   c. 21-hydroxylase

_____15. The sex that an individual considers himself or herself to be is his or her
   a. sex orientation   d. sexual inversion
   b. gender identity   e. gender preference
   c. gender assignment

True/False

_____1. An individual's gender identity is determined by genes alone.

_____2. At the onset of puberty there is a tremendous increase in gonadal hormones.

_____3. The androgen insensitivity syndrome victim is typically raised as a male because the individual began life as an embryo with an XY chromosomal combination.

_____4. It is possible to masculinize the brain of the neonatal female finch by injecting her with estrogens.

_____5. All normal human embryos have both a Mullerian duct and a Wolffian duct.

_____6. On the basis of the neural circuitry involved, one would predict that a trauma that produced the severing of the cord at its uppermost level from the brain would make it impossible for a male victim to ever experience penile erection.

_____7. The enzyme 5-alpha-reductase is necessary for full prenatal development of the male external genitalia.

_____8. Human reproductive behavior can best be described as a well-coordinated series of reflexive behaviors.

_____9. Even though there is a definite lack of data available, it seems likely that human male and female sexual motivation is heavily influenced by levels of gonadal hormones.

_____10. According to the Ellis and Ames (1987) theory, homosexuality is viewed primarily as a product of intrauterine sexual differentiation of the brain.

_____11. The chance that one twin will be homosexual if the other is turns out to be no higher in identical twins than in fraternal twins.

_____12. An individual's gender identity and gender assignment may not agree with his or her genetic gender.

_____13. Studies of rats and lower primates strongly suggest the existence of a link between the hormone testosterone and aggressive behavior.

_____14. It is not until the fetal period of development that gonads first begin to form.

_____15. The human menstrual cycle is triggered by the secretion of the luteinizing hormone.

12.1

activational effect

(494)

12.2

adrenogenital syndrome

(492)

12.3

alpha fetoprotein

(494)

12.4

androgen-induced hermaphrodism

(492)

12.5

androgen insensitivity syndrome

(490)

12.6

androgens

(483)

12.7

anterior pituitary gland

(485)

12.8

brain differentiation

(493)

12.9

chromosomes

(483)

12.10

corpus luteum

(488)

12.6

A family of hormones derived from cholesterol and produced and secreted by the adrenal cortex and gonads. Testosterone is one member of this family.

12.7

The part of the pituitary that produces and secretes both the follicle-stimulating hormone and the luteinizing hormone in response to the releasing factors secreted by cells in the hypothalamus.

12.8

The developmental processes that lead to sex-specific brain circuits.

12.9

Groupings of genes arranged into 23 pairs.

12.10

An endocrine gland developed from a ruptured ovarian follicle under the influence of the luteinizing hormone; secretes progesterone.

Copyright 1990 by Wadsworth, Inc.

12.1

According to Phoenix, the activational effect is the result of the effect of testosterone on the masculinized brain circuitry of the adult male. Specifically the activational effect refers to the high rate of male behavior.

12.2

Masculinization of the external genitalia of a developing XX fetus brought about by overproduction of androgens by the child's own adrenal cortex. It is caused by a genetically produced lack of the enzyme 21-hydroxylase.

12.3

A circulating chemical in the bloodstream of neonates that temporally binds estrogen so that it cannot cross the blood-brain barrier and affect the nervous system.

12.4

Masculinization of external genitalia of a developing XX fetus due to the mother's development of an adrenal cortical tumor, resulting in excessive androgen production. Because androgen production occurs late, the developing Mullerian duct is unaffected.

12.5

A condition in which the tissue of a developing XY fetus becomes insensitive to testosterone resulting in the Wolffian duct remaining undeveloped. Thus neither set of genitalia develops as Mullerian duct-inhibiting factor is produced.

12.11

dihydrotestosterone (DHT)

(492)

12.12

dimorphism

(483)

12.13

embryo

(483)

12.14

estrogens

(483)

12.15

estrous cycle

(489)

12.16

fallopian tubes

(485)

12.17

follicle

(488)

12.18

follicle-stimulating hormone (FSH)

(485)

12.19

gender assignment

(490)

12.20

gender identity

(489)

12.16

Tubes that transport the ova from the ovaries to the uterus.

12.11

An androgen that encourages the development of the external male genitalia.

12.17

Small pockets of cells within the ovaries stimulated by the follicle-stimulating hormone to mature the ova within it.

12.12

Body differences between the sexes.

12.18

A gonadotropic hormone that stimulates the ovarian follicle to mature the ovum. Together with LH it stimulates the gonads to suddenly increase their secretions at puberty.

12.13

The term given the developing human from the 3rd to the 12th prenatal week; during this period the gonads begin to form.

12.19

The gender of an individual as determined by the obstetrician. It appears on the birth certificate.

12.14

The female sexual hormones that are secreted by the ovaries. They function to develop female sex characteristics.

12.20

The sex that an individual considers herself/himself.

12.15

Hormonal and physical changes in the reproductive system and changes in sexual receptivity of most female mammals other than primates.

Copyright 1990 by Wadsworth, Inc.

12.21 genes (483)	12.26 intersexual (491)
12.22 gonadotrophin-releasing factors (GRF) (485)	12.27 LH surge (506)
12.23 gonads (482)	12.28 lordosis (498)
12.24 hermaphrodism (482)	12.29 luteinizing hormone (LH) (485)
12.25 21-hydroxylase (492)	12.30 medial forebrain bundle (MFB) (499)

12.26

An individual in which conflicts have arisen among the six factors determining gender identity.

12.27

The normal rise in luteinizing hormone resulting from the combined effects of estrogen and luteinizing hormone releasing factor.

12.28

Intercourse posture adopted by the female mammal in which she arches her back and moves her tail to one side to facilitate mounting.

12.29

A gonadotropic hormone that causes ovulation and later in the cycle causes the ovarian follicle to become a corpus luteum.

12.30

A major tract consisting of the axons of cells in the medial preoptic area. It terminates in the ventrotegmental area. With the VTA, it provides the pleasurable feelings associated with sexual behavior in males and maternal behavior.

Copyright 1990 by Wadsworth, Inc.

12.21

Individual segments of DNA that are organized into groupings called chromosomes. They contain the complete set of building plans for an entire organism.

12.22

Hormones produced by the hypothalamus that cause the anterior pituitary gland to secrete the gonadotropic hormones.

12.23

Testes or ovaries.

12.24

Having both sexes in the same body.

12.25

An enzyme that normally converts some progesterone to cortisol, a hormone involved in resisting stress.

12.31 medial preoptic area (MPOA) (498)

12.32 masculinization (494)

12.33 menstrual cycle (487)

12.34 morphology (483)

12.35 mounting (498)

12.36 Mullerian ducts (485)

12.37 Mullerian inhibiting factor (MIF) (485)

12.38 organizational effect (494)

12.39 ovaries (483)

12.40 ovulation (488)

12.36

The embryonic system that develops into the internal female sex organs, including the fallopian tubes and uterus.

12.37

A defeminizing hormone secreted by the Sertoli cells; it prevents the development of the Mullerian duct.

12.38

According to Phoenix, the testosterone effect wherein this hormone determines that male circuitry will be established in the new brain. This process, called masculinization, takes place before birth or around the time of hatching.

12.39

Female gonads.

12.40

The release of the ovum from the follicle, which is triggered by a sudden increase in luteinizing hormone.

12.31

A group of sexually differentiated neurons that contain circuits that control mounting and erection in the male rat and nest building, nursing, and pup retrieval in the female.

12.32

Induction of male morphology (in the brain or the rest of the body) by hormones.

12.33

The hormonal and physical changes in the reproductive system of most female primates that occurs on a 28-day cycle.

12.34

The shape, structure, or appearance of the body.

12.35

The important copulatory behavior in the mammalian male.

Copyright 1990 by Wadsworth, Inc.

12.41 progesterone	12.46 secondary sex characteristics
(488)	(487)
12.42 progesterone-induced hermaphrodism	12.47 seminal vesicle
(491)	(485)
12.43 puberty	12.48 Sertoli cells
(485)	(485)
12.44 levator ani muscle	12.49 sexual inversion
(496)	(505)
12.45 secondary impotence	12.50 sexual orientation
(498)	(505)

12.46

Physical features that are developed after the onset of puberty and are characteristic of the sexually mature male or female. Examples include development of breasts, pubic hair, and facial hair and enlargement of the voice box.

12.47

The sac that holds the sperm until they are ejaculated.

12.48

Cells generated by the Y-chromosome. Their function is to secrete the chemical Mullerian-duct inhibiting factor, which prevents the development of the Mullerian duct.

12.49

Choice of a same-sexed partner.

12.50

The choice of a sexual partner.

12.41

A hormone secreted by the corpus luteum that prepares the uterus for the implantation of the ovum and inhibits female sexual receptivity.

12.42

Masculinization of external genitalia of a developing XX embryo brought about by the mother's use of the synthetic steroid progestin.

12.43

The period that begins adolescence, somewhere around the age of 11 for girls or 13 for boys. Also the period during which the person acquires the ability to reproduce.

12.44

A muscle that aids the bulbocavernosus in the ejaculation of sperm and in the maintenance of an erection.

12.45

A male sexual dysfunction in which anxiety renders the person incapable of having or keeping an erection during intercourse.

Copyright 1990 by Wadsworth, Inc.

12.51

spinal nucleus of the bulbocavernosus

(496)

12.52

testes

(483)

12.53

testosterone

(483)

12.54

uterus

(485)

12.55

vas deferens

(485)

12.56

ventromedial hypothalamus (VMH)

(498)

12.57

ventrotegmental area (VTA)

(499)

12.58

Wolffian duct

(485)

12.59

X-chromosome

(483)

12.60

Y-chromosome

(483)

12.56

Area of the hypothalamus that controls female receptivity behavior.

12.51

A cluster of neurons located in the lower spinal cord that innervates the predominately male muscles--the bulbocavernosus and the levator ani.

12.57

Region of the midbrain tegmentum that receives fibers from the medial preoptic area via the medial forebrain bundle. Probably mediates the pleasure of sexual activities and maternal behavior.

12.52

Male gonads.

12.58

The embryonic system that develops into the internal male sex organs, including the vas deferens and the seminal vesicles.

12.53

A sex hormone secreted by the testes that is responsible for the development of male secondary sex characteristics and the production of sperm.

12.59

Sex-determining chromosome. A pair of X-chromosomes are needed to produce a female.

12.54

Part of the female reproductive system within which fertilized eggs will mature into fetuses.

12.60

Sex-determining chromosome. A Y-chromosome must be paired with an X-chromosome to produce a male.

12.55

Tubes that carry the sperm from the testes to the seminal vesicles.

Copyright 1990 by Wadsworth, Inc.

CHAPTER THIRTEEN
EMOTION AND STRESS

READ-WRITE-REVIEW

Read pages 514-521 and summary statements 1-3 on page 540, then answer each of the following questions in this section.

---

1. What difficulties do physiological psychologists face in attempting to answer the question, "What sort of brain mechanisms are emotions, and where are they located?" (514)

    a. List and briefly identify the three dimensions that underlie emotions and may represent real brain processes. (515)

    b. Identify the part or parts of the brain circuitry that can be associated with each of these dimensions. (515)

2. What kind of useful distinction can be made between fear and anxiety? (517)

3. Egaz Moniz was the first to suggest surgery as a way of relieving the debilitating effects of anxiety suffered by psychotic patients. What did he propose to remove surgically? (517)

    a. What name is attached to this surgical procedure? (517)

    b. Beside relieving the anxiety of the psychotic patient, what other effects were produced by the surgery? (517-518)

    c. What happened in the 1950s that greatly reduced the frequency of this surgical procedure? (517)

4. Locate the amygdala. (518)

    a. How is the amygdala related to the orbitofrontal cortex? (518)

    b. What did Kluver and Bucy (1938, 1939) find when they bilaterally amygdalectomized their rhesus monkey subjects? (518)

    c. Stimulation of the amygdala and the area around it has been observed in humans under what conditions? (520)

    d. What kinds of behavioral changes are observed in these two conditions? (520)

e. More recently, researchers have selectively lesioned or stimulated individual amygdaloid nuclei with what results? (520)

f. What is the probable contribution of the amygdala to fear? (520)

g. What makes the amygdala such a perfect structure for this role? (520)

h. Below is a frontal section of the brain just posterior to the optic chiasm. Locate and label the three divisions of the amygdala. (519)

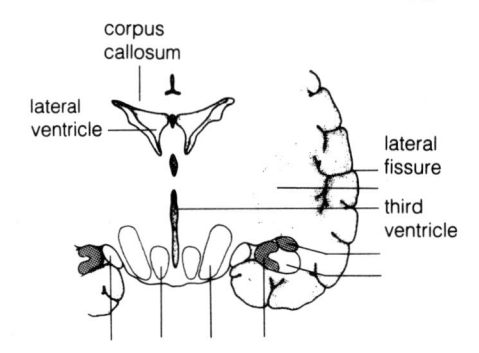

5. How does the amygdala exert its control over the emotion response if the response circuits are located in the brain stem and spinal cord? (520)

   a. The presence of fear or anxiety can be objectively measured by what changes? (520)

   b. What is HACER? (520)

   c. What happens when this area is lesioned? (520)

   d. What is the role of the medial hypothalamus in fear? (521)

   e. Axons of the medial hypothalamus go where? (521)

   f. What is the function of this area in fear? (521)

Read pages 521-524 and summary statement 4 on page 540, then answer each of the following questions in this section.
---

1. What role does the sympathetic nervous system play in fear and anger? (521-522)

2. The class of drugs that relieve anxiety is called what? (522)

   a. Who discovered the barbiturates and from what are they derived? (522)

   b. What symptoms do these drugs produce? (523)

   c. How do barbiturates affect transmission and how is this effect brought about? (523)

d. Why are barbiturates considered a poor solution to the problem of anxiety? (523)

e. Another set of drugs that relieve anxiety was discovered in 1957. What is this set called? (523)

f. What are two examples of this set? (523)

g. What is the effect of these drugs on neural transmission? (523)

h. Exactly what do these drugs do that potentates activity at the GABA synapse? (523)

i. If chlordiazepoxide is injected directly into the rat's periaqueductal gray area, significantly higher levels of shock are needed to induce fleeing. The same effect can be obtained with injections of GABA. What do these results imply? (524)

Read pages 524-531 and summary statements 5-6 on page 541, then answer each of the following questions in this section.
---

1. List and describe Moyer's (1976) seven categories of mammalian aggressive behavior. (524)

2. Fear-induced aggression is almost always preceded by what? (524-525)

    a. What are some behaviors characteristic of fear-induced aggression? (525)

    b. Trace the structures involved in fear-induced aggression and indicate the role played by each. (525)

3. Describe the behaviors exhibited by the resident male when confronted by a strange male. (525)

    a. Trace the structures involved in intermale aggression and indicate the role played by each. (526-527)

4. What is missing in the behaviors observed in predatory aggression? (527)

    a. Trace the structures involved in predatory aggression and indicate the role played by each. (527-528)

291

5. Irritable aggression in mammals most closely resembles what emotions in humans? (528)

   a. What structures in the nervous system play a role in this form of aggression and what function does each serve? (529-530)

Read pages 531-540 and summary statements 7-12 on page 541, then answer each of the following questions in this section.
---

1. What is stress? (531)

   a. According to Hans Selye if stress continues long enough it will produce a set of conditions he called what? (531)

   b. What is the immune system and what has it to do with the symptoms of prolonged stress? (531-532)

   c. Under conditions of prolonged stress what happens to the adrenal cortex? (532)

   d. Another symptom that occurs under conditions of prolonged stress is ulcers. What happens to cause the ulcers? (532)

   e. According to Selye the body reacts to prolonged stress by going through three stages. List and identify these three stages. (532)

2. What are psychosomatic disorders? (532)

   a. The recent emphasis researchers have placed on stress has led to the concept of multiple causation. Explain this idea. (533)

3. During any kind of stress the pituitary-adrenal cortex response occurs. Describe this response in detail. (534-535)

   a. Depending on the circumstances, this response is under the control of a number of various parts of the body, including the paraventricular nucleus. Locate this nucleus. (534)

   b. Under what conditions does this control unit activate? (534)

   c. What does the paraventricular nucleus do under these conditions? (534)

4. What is an antigen and what is its function? (535)

   a. To deal with these antigens the body must make what? (535)

   b. What purpose do these structures serve? (535)

c. What purpose do the lymphocytes and leucocytes serve? (535)

d. What is it that makes you immune to a particular disease? (536)

e. What part of the immune system is of most interest to stress researchers? (536)

5. Consider the Kasi et al. (1979) study involving the Epstein-Barr virus and West Point cadets. Describe briefly the research stratagem employed in this study. (536-537)

   a. What were the findings of this study? (537)

   b. What is the best explanation of these results? (537)

6. List five factors that interact with stress to produce a level of immuno-suppression, and in each case indicate the effect of the factor. (538)

7. Stress, such as that brought about by being defeated in combat, affects the secretion of what two substances? (538)

   a. What effects do each of these substances have on the body? (538)

   b. What is 3 alpha, 5 alpha, tetrahydrodeoxy corticosterone? (540)

   c. What are the effects of this substance? (540)

PRE-EXAM QUIZ

Multiple-Choice
Select the choice that best completes the stem in each question and indicate your selection in the appropriate space to the left of the question.

_____ 1. One of the three dimensions most states we call emotion contain is appetitive-aversive. This dimension is associated with which of the following brain circuitries?
   a. medial forebrain bundle
   b. amygdala
   c. periventricular system
   d. reticular formation
   e. more than one of the above

_____ 2. The role of the amygdala in approach-avoidance is to
   a. tie the emotions to the internal environment of the body
   b. select the appropriate emotional response using past experience
   c. analyze incoming sensory information
   d. more than one of the above
   e. none of the above

_____ 3. In the surgical technique prefrontal lobotomy
   a. the anterior portion of the frontal lobe is removed
   b. the connections between the frontal lobe and the rest of the brain are severed
   c. the orbitofrontal cortex is removed
   d. the orbitofrontal cortex-limbic system connections are cut
   e. none of the above

_____ 4. Which of the following appears to be an organizer of striate muscle fear behaviors?
   a. medial hypothalamus
   b. motor cortex
   c. cerebellum
   d. periaqueductal gray area
   e. tegmental area

_____ 5. The type of aggression that probably is accompanied by the conscious experience we call anger or rage is called
   a. predatory aggression
   b. instrumental aggression
   c. irritable aggression
   d. intermale aggression
   e. sex-related aggression

_____ 6. A kind of aggression that might also be named territorial aggression is
   a. intermale aggression
   b. irritable aggression
   c. sex-related aggression
   d. fear-induced aggression
   e. instrumental aggression

_____ 7. Lesions in this region abolish intermale aggression but have no effect on other kinds of aggression. The region is the
   a. corticomedial amygdala
   b. ventromedial hypothalamus
   c. periaqueductal gray region
   d. ventrotegmentum
   e. medial anterior hypothalamus

_____ 8. In this type of aggression there is little or no outward display of emotion.
   a. intermale aggression
   b. maternal aggression
   c. predatory aggression
   d. sex-related aggression
   e. none of the above

_____ 9. If you are immune to a disease it means that you already have _____ for the infective organism.
   a. leucocytes
   b. antibodies
   c. lymphocytes
   d. antigens
   e. none of the above

_____ 10. THDOC is a breakdown product of
   a. barbiturates
   b. glucocorticoids
   c. adrenocorticotropic hormone
   d. gamma-amino-butyric acid
   e. none of the above

_____ 11. Which of the following is not one of the three dimensions that appear to underlie all emotions?
   a. arousal
   b. approach-avoidance
   c. appetitiveness-aversiveness
   d. acute-chronic
   e. none of the above

_____ 12. Barbiturates produce their depressive effect on the nervous system by
   a. potentiating the inhibition induced by GABAergic neurons
   b. interfering with the sodium channels
   c. blocking the reuptake of norepinephrine by the presynaptic neurons in the raphe nucleus
   d. blocking cholinergic receptor sites in the prefrontal cortex
   e. all of the above

_____ 13. One explanation of how stress affects the immune system functioning has to do with the fact that _____ suppresses the formation of _____, which is necessary if the immune system is to function properly.
   a. adrenalin; proteins
   b. glucocorticoids; carbohydrates
   c. adrenalin; carbohydrates
   d. glucocorticoids; proteins
   e. none of the above

_____ 14. The literally hundreds of mice experiments concerning the link between stress and cancer would support which of the following therapy stratagems?
   a. daily injections of adrenocorticotropic hormone
   b. a diet high in protein substances
   c. a carbohydrate-rich diet
   d. a stress-reduced or stress-free environment
   e. more than one of the above

_____ 15. In an aggressive interaction the defeated will experience
   a. an increase in opioid transmitters
   b. an increase in ACTH secretion
   c. an increase in the production of benzodiazepine receptors
   d. a decrease in testosterone output
   e. all of the above

True/False

_____ 1. It is likely that almost all diseases have a psychosomatic component.

_____ 2. Antibodies are to antigens as receptor sites are to neurotransmitters.

_____ 3. Anxiety inhibits aggression.

_____ 4. Level of arousal, one of the dimensions associated with almost all emotions, is associated with the periventricular system.

_____ 5. It was the introduction of the tranquilizers and antipsychotic drugs in the 1950s that drove the frequency of prefrontal lobotomies way down.

_____ 6. Kluver and Bucy (1938, 1939) were among the first to demonstrate a definite cortical role in emotion when they demonstrated the removal of the frontal cortex in rhesus monkeys.

_____ 7. Research data suggest that HACER may be limited to the control of autonomic responses.

_____ 8. Benzodiazepines such as chlordiazepoxide and diazepam relieve anxiety better than do barbiturates and have less of a sedative effect.

_____ 9. Although we are certain that the amygdala is involved with irritable aggression, it is not possible, as yet, to point out which part or parts are critical.

_____10. The major function of the periaqueductal gray area in aggression is that of organizing the motor patterns for the species-typical behaviors.

_____11. EEG recordings in humans through deep electrodes revealed that during aversive emotions there was a consistent pattern of spindle-like bursts in the hippocampus and nearby amygdala.

_____12. The antigens of the immune system are of particular interest to stress researchers.

_____13. Studies comparing cancer patients with healthy controls showed that the former had experienced more stressful incidents in the year or two preceding cancer symptoms onset.

_____14. All types of acute stressors will adapt, but practically none of the chronic stressors will adapt.

_____15. The longer a stress lasts, the greater the immunosuppression.

13.1 acute stress (583)

13.2 adaptation (538)

13.3 adrenal cortex (532)

13.4 adrenocorticotropic hormone (ACTH) (534)

13.5 alarm reaction (532)

13.6 amygdala (518)

13.7 anterior pituitary (534)

13.8 antibody (535)

13.9 antigen (535)

13.10 anxiolytic drugs (522)

13.6

A cluster of nuclei located just beneath the cortex near the tip of the temporal lobe; part of the limbic system involved in approach-avoidance decisions.

13.7

The part of the "master" gland that secretes, among other hormones, ACTH.

13.8

A recognition protein made by the body in the bone marrow and thymus that will find the corresponding antigen, bind to it, and thereby tag it for destruction.

13.9

Any foreign protein that can act as a label. Antigens are found in the outer jackets of a virus or microorganism and are different from any found in normal cells.

13.10

Drugs that relieve anxiety.

Copyright 1990 by Wadsworth, Inc.

13.1

The type of stress that comes and goes in a relatively short time.

13.2

The return of ACTH and glucocorticoid levels to normal after a number of days or weeks of daily exposures to the stressor.

13.3

The outside layer of the adrenal gland.

13.4

Hormone secreted during any kind of stress by the anterior pituitary. Travels by way of the bloodstream to the adrenal cortex where it stimulates the release of hormones called glucocorticoids.

13.5

First stage of Selye's general adaptation syndrome. It lasts only a few hours, during which the stress hormones are mobilized.

13.11

appetitive

(515)

13.12

approach-avoidance tendency

(515)

13.13

aversion system

(517)

13.14

aversive

(515)

13.15

barbiturates

(522)

13.16

basolateral nuclear group

(518)

13.17

benzodiazepines

(523)

13.18

cardiovascular responses

(520)

13.19

central nucleus

(518)

13.20

chlordiazepoxide

(523)

13.16

One of the divisions of the amygdala, stimulation of which in humans elicits feelings or fear and anxiety together with physical symptoms of fear such as heart rate and blood pressure.

13.17

A set of anxiolytic drugs that is better than barbiturates. It is possible that these drugs act directly on the anxiety circuits of the brain, probably by arousing the cortex and limbic system during stress.

13.18

Heart-rate and blood-vessel changes.

13.19

A division of the amygdala, stimulation of which, in cats, produces fear and attempts to escape.

13.20

A benzodiazepine.

Copyright 1990 by Wadsworth, Inc.

13.11

Something good, desirable; something you have an appetite for.

13.12

A response tendency. A motivation to move toward some stimuli and away from others.

13.13

A set of nuclei and tracts that may decide whether or not a particular stimulus is undesirable (aversive) and whether it should be avoided (fear or disgust) or attacked (aggression); includes the paraventricular system.

13.14

Bad, undesirable, unwanted.

13.15

Drugs that were discovered by von Bayer that have been used for decades as sedatives and anxiolytics. They are derivatives of the chemical, barbituric acid.

13.21

chronic stress

(538)

13.22

clinical level infection

(535)

13.23

corticomedial nuclear group

(518)

13.24

corticotropin-releasing factor (CRF)

(534)

13.25

diazepam

(523)

13.26

exhaustion

(532)

13.27

fear-induced aggression

(524)

13.28

GABA-modulin

(523)

13.29

general adaptation syndrome (GAS)

(531)

13.30

glucocorticoids

(534)

13.26

Final stage of Selye's general adaptation syndrome in which defenses are used up. If stress continues after the stage of exhaustion has been reached, death results.

13.27

A set of responses that occurs when a stimulus has frightened an animal and it tries to escape.

13.28

A chemical that attaches to its sites on the satellite receptors of a GABA neuron. When these sites are occupied by this chemical GABA, receptor sites are blocked, thus preventing the transmitter from inhibiting the postsynaptic cell.

13.29

A set of conditions produced by a long duration processes within the body which are initiated by the application of a stressor.

13.30

Hormones released by the adrenal cortex that circulate in the blood to all the cells of the body, where they have a number of effects on cell chemistry important to stress resistance.

Copyright 1990 by Wadsworth, Inc.

13.21

Stress that continues over days, weeks, or even years.

13.22

An infection that has progressed far enough to have obvious disease symptoms.

13.23

A division of the amygdala.

13.24

Hormone secreted by certain cells in the paraventricular nucleus of the hypothalamus that stimulates the anterior pituitary to release adrenocorticotropic hormone.

13.25

A benzodiazepine.

13.31

HACER

(520)

13.32

immune system

(532)

13.33

immunity

(536)

13.34

immunosuppression

(537)

13.35

instrumental aggression

(524)

13.36

intermale aggression

(524)

13.37

irritable aggression

(524)

13.38

lateral attack

(525)

13.39

leucocyte

(535)

13.40

level of arousal

(515)

13.36

A set of responses employed by a resident male when a strange male roams into his territory.

13.37

A set of responses that is probably accompanied by the conscious experience labeled anger or rage and usually occurs as the result of frustration, pain, or deprivation.

13.38

Threat posture of the resident male in intermale aggression. In this posture the resident male places his body at right angles across the front of the stranger, pushing and shoving belligerently.

13.39

Cells that continually swarm through the body scavenging dead or tagged tissue.

13.40

How awake, excited, or bored you are; one aspect of emotion.

13.31

An acronym for hypothalamic area for conditioned emotional responses. Apparently HACER may be limited to control of autonomic responses.

13.32

Body's apparatus for resisting diseases and tumors.

13.33

A condition in which antibodies for a disease have already been acquired in sufficient quantities to prevent a clinical level infection.

13.34

Suppression of antibody and leucocyte production.

13.35

Any increase in frequency or extremeness of any of the genetically endowed types of aggression with species-typical responses patterns due to reinforcement by circumstances.

Copyright 1990 by Wadsworth, Inc.

13.41

lymphocyte

(535)

13.42

maternal aggression

(524)

13.43

medial forebrain bundle

(515)

13.44

medial hypothalamus

(521)

13.45

multiple causation

(533)

13.46

orbitofrontal cortex

(518)

13.47

paraventricular nucleus (PVN)

(534)

13.48

periaqueductal gray (PAG)

(521)

13.49

periventricular system

(515)

13.50

piloerection

(525)

13.46

Considered to be the "limbic frontal lobe," its role may be to connect the emotion areas of the limbic system into the planning areas of the prefrontal cortex.

13.47

Hypothalamic nucleus that is strongly connected to the aversion system by way of the ventromedial hypothalamus. During stress certain cells in the paraventricular nucleus are stimulated to secrete a hormone called corticotropin-releasing factor.

13.48

A midbrain area that probably contains the motor circuits for many species typical behavioral patterns.

13.49

Group of nuclei lying just medial to the medial forebrain bundle that apparently label stimuli as aversive.

13.50

Response seen in fear-induced aggression. It is a reflexive fluffing up of the fur to make the animal appear larger.

13.41

A type of leucocyte with antibodies embedded in its cell membrane. Each is specialized for identifying and destroying anything bearing one specific antigen.

13.42

A set of responses displayed by a mother in the nesting area just before delivering the young and afterward until the offspring are capable of defending themselves.

13.43

A large bundle of tracts connecting parts of the brain stem with the limbic system and striatum; contains parts of the reinforcement system.

13.44

Area just medial to HACER and probably overlapping it. This area appears to be an organizer of striate muscle fear behaviors, especially escape responses.

13.45

The principle that a disease usually is caused by two factors working concurrently; especially a physical factor interacting with a stressor.

Copyright 1990 by Wadsworth, Inc.

13.51

predatory aggression

(524)

13.52

prefrontal lobotomy

(517)

13.53

psychosomatic disorders

(517)

13.54

quiet-biting attacking

(527)

13.55

resistance

(532)

13.56

reticular formation

(515)

13.57

satellite receptors

(523)

13.58

sex-related aggression

(524)

13.59

stress

(531)

13.60

subclinical infection

(535)

13.56

A column of gray matter extending up through the center of the brain stem; its cells send nonspecific facilitation and inhibition to the cortex and spinal cord.

13.51

A set of responses that a mammal uses to kill prey for food.

13.57

Receptor sites that are attached to and modulate other receptors; for example, satellite receptors that bind GABA-modulin can block the $GABA_a$ receptor from binding GABA.

13.52

A surgical technique developed by Egaz Moniz to relieve the debilitating anxiety of psychotic patients. With the appearance of antipsychotic drugs and tranquilizers, use of the procedure became much less frequent.

13.58

A set of responses that occurs between male and female as a normal part of the mating process.

13.53

Conditions of organic damage stemming in part from emotion problems.

13.59

A wide variety of life conditions that range from emotional states through disease and injury to being too cold or too hot. Stress can be acute, coming and going in a relatively brief time, or chronic, continuing over a prolonged period of time.

13.54

Predatory aggression in the cat, so named because all the behavior involved is carried out with so little display of emotionality.

13.60

An infection that has not yet progressed far enough to have obvious disease symptoms.

13.55

Second stage of Selye's general adaptation syndrome, which can go on for days or weeks, which represents full mobilization.

Copyright 1990 by Wadsworth, Inc.

13.61

THDOC (3 alpha, 5 alpha, tetrahydrodeoxy corticosterone)

(540)

13.61

A breakdown product of glucocorticoids. It mimics a barbiturate drug by binding with GABA receptors to enhance inhibition.

CHAPTER FOURTEEN
LEARNING

READ-WRITE-REVIEW

Read pages 546-550 and summary statements 1-3 on page 582, then answer each of the following questions in this section.
---

1. Learning is a concept that refers to a group of related abilities, all of which have what in common? (546)

    a. Identify some of the forms or types of learning. (546)

    b. What reason can you give for believing that the origins of our ability to learn lie millions of years in the past? (546)

2. What is habituation? (547)

    a. How might habituation have been of value to that tube worm on the sea-floor with its uncooperative neighbors? (547)

    b. Demonstrate how a human might benefit from this very simple form of learning. (547)

    c. What is the startle response? (547)

    d. What is the orienting reflex and how is it related to the startle response?

    e. What is sensitization? (547-548)

    f. What is dishabituation and how is it related to sensitization? (548)

3. What is associative learning? (548)

    a. What association, if any, is being made in classical conditioning? (548-549)

    b. In operant conditioning? (549)

4. Define the terms "unconditioned stimulus," "unconditioned response," "conditioned stimulus," and "conditioned response." (548-549)

    a. In classical conditioning what connection is learned? (548)

    b. In classical conditioning what connection is genetically determined? (548)

5. What is the most significant difference between classically conditioned and instrumentally conditioned responses? (549)

a. List and identify three different ways in which the consequences can be arranged in an instrumental learning task. (549)

b. Describe a passive avoidance learning task. (549)

c. Describe an active avoidance learning task. (549)

d. Describe a discrimination learning task. (549)

Read pages 550-557 and summary statements 4-7 on page 582, then answer each of the following questions in this section.
---

1. Lashley (1961), mounted a research program aimed at locating the engram. What is this engram Lashley was looking for? (550)

    a. Describe the method Lashley employed to locate this engram. (550)

    b. Using this technique what did Lashley expect to find specifically? (550)

    c. What did Lashley actually find? (550)

    d. Based on these findings Lashley came to what conclusion? (550)

    e. This conclusion he called the _____. (550)

    f. What probably caused Lashley to obtain such results? (550-551)

2. Lashley searched for the engram in the cerebral cortex, but had he been looking for an engram formed by habituation, probably the simplest form of learning, would you expect him to be looking in the same place? (551)

    a. Why or why not? (551)

    b. What is *Aplysia* and why is it such a popular subject for physiological psychologists? (551-552)

    c. Kandel's (1979) study of the *Aplysia* demonstrated what kind of learning? (552)

    d. What response of the *Aplysia* did Kandel study in this piece of research? (552)

    e. Explain specifically why this change in responding occurs. (553)

    f. What is this called? (553)

3. Kandel (1979) discovered that the nervous system of the *Aplysia* was also capable of what other kind of learning? (553)

    a. What is presynaptic facilitation? (554)

    b. What role does presynaptic facilitation play, and which of the neurons in this siphon reflex is especially important in the presynaptic facilitation process? (554)

    c. What neurotransmitter is released by this neuron? (554)

d. Describe what happens when a molecule of this neurotransmitter substance fits into a receptor site on the terminal of a sensory neuron until cyclic adenosine monophosphate is produced. (554-555)

e. Explain precisely how cyclic adenosine monophosphate can influence the events in the sensory neuron terminal. (555)

f. What reason can you give for such a complicated and rather indirect process? (556)

4. Demonstrate that it is possible for learning to occur within the mammalian spinal cord. (556)

   a. Describe the acoustic startle reflex response. (556)

   b. Describe the neural mechanism behind the acoustic startle reflex response. (556)

   c. The acoustic startle reflex is what kind of reflex? (556)

   d. There appears to be enough evidence to suggest the existence of two types of habituation. Identify these two varieties and differentiate between them. (557)

   e. In looking for the locus of the habituation engram for the acoustic startle reflex, what two brain areas appear to be involved in long-term habituation, and how do they relate to the startle reflex arc? (557)

   f. The human organism possesses the highest structures and the largest hierarchy of any known nervous system, and thus it is quite possible that the cortex is employed even in this very simple kind of learning. What evidence can you cite that would refute such a hypothesis? (557)

Read pages 557-566 and summary statements 8-9 on page 582, then answer each of the following questions in this section.
---

1. Describe how one might go about conditioning the paw flexion response in the cat using the following diagram. (558)

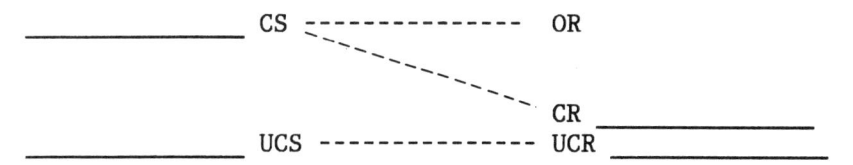

   ```
   _____ CS -------------- OR
                    ╲
                     ╲
                      ╲  CR _____
   _____ UCS -------------- UCR _____
   ```

   a. Once conditioning has been established what would happen if you lesioned the red nucleus? (558-559)

   b. Locate the red nucleus and trace both the neural input and the neural output. (558)

   c. What is sprouting and what has it to do with the functioning of the red nucleus? (559)

d. In Tsukahara's (1981) classical conditioning study of the forepaw flexion in the cat, when the CS was an electrical stimulus to the corticorubral tract, where did the connections show improvement? (559)

   e. What two possible explanations can be given for this finding? (559)

   f. Which explanation does Tsukahara favor and why? (559)

2. Identify and describe the simple, easily controlled example of classical conditioning that Thompson et al.(1984) needed for a long series of ablation and single-cell recording experiments. (559)

   a. Thompson et al.(1984) found what two structures to be most involved in the development of this association? (560)

   b. Of these two structures, which one actually becomes two separate structures in the human, and what are these two structures called? (560)

   c. The finding that lesioning these areas caused the established CR to be lost was not interpreted as being due to the fact that the lesioning destroyed the original reflex arc: Why? (561)

   d. Marr and Albus make use of what anatomical structure in trying to explain nictitating membrane reflex conditioning? (561)

   e. Why is this structure considered to be ideal, from an anatomical standpoint, for forming associations between stimuli and reflexes? (561)

   f. Explain how the original circuitry of the basic reflex arc for the nictitating membrane reflex is formed. (561)

   g. Explain the way in which neural circuitry might be laid out to accommodate the development of an association during the classical conditioning of the nictitating membrane reflex. (561-562)

   h. According to the Marr-Albus theory, at what point in the classical conditioning of the nictitating membrane reflex do the Purkinje cells of the cerebellar cortex begin to play an active role? (562)

   i. First in a lesioning study and later in a study in which he removed the cerebellar cortex, what did Thompson (1986) demonstrate? (562)

   j. Thompson's findings led him to conclude that the site of the formation of the essential association in the conditioning of the nictitating membrane reflex is where? (562)

   k. Describe Yeo's findings regarding the effects of cerebellar cortical removal on classical conditioning of the nictitating membrane reflex, and tell what these findings suggest. (562)

1. Describe the timing relationship between the CR and the CS and UCS that is commonly observed in classical conditioning. (562)

m. How might this standard phenomenon make it easier to understand or explain Thompson's findings in a lesioning study and later in a study in which he removed the cerebellar cortex? (562-563)

n. What does the red nucleus have to do with the classical conditioning of the nictitating membrane reflex? (563)

o. What conclusion can you safely draw concerning classical conditioning, having read the material on paw flexion and nictitating membrane reflexes? (563)

p. What is a conditioned emotional response? (563)

3. How might you interpret the development of a conditioned response in terms of survival value? (563)

   a. Distinguish between trace conditioning and delay conditioning. (563)

   b. Why is it logical to expect that trace conditioning might require a more highly evolved brain structure than the brain stem? (564)

   c. What evidence is there to suggest that such a brain structure is important in the development of a trace conditioned response, and what is this structure? (564)

   d. What is discrimination-reversal learning? (564)

   e. Under what conditions would the subject in a discrimination-reversal task be unable to master the reversal? (564)

   f. Trace the firing of the hippocampal cells throughout the discrimination-reversal task. (564)

   g. Describe the four apparent stages of the discrimination-reversal learning task and the brain mechanism associated with each state. (564)

   h. Describe the general principle that this illustrates. (564-565)

   i. What reasons can you provide for this? (560)

Read pages 566-571 and summary statements 10-13 on page 583, then answer each of the following questions in this section.
---

1. Define instrumental conditioning and explain why it is so much more complex than classical conditioning. (566)

315

a. What evidence can you provide that suggests that instrumental conditioning can occur without the benefit of cortical activity? (566)

b. Describe the extinction process in instrumental conditioning. (567)

c. What evidence is there to suggest that the hippocampus is heavily involved in the extinction of an instrumental response? (567)

d. What is meant by the term "perseveration"? (567)

e. What is a differential reinforcement of low rates of responding (DRL) schedule? (568)

f. How does the behavior of hippocampally damaged rats differ from normal rats when faced with a DRL schedule? (568)

g. How did Schmaltz and Isaacson (1966) alter the standard procedure for training rats on a DRL schedule, and what results did they obtain? (568)

h. How did they interpret the DRL results? (568)

2. List those brain areas that directly or indirectly receive hippocampal output. (568-569)

   a. Experiments have demonstrated that lesioning of which of these areas will impair active-avoidance learning? (569)

   b. Lesioning of which of these areas will mimic hippocampal damage and result in making passive-avoidance learning more difficult? (569)

   c. What effect would damage to this area have on active avoidance learning? (569)

   d. What does this suggest about active-avoidance learning in general? (569)

   e. According to Sagvolden and Holth (1986), what role is played by the septum in active-avoidance learning? (570)

   f. Describe and locate the amygdala. (570)

   g. Studies suggest what concerning the function of the amygdala? (570)

   h. What part of the amygdala has been shown to be important in taste aversion? (570)

   i. What is lesioned in a thalamotomy and what is the purpose of such a surgical procedure? (570)

   j. There is evidence to suggest that in addition to active-avoidance learning, the dorsomedial nucleus of the thalamus is also involved in what other behaviors? (571)

k. What is the concept of distributed learning and how does it relate to instrumental conditioning? (571)

Read pages 571-581 and summary statements 14-17 on page 583, then answer each of the following questions in this section.
---

1. What reasons are there for the various usages of the term "reinforcement"? (571)

    a. How is the term used in this book? (571)

2. Briefly discuss the major events that led to the research efforts of Olds and Milner (1954). (571)

    a. What happened in the open box experiment that led these researchers to focus their attention on a single animal and eventually redesign the task? (571)

    b. Describe the T maze task employed by Olds and Milner. (571)

    c. What results did this research team obtain from the T maze test? (571-571)

    d. Describe the self-stimulation of the brain technique developed by Olds. (572)

3. Identify brain area sites that act as reward centers. (572)

    a. How do these areas differ? (572)

    b. Describe in general terms the type of research study employed to determine whether or not all these brain areas feed into one reward center so that stimulating them triggers activity in that center. (572)

    c. What conclusions can be drawn from the results of such studies? (572)

    d. Of the brain areas that act as reward centers, which area is the best for obtaining a reward effect from electrical stimulation? (572)

    e. With what other behavioral activity is this area known to be involved? (572)

    f. What findings can you cite that strongly suggest that the rewarding effect of electrical stimulation delivered to this area comes from the fact that circuits involved in eating and drinking are being stimulated? (572)

    g. Why did Olds and Fobes (1981) conclude that it was impossible at that time to determine if self-stimulation of the brain works because it activates the same circuits as those activated by food or water? (572-573)

4. To what conclusion was Olds forced to arrive based on his reward-mapping experiments? (573)

    a. To where do the axons of the medial forebrain bundle project? (573)

    b. Olds' theory of reward and punishment placed punishment in a tract called the _____ and the reward function in the _____. (574)

317

c. According to Olds, what was the primary event in reinforcement? (574)

d. Although it is apparent today that it is impossible that all conceivable sensory-motor associations take place at synapses with hypothalamic neurons, Olds was correct in what two respects? (574)

5. It was the effect of what drug on the rate of responding for SSB that lead Stein (1968) to propose the norepinephrine hypothesis? (574)

   a. Of the five clusters of noradrenergic cells in the brain, how many lie within the brain-stem reticular formation? (575)

   b. Of these five clusters which is the largest? (575)

   c. What specific reward effect does cocaine have? (575)

   d. What type of drug is chlorpromazine and what effect does it have on self-stimulation of the brain? (575)

   e. How does chlorpromazine affect catecholamine transmitters? (575)

   f. Of what importance to Stein's norepinephrine hypothesis is the fact that amphetamine, cocaine, and chlorpromazine also facilitate or block dopamine transmission? (575)

   g. What research evidence can you cite that suggests that the relationship between the norepinephrine system and reinforcement is far from a simple one? (576)

6. What are the two major dopaminergic pathways of the brain? (576)

   a. Which of these pathways originates in the ventrotegmental area of the midbrain? (576)

   b. Which of these pathways appears to be more concerned with motor control? (577)

   c. Which of these pathways relates to motivation and reinforcement? (577)

7. Wise (1980) demonstrated that dopamine-blocking drugs not only decrease the rewarding quality of food and water for rats but also eliminate their bar pressing for SSB. What problems do researchers face when they attempt to interpret this kind of data? (577-578)

   a. One attempt to overcome this problem has involved the use of the double-extinction method. Describe this method. (578)

   b. How did Spyraki et al. (1982) attempt to deal with the same problem? (578)

   c. How would you summarize the findings of those dopamine-blocking drug studies that controlled for the effects of motor disability? (578)

d. Describe the procedure used to discover that the fibers stimulated in SSB that produce the reward effect are those that descend from the cerebrum to the brain stem. (578)

e. Suggest possible points of origin for these descending fibers. (578-579)

f. Describe how ibotenic acid has played a role in locating one point of origin of these descending fibers. (579)

g. Where do many of these descending reward fibers terminate? (579)

h. Because of its anatomical connections to both the striatum and the ventrotegmental area of the midbrain, the _____ might serve as the point in the nervous system where motivational factors like reinforcement select which behaviors the striatum will elicit. (579)

i. What neurotransmitter is clearly involved in those synapses on the cells that compose this structure? (579)

j. Beginning with those points that are directly stimulated and using current information, trace the dopamine reinforcement system.

8. Most of the SSB areas in the cerebrum are cell groups that connect to the ventrotegmental area through the medial forebrain bundle; however, there is one notable exception. What is this exception? (580)

   a. Based on radioactive 2-DG studies, we know that SSB of this area results in the activation of the _____, _____, and _____, but not the _____. (580)

   b. What behavioral differences exist between animals self-stimulating in their medial frontal cortex and animals self-stimulating in their lateral hypothalamus? (580)

   c. Studies have shown that suppression of medial frontal cortical SSB can be achieved by cutting what pathways? (581)

   d. Trace the prefrontal reward path as suggested by Stellar and Stellar (1985). (581)

PRE-EXAM QUIZ

Multiple-Choice
Select the choice that best completes the stem in each question and indicate your selection in the appropriate space to the left of the question.

_____ 1. Continuing to make a response long after it has ceased to serve any purpose is called
   a. perseveration
   b. dishabituation
   c. extinction
   d. habituation
   e. sensitization

_____ 2. According to the Marr-Albus theory of nictitating membrane reflex conditioning, the association formed is found in the _____.
   a. dentate nucleus
   b. red nucleus
   c. cerebellar cortex
   d. substantia nigra
   e. nucleus interpositus

_____ 3. Stein (1968) proposed that part or all of the _____ is/are responsible for the brain mechanism of reinforcement.
   a. mesolimbic system
   b. noradrenergic cells within the brain-stem reticular formation
   c. periventricular system
   d. nigrostriatal system
   e. more than one of the above

_____ 4. Which of the following brain structures plays an important role in the learning of preferences and aversions concerning the choice of what to eat, what to drink, and with whom to mate?
   a. red nucleus
   b. dentate nucleus
   c. substantia nigra
   d. ventrotegmental area
   e. amygdala

_____ 5. Which of the following is the most significant difference between classical conditioned responses and instrumental conditioned responses?
   a. the former involves the learning of emitted responses; the latter involves elicited responses
   b. the former are goal oriented; the latter are not
   c. the former involves the learning of elicited responses; the latter involves emitted responses
   d. the former are not goal oriented; the latter are
   e. none of the above

_____ 6. The brain area that yields the highest rates of self-stimulation of the brain in rats is the
   a. amygdala
   b. lateral hypothalamus
   c. entorhinal cortex
   d. septum
   e. caudate nucleus

_____ 7. Habituation of the gill withdrawal reflex in Aplysia is probably due to
   a. an increase in the amount of serotonin released by the motor neurons
   b. an increase in calcium ion influx into the terminals of the sensory neurons
   c. a decrease in calcium ion influx into the terminals of the sensory neurons
   d. an increase in the amount of serotonin released by the motor neurons
   e. a decrease in calcium ion influx into the terminals of the motor neuron

_____ 8. Which of the following research tasks has been used to deal with the problem of motor disability interfering with the interpretation of dopamine-blocker experiments?
   a. delayed object alternation
   b. trace conditioning
   c. passive-avoidance technique
   d. double-extinction procedure
   e. discrimination-reversal learning

_____ 9. _____ is probably the most basic form of learning.
   a. classical conditioning
   b. habituation
   c. instrumental conditioning
   d. operant conditioning
   e. none of the above

_____ 10. Which of the following brain areas appears to be involved in enabling the organism to use classical conditioning in the more natural circumstances that one would find outside the controlled environment of the laboratory?
   a. red nucleus
   b. dentate nucleus
   c. pons
   d. hypothalamus
   e. none of the above

_____ 11. The process in which an aversive stimulus sensitizes a reflex that has already undergone habituation is called
   a. rehabituation
   b. extinction
   c. dishabituation
   d. double-extinction
   e. none of the above

_____ 12. Microelectrode recordings from rat hippocampal cells during discrimination training reveal that when the rat mistakenly responds to the CS-, the hippocampal neurons _____, indicating that the hippocampus had not yet learned the discrimination.
   a. fire before the response began just as though the tone had been the CS+
   b. fire after the response is over just as though the tone had been the CS+
   c. fire both before and after the response just as though the tone had been the CS+
   d. fire during the response just as though the tone had been the CS+
   e. none of the above

_____ 13. _____ involves training the animal to withhold a response that used to be reinforced but now leads to punishment.
   a. extinction
   b. active-avoidance training
   c. dishabituation
   d. passive-avoidance conditioning
   e. none of the above

_____ 14. It is possible that a secondary reinforcement system exists that, in the rat, would include all but one of the following brain areas. Which of the following would NOT be a part of this system?
   a. entorhinal cortex
   b. sulcal cortex
   c. hippocampus
   d. ventrotegmental area
   e. lateral hypothalamus

_____ 15. A conditioning procedure in which there is a time lag between the CS and the UCS is called
   a. discrimination conditioning
   b. trace conditioning
   c. operant conditioning
   d. delayed conditioning
   e. none of the above

True/False

_____ 1. Most of our data concerning the brain mechanisms of reinforcement have come from research employing self-stimulation of the brain.

_____ 2. The phenomenon of sensitization is the opposite of facilitation.

_____ 3. Conditioning is a form of associative learning.

_____ 4. The lesioning of the dorsomedial nucleus of the hypothalamus, called a thalamotomy, is used for the relief of psychotic symptoms such as tension, anxiety, and agitation.

_____ 5. Correct timing of the CR, in relation to the UCS, is probably learned in the cerebellar cortex.

_____ 6. Once activated by the receptor molecule, adenylate cyclase reacts with adenosine triphosphate and splits off two of its phosphate groups, leaving a molecule called cyclic adenosine monophosphate.

_____ 7. The one idea that clearly emerges from the mass of experiments on instrumental conditioning is that learning is not a specialized function of a single brain area or even a select few.

_____ 8. Cocaine increases the rate of self-stimulation of the brain by modulating dopaminergic synaptic transmission.

_____ 9. Rats with cerebellar cortex damage tend to perseverate in making unreinforced responses in extinction, passive-avoidance learning, discrimination reversal, and DRL performance.

_____ 10. Because of its simple nervous system, *Aplysia* is a popular laboratory subject in many physiological psychology laboratories.

_____ 11. The cerebellar vermis is the midline portion of the cerebellum that plays an important role in reinforcement.

_____ 12. Olds (1981) searched for the engram in the rat brain but found that learning appeared to be distributed more or less evenly throughout the cortex.

_____ 13. Ibotenic acid selectively kills the axons passing through an area without harming any of the cell bodies.

_____ 14. Sprouting is a response to brain damage in which cells that have lost some inputs make new synapses with nearby axons through their growth of the telodendria and terminals.

_____ 15. Reinforcement is an event that lowers the subsequent probability of the response it follows.

14.1

acoustic startle reflex

(556)

14.2

active-avoidance learning

(549)

14.3

adenylate cyclase

(554)

14.4

amphetamines

(574)

14.5

amygdala

(570)

14.6

anterior nucleus of the thalamus

(569)

14.7

Aplysia

(551)

14.8

associative learning

(548)

14.9

cerebellar vermis

(557)

14.10

chlorpromazine

(575)

14.6

One of a number of structures that receives input from the hippocampus and is involved in memory. It also sends output to the cingulate gyrus, thus providing an indirect route from the hippocampus to the cingulate gyrus.

14.7

A rather large marine snail with a nervous system that contains only about 15,000 neurons, many of which have been named and their connections listed in a catalogue of cells.

14.8

Learning in which associations are formed between two stimuli or between a stimulus and a response. Classical and instrumental conditioning are forms of associative learning.

14.9

The midline portion of the cerebellum.

14.10

An antipsychotic drug that has its effects by blocking the receptor sites for catecholamine transmitters such as norepinephrine and dopamine.

Copyright 1990 by Wadsworth, Inc.

14.1

A defensive reflex that tends to curl the body into a hunched-over, protective posture with the head down when a sudden, loud noise occurs.

14.2

A form of instrumental learning in which a warning signal immediately precedes the onset of an aversive stimulus, allowing the animal an opportunity to escape the aversive stimulus.

14.3

An enzyme located on the inside surface of the cell membrane where it is in contact with all chemicals floating around in the intercellular fluid. The purpose of this enzyme is to react with adenosine triphosphate, splitting off two of its phosphate groups and leaving a molecule called cyclic adenosine monophosphate.

14.4

A family of drugs that has the ability to stimulate the nervous system, which it accomplishes through its effects on noradrenergic neurons.

14.5

A collection of nuclei in the anterior temporal lobe at the forward tip of the hippocampus. It has strong connections with the motivational-emotional areas of the hypothalamus and seems to be involved with making associations between environmental stimuli and internal motivational states like hunger and fear.

14.11

cingulate gyrus

(568)

14.12

cocaine

(575)

14.13

conditioned emotional response (CER)

(563)

14.14

conditioned response (CR)

(549)

14.15

conditioned stimulus (CS)

(549)

14.16

continuous reinforcement schedule

(568)

14.17

cyclic adenosine monophosphate (cAMP)

(555)

14.18

delay conditioning

(563)

14.19

dentate nucleus

(560)

14.20

diagonal band of Broca

(578)

14.16

A reinforcement schedule that provides one reinforcer each time the response is made.

14.11

A structure of the limbic system that receives input from the hippocampus. Lesioning this structure impairs active-avoidance learning.

14.17

A substance made in the postsynaptic terminal only in response to an impulse arriving at the synapse between the interneuron and the sensory neuron terminal. It is formed from adenosine triphosphate in the presence of adenylate cyclase by splitting off two of its phosphate groups.

14.12

A drug that acts as a stimulant and is known to exert its effects through its influence on the catecholamine transmitters norepinephrine and dopamine.

14.18

A conditioning procedure in which there are several seconds between the beginning of the conditioned and unconditioned stimuli, but later the stimuli overlap.

14.13

An overall emotional reaction that occurs in response to any novel aversive stimulus. It has been suggested that the nictitating membrane initially may have been one part of this overall response.

14.19

A structure located in the cerebellum of the rabbit. It is one of two structures involved in the development of the nictitating membrane reflex.

14.14

A response elicited by the conditioned stimulus after it has been sufficiently paired with the unconditioned stimulus. The conditioned response resembles but is not identical to the unconditioned response.

14.20

An area near the anterior hypothalamus. Lesioning of this area has been reported to hinder the self-stimulation of the brain effect, which suggests that reward fibers may originate here.

14.15

A previously neutral stimulus that over time comes to elicit the conditioned response when paired with the unconditioned stimulus.

Copyright 1990 by Wadsworth, Inc.

14.21 discrimination learning (549)

14.22 discrimination-reversal learning (564)

14.23 dishabituation (548)

14.24 distributed learning (571)

14.25 dopaminergic fibers (575)

14.26 dorsomedial nucleus of the thalamus (570)

14.27 double-extinction method (578)

14.28 DRL schedule (568)

14.29 emitted responses (549)

14.30 engram (550)

14.26

Thalamic nucleus, which receives its major input from the amygdala. In humans neurosurgeons have often lesioned this area in order to relieve psychotic symptoms.

14.21

A process whereby the organism learns to respond differently to stimuli that are differently reinforced.

14.27

Research method designed to get around the fact that a dopaminergic blocker works on both the nigrostriatal motor projection and the mesolimbic path. A subject trained to press a bar in 2 operant chambers, is given a dopaminergic blocker and then put in the first chamber, where it bar presses until the rate drops to zero, at which time it is put in the second chamber.

14.22

Classical discrimination conditioning in which after the subject has learned to respond to the conditioned stimulus followed by the unconditioned stimulus and not the CS presented alone, the stimuli are reversed so that what was the CS+ becomes the CS-. The subject has to unlearn what he initially learned and learn the new discrimination.

14.28

Differential reinforcement of low rates of responding schedule in which the first response is reinforced, followed by a waiting period during which the subject must not make the response or the waiting begins all over again. Once the delay is over and the animal has not responded, the subject will be reinforced for the next response.

14.23

Refers to the recovery of the strength of a habituated response when a novel stimulus is presented prior to the habituating stimulus.

14.29

Responses that cannot be elicited directly by any stimulus.

14.24

The idea that learning is not a specialized function of a single brain area or even a select few. Rather it appears that most of the areas of the nervous system are modifiable to some degree.

14.30

According to Karl Lashley, a hypothetical physical change that occurs somewhere in the brain when a piece of information is stored. A memory trace.

14.25

Axons that use dopamine as the neurotransmitter.

Copyright 1990 by Wadsworth, Inc.

14.31

extinction procedure

(567)

14.32

habituation

(547)

14.33

incentive-learning

(570)

14.34

mammillary bodies

(569)

14.35

Marr-Albus theory

(562)

14.36

medial forebrain bundle (MFB)

(573)

14.37

mesolimbic pathway

(576)

14.38

negative reinforcement

(549)

14.39

nictitating membrane reflex (NMR)

(559)

14.40

nigrostriatal pathway

(576)

14.36

A bundle of fibers that send branches to all areas from which self-stimulation of the brain can be obtained by using lateral hypothalamus electrodes. It contains millions of axons of brain-stem neurons projecting to the limbic system, striatum, and neocortex and axons of neurons in those areas projecting back to the stem.

14.37

A major dopaminergic pathway of the brain. It originates in a group of cells located in the ventrotegmental area of the midbrain, and it projects upward through the medial forebrain bundle to terminate primarily in the limbic structures of the cerebrum and in the prefrontal cortex. It is related to the functions of motivation and reinforcement.

14.38

The procedure used to increase the probability that a response will recur by removing an aversive stimulus after the response occurs.

14.39

A defensive reflex found in rabbits. The inner eyelid called the nictitating membrane is closed and the eyeball is retracted when something touches the very sensitive cornea of the eye.

14.40

A major dopaminergic pathway of the brain. It appears to be more concerned with motor control.

Copyright 1990 by Wadsworth, Inc.

14.31

The way in which extinction is produced. In instrumental conditioning, this involves stopping the reinforcement of the learner for making a correct response.

14.32

The ability to stop responding to a repetitive stimulus that is meaningless in terms of any existing need such as mating, feeding, or safety.

14.33

The motivational learning aspect in active-avoidance conditioning. It is the learning to be motivated by the warning signal.

14.34

Structures of the hypothalamus that receive input from the hippocampus. Some of its output goes to the cingulate gyrus providing an indirect route between the hippocampus and the cingulate gyrus.

14.35

A nictitating membrane reflex conditioning theory that holds that the Purkinje cells do not begin to react to the cochlear input (CS) until after this input has occurred together with the somatosensory input (UCS) a number of times.

14.41

noradrenergic neurons

(574)

14.42

nucleus interpositus

(560)

14.43

operant conditioning

(566)

14.44

passive-avoidance conditioning

(549)

14.45

periventricular system

(574)

14.46

perseveration

(567)

14.47

positive reinforcement

(549)

14.48

presynaptic facilitation

(554)

14.49

principle of equipotentiality

(550)

14.50

punishment

(549)

14.46

Continuing to make a response long after it has ceased to serve any purpose.

14.41

The neurons that employ norepinephrine as a neurotransmitter and through which amphetamines have their stimulating effect on the nervous system.

14.47

Increasing the probability of an occurrence of a response by following it with a desirable stimulus.

14.42

A structure located in the cerebellum of the rabbit. In the human, the nucleus interpositus becomes two structures--the nucleus globosus and the nucleus emboliformis. This structure is one of two that seems to be involved in the development of the nictitating membrane reflex.

14.48

An increase in the efficacy of a synapse induced by a third neuron that has a terminal synapsing on the terminal of the presynaptic cell.

14.43

A form of instrumental conditioning in which there are no trials and the subject is free to make the response anytime it is in the operant chamber.

14.49

Lashley's principle, which holds that most of the cortex works, not as a collection of separate and discrete areas each with its own task, but as an undifferentiated whole.

14.44

Instrumental conditioning in which a passive response is learned.

14.50

Any noxious stimulus that follows an operant response, which will bring about a decrease in the probability of that response.

14.45

A tract lying alongside the medial forebrain bundle. It passes through the medial hypothalamus and connects brain-stem areas with higher structures such as the amygdala. Olds placed the punishment function in this system.

Copyright 1990 by Wadsworth, Inc.

14.51

Purkinje cells

(561)

14.52

red nucleus

(558)

14.53

schedule

(568)

14.54

self-stimulation of the brain

(572)

14.55

sensitization

(548)

14.56

septal nucleus

(569)

14.57

sprouting

(559)

14.58

startle response

(547)

14.59

synaptic depression

(553)

14.60

thalamotomy

(570)

14.56

A structure that receives input from the hippocampus. Lesioning this area mimics hippocampal damage by making passive-avoidance learning more difficult and can also impair active-avoidance learning.

14.57

A process by which new synapses are established. These synapses are functional, although the new input may not be able to accomplish the same results as the original correct input. This process can occur sometimes even in the absence of damage.

14.58

A mammalian reflex to a sudden, unexpected loud noise.

14.59

A decrease of calcium influx into the presynaptic terminals of the sensory neurons of the siphon of *Aplysia* resulting in habituation.

14.60

Surgery to relieve psychotic symptoms of emotional tension, anxiety, and agitation by lesioning the dorsomedial nucleus of the thalamus.

14.51

Cerebellar cortical cells that receive input from the inferior olivary nucleus and from the cochlea. In turn these cells cells project to the dentate nucleus and nucleus interpositus in the rabbit. According to the Marr-Albus theory these cells play a role in nictitating membrane reflex conditioning.

14.52

A part of the motor system located near the substantia nigra at the top of the midbrain. It receives input from the cerebellum and cortex and its fibers project down into the cord to the motor neurons of the ventral horn.

14.53

A set of rules for when reinforcement will be delivered.

14.54

A research technique in which the delivery of a train of electrical pulses to electrodes implanted in the brain of the organism is accomplished by the subject's own performance. (e.g., pushing a bar in an operant chamber).

14.55

The enhancement of a reflex following a number of recent experiences with strong or noxious stimuli.

Copyright 1990 by Wadsworth, Inc.

14.61

trace conditioning

(563)

14.62

unconditioned response (UCR)

(548)

14.63

unconditioned stimulus (UCS)

(548)

14.64

ventrotegmental area (VTA)

(576)

14.61

A difficult type of classical conditioning in which there is an actual gap between the offset of the conditioned stimulus and the onset of the unconditioned stimulus. It seems possible that this type of conditioning might exceed the capacity of the brain-stem.

14.62

The response that normally is elicited by the unconditioned stimulus in classical conditioning.

14.63

The normal stimulus that elicits the response to be conditioned in classical conditioning.

14.64

A midbrain nucleus with dopaminergic cells whose axons form the mesolimbic portion of the medial forebrain bundle. It is an important part of the reinforcement system.

Copyright 1990 by Wadsworth, Inc.

CHAPTER FIFTEEN
THE HIPPOCAMPUS IN LEARNING AND MEMORY

READ-WRITE-REVIEW

Read pages 588-597 and summary statements 1-2 on page 608, then answer each of the following questions in this section.

---

1. List three methods that have been used to study the function of the hippocampus. (588)

    a. Describe a macroelectrode. (588)

    b. What is picked up at the tip of the macroelectrode? (588)

    c. Because these voltage charges are so small they must first be amplified and then written out by a machine to produce a record. What is this record called? (588)

    d. Describe theta rhythm. (589)

    e. According to research data, under what conditions has hippocampal theta been recorded? (589)

    f. Based on this research data, under what conditions has hippocampal theta been recorded? (589)

2. What research technique in hippocampal research has provided the most interesting results? (589)

    a. According to O'Keefe and colleagues (1978) there exists within the hippocampus a type of cell not related to theta rhythm. What name have they given it? (589)

    b. What are the receptive fields of these cells? (589)

    c. Describe the experimental conditions under which this type of cell was discovered. (589-590)

    d. Based on a number of experiments (O'Keefe & Black, 1978; O'Keefe & Nadel, 1978) what conclusion did O'Keefe and Nadel (1978) arrive at concerning hippocampal function and the role of these cells? (590)

    e. What evidence can you suggest to support the notion that these cells are specific to places as such and not merely to individual stimulus cues? (590-591)

f. What kinds of information does this cell need in order to cause it to fire? (591)

   g. What happens to the firing of this cell if it only receives part of this information? (591)

3. Trace the path taken by sensory information from the neocortical area of the temporal lobe through the hippocampus. (592)

4. Identify the functions of each of the components of the hippocampus in the formation of sensory maps. (593)

5. What is perseveration? (593)

   a. In a discrimination reversal of the nictitating membrane response what does one see in the hippocampal neurons? (593)

   b. How might one extend O'Keefe and Nadel's (1978) theory of hippocampal sensory maps to explain what happens in nictitating membrane reversal conditioning? (594)

6. Kubie and Ranck (1983) employed microelectrode recordings to study the activity of the place cells of the hippocampus in a variety of environments including a radial arm maze, an operant chamber, and a home cage. What is a radial arm maze? (594-595)

   a. What learning tasks were provided for the rats in each environment? (595)

   b. The largest percentage of hippocampal place cells became active in all three environments. What was the surprising finding concerning these cells? (595)

   c. How do the Kubie and Ranck findings fit in with the O'Keefe and Nadel theory? (595)

   d. What is meant by the "background firing" of these place cells? (595)

   e. How did Kubie and Ranck (1984) interpret this background firing? (595)

   f. What reason might one give for this background firing? (595)

Read pages 597-599 and summary statement 3 on page 608, then answer each of the following questions in this section.
---

1. In what way does the associational context theory presented in the text agree with the theory proposed by O'Keefe and Nadel? (597)

   a. What kinds of stimuli have been shown by research to be mapped by the hippocampal cells? (597)

   b. According to context theory what is the function of the hippocampus? (597)

338

c. Eichenbaum et al.(1987) carried out a rat hippocampal recording study that provided results that would have been most difficult to explain on the basis of the spatial mapping idea. These experimenters placed their rats in a large box with a goal cup at one end, where food reinforcement was delivered, and a stimulus-sampling port at the other end, where odors (S+ and S-) were delivered. What results were obtained that could not be explained satisfactorily by spatial mapping? (597-598)

d. Why were such findings so difficult to explain in terms of spatial mapping? (598)

e. How could these results be interpreted by context theory? (598)

f. Can we conclude that the hippocampus is not involved in the construction of spatial maps? (598)

2. In the context theory proposed by Teyler and DiScenna (1986) the hippocampus functions as what? (598)

a. According to this form of context theory where are the stimulus engrams stored? (598)

b. According to Teyler and DiScenna what is found within the hippocampus? (598)

c. While taking an exam this morning you encountered a question you could not answer even though you distinctly remember studying the material. During the test you remembered not only the page but the place on the page where the topic was discussed. You remembered reviewing that material the previous afternoon while eating a candy bar and listening to the latest top 40 release. Finally, just before the end of the time limit, you remembered the material necessary to answer the question. How would the Teyler and DiScenna theory explain this episode? (598-599)

Read pages 599-604 and summary statements 4-5 on page 608, then answer each of the following questions in this section.
---

1. Lesions to both CA3 and the _____ have the same effect on memory. What effect on memory would such lesions produce? (599)

a. What might lead you to predict such a similarity? (599)

b. From what two brain areas does the hippocampus receive drive-related arousal information? (599)

c. What appears to be the role of the medial septal nucleus input to the CA3 cells? (599)

d. Explain why damage to the medial septal nucleus appears to impair a rat's memory. (599)

e. Identify a second major input to the CA3 cells of the hippocampus. (599)

f. What type of information is carried via the prefrontal path? (599)

g. What would the cognitive map stored in the CA3 pyramidals be like without the septal input? (600)

2. By what indirect route does the motivational arousal information from the septal nucleus reach the CA3 pyramidal cells? (600)

   a. Identify the steps in this indirect route. (600)

   b. What function does Routtenberg (1984) ascribe to this indirect route? (600)

   c. What research evidence supports Routtenberg's notion concerning the function of this indirect route? (600-601)

   d. Why is it important for survival that the organism have a quick erasure mechanism? (601)

3. Describe the evoked response technique. (601)

   a. How did Deadwyler et al.(1981) employ this technique in their study of the role of the dentate nucleus? (601)

   b. In the Deadwyler et al. study what was represented by the N_1 wave seen in the typical average evoked response recording of electrical activity in the dentate gyrus? (602)

   c. What was represented by the N_2 wave? (602)

   d. From where did the N_1 input come? (603)

   e. From where did the N_2 input come? (603)

   f. How does Graham (the author of your text) propose that the Deadwyler results be combined with the findings of Routtenberg? (603-604)

Read pages 604-608 and summary statements 6-7 on page 608, then answer each of the following questions in this section.
---

1. Olton (1983) proposed that there were two forms of memory. Identify and describe these two memories. (604)

   a. Which of the two kinds of memory is associated with the hippocampus? (604)

   b. In the Olton (1979) study the investigator attempted to compare the predictive ability of the cognitive maps concept of O'Keefe and Nadel with the predictive ability of his own concept of memory. What piece of experimental apparatus did he employ? (604)

340

c. What manipulations did Olton make during this study that ensured that the O'Keefe and Nadel model would predict that the hippocampus was not involved in learning not to re-enter arms? (604)

d. In this study the rats learned to visit each of the four arms without returning to any that had already been stripped of food, despite the fact that they were limited to only cues within the arms. Olton and his colleagues then lesioned the fornix in both hemispheres of the brain. What effect did this lesion have? (604)

e. What did the results of the study suggest concerning the role of the hippocampus? (604-605)

f. Describe the apparatus employed in a second study by Olton and Papas (1979). (605)

g. According to Olton, as the rats gained experience with the environment _____ memory should have enabled them to avoid those arms that had been baited but had already been stripped of food, whereas _____ memory enabled the subjects to avoid the unbaited arms. (605)

h. Under the experimental conditions established in the Olton and Papas (1979) study, what would the cognitive maps theory predict concerning the effects of lesioning the fornix of the experimental animals? (605)

i. What prediction would you make based on the working memory concept? (605)

j. What were the results obtained by Olton and Papas (1979) following fornix lesioning? (605)

k. Describe the typical delayed spatial alternative task. (605)

l. How does the typical delayed object alternation task differ from the delayed spatial alternative task? (605-607)

m. Employing the 2-deoxyglucose technique during the learning of a delayed object alternation task and a delayed spatial alternation task, Friedman and Goldman-Rakic (1988) obtained what results? (607)

n. The Friedman and Goldman-Rakic (1988) results support what theory? (607)

o. Murray and Mishkin (1984, 1986) obtained data that disagree with the conclusions arrived at by Friedman and Goldman-Rakic (1988). Identify the discrepancies between the findings of these two studies. (607)

p. Discuss those studies that have offered convincing evidence against the hypothesis that the hippocampus is the site of working memory. (607)

2. Compare context memory and a spatial map. (607-608)

PRE-EXAM QUIZ

Multiple-Choice
Select the choice that best completes the stem in each question and indicate your selection in the appropriate space to the left of the question.

_____ 1. Which of the following best describes those brain waves called theta rhythm?
   a. small, irregular waves with a frequency of 13-20 Hz.
   b. relatively regular waves with a frequency of 7-9 Hz.
   c. large, irregular waves with a frequency of 1-4 Hz.
   d. relatively regular waves with a frequency of 4-5 Hz.
   e. none of the above

_____ 2. Hippocampal theta occurs under all but one of the following conditions. Under which condition would you not expect hippocampal theta to occur?
   a. early stages of condition
   b. presentation of a habituated stimulus
   c. when the animal is swimming
   d. presentation of a novel sound
   e. more than one of the above will not lead to the production of hippocampal theta

_____ 3. The major reason O'Keefe and Nadel (1978) rotated the T maze and the locational cues between each pair of trials was to
   a. change the location of the food reinforcer
   b. decrease the effectiveness of the locational cues
   c. eliminate the possibility of turn learning
   d. decrease the effectiveness of locational cues from outside the experimental enclosure
   e. more than one of the above

_____ 4. The first stage of the three-stage hippocampal three-stage analyzer is the
   a. CA1   d. CA3
   b. dentate gyrus   e. fornix
   c. entorhinal cortex

_____ 5. Kubie and Ranck (1983) used microelectrode recordings from hippocampal place cells and employed three different environments, each with a different task for the rat to perform. The most surprising finding of this study was that
   a. some of the place cells became active to stimulus cues outside the learning environment
   b. each place cell was specific to a single space in a single environment
   c. the majority of hippocampal place cells were active in all three environments
   d. the same place cell simultaneously developed selectively for a different place within different environments
   e. none of the above

_____ 6. According to the _____ theory, the hippocampus becomes the "secretary" of the brain, recording all environmental stimuli, internal stimuli, emotions, drives, and responses that occurred during any one episode of time. It then associates these events with one another so that they form a memory of the framework in which the primary stimulus and response occurred.
   a. spatial maps   d. reference memory
   b. working memory   e. none of the above
   c. context

_____ 7. A major input to the CA3 pyramidal cells comes from the _____. This input consists of drive-related arousal, which appears to keep the CA3 cells appraised of the relative importance of stimuli present in the environment.
   a. entorhinal cortex
   b. corpus striatum
   c. inferotemporal cortex
   d. limbic cortex
   e. medial septal nucleus

_____ 8. According to Routtenberg (1984) the indirect route from the entorhinal cortex through the _____ to the CA3 pyramidal cells is involved in the process of forgetting.
   a. dentate gyrus
   b. locus coeruleus
   c. fornix
   d. hypothalamus
   e. reticular formation

_____ 9. The synapses between dentate gyrus granule cells and CA3 pyramidal cells employ _____ as the neurotransmitter.
   a. acetylcholine
   b. serotonin
   c. norepinephrine
   d. dopamine
   e. none of the above

_____ 10. It contains all the constant, stable engrams. It is
   a. context memory
   b. working memory
   c. indexing memory
   d. reference memory
   e. none of the above

_____ 11. Employing a 17-arm radial maze in which room cues were readily available, Olton and Papas (1979) placed food in only eight of the arms (the same arms on each trial). According to these investigators _____ memory should enable the animal to ignore the nine unbaited arms, and _____ memory would tell it which of the baited arms to avoid because they had already been stripped of food.
   a. working; referencing
   b. referencing; context
   c. context; working
   d. indexing; referencing
   e. referencing; working

_____ 12. In a reversal learning or extinction situation, the size of N reflects
   a. the amount of ongoing neural activity in the hippocampus
   b. the probability that a response will be followed by reinforcement
   c. the neural activity in the medial septal nucleus
   d. the probability that a response will not be followed by reinforcement
   e. more than one of the above

_____ 13. Basket cells
   a. can be used to explain the background firing of place cells
   b. are interneurons found in the reticular formation
   c. are the primary type of cell found in the dentate gyrus
   d. are the primary type of cell found in the entorhinal cortex
   e. more than one of the above

_____ 14. The memory indexing system is a variation of which of the following?
   a. spatial mapping theory
   b. working memory theory
   c. context theory
   d. reinforcement theory
   e. none of the above

_____ 15. It is a type of hippocampal neuron that responds selectively to different places in the environment. It is a
   a. granule cell
   b. pyramidal cell
   c. glial cell
   d. Golgi II cell
   e. none of the above

True/False

_____ 1. Theta rhythm studies suggest that the hippocampus systematically monitors both the ongoing sensory events and the motor events that are being attended and that demand, or may demand, voluntary adjustments.

_____ 2. Studies of single-cell recordings of hippocampal neurons have done more to inspire the creation of theories to explain hippocampal function than any other research approach.

_____ 3. The receptive fields of the hippocampal place cells are actual places in the animal's environment.

_____ 4. O'Keefe et al.(1978) found that even through some of the external cues were removed from the enclosure surrounding the T maze, the rat's place cells were still as accurate in detecting the location of the food in the maze.

_____ 5. Destruction of CA1 neurons makes it impossible to learn the maze when correct responding depends on the ability to discriminate places in the environment.

_____ 6. According to O'Keefe and Nadel (1978) all the sensory inputs necessary to create a cognitive map are received in the entorhinal cortex of the hippocampus.

_____ 7. Each time the animal's environment changes, a different cognitive map is established in the hippocampus.

_____ 8. According to Kubie and Ranck (1984) the background firing of a place cell is somehow specific to all the surrounding stimuli of the environment.

_____ 9. According to indexing theory, the engrams for any particular episode can be found in the hippocampus.

_____ 10. Neither the entorhinal input nor the medial septal nucleus alone can activates the CA3 pyramidal cells.

_____ 11. The indirect route through the granule cells of the dentate gyrus to the CA3 cells prevents response perseveration.

_____ 12. Both N_1 and N_2 are recorded from and generated within the hippocampus.

_____ 13. Friedman and Goldman-Rakic (1988) found that the hippocampus showed significantly higher levels of activity during the learning of both the delayed spatial alternation task and the delayed object alternation task. Contrary to what the working memory theory would predict, the researchers found no difference in activity levels between the two tasks.

_____ 14. The idea that the hippocampus provides a working memory is in direct conflict with the idea that it provides an indexing mechanism.

_____ 15. N_1 may be the neural signal that triggers the erasure mechanism to remove a reinforcement association from some part of the cognitive map.

15.1 CA1 (592)	15.6 delayed spatial alternation task (606)
15.2 CA3 (592)	15.7 dentate gyrus (592)
15.3 context (597)	15.8 erasure mechanism (601)
15.4 context theory (597)	15.9 evoked response technique (601)
15.5 delayed object alternation task (605)	15.10 granule cells (592)

15.6

Employed in the study of working memory of primates. The animal is forced to make a choice between two stimuli. After the animals chooses, there is a delay, during which the animal must keep a memory of which stimulus, the one on the left or on the right, was correct so that it can choose the alternate stimulus next time.

15.7

A serrated strip of gray matter lying under the medial border of the hippocampus. According to the O'Keefe and Nadel theory it receives all the sensory input necessary to create a cognitive map.

15.8

A term denoting the dentate gyrus, which is part of the indirect pathway between CA3 and the entorhinal cortex and which produces a quick form of forgetting. It provides a quick method of changing the reinforcement aspect of cognitive maps.

15.9

Technique that employs a macroelectrode to record the composite activity of thousands of neurons simultaneously. All surrounding nerve impulses within the range of the electrode tip are blended into a single voltage level that fluctuates from moment to moment as the pattern of action potentials and postsynaptic potentials changes.

15.10

Cells located in the dentate gyrus that project their fibers to a crescent-shaped area of pyramidal cells called CA3.

Copyright 1990 by Wadsworth, Inc.

15.1

An area of pyramidal cells located in the hippocampus. It receives input from both CA3 and the commissural fibers crossing the midline from the hippocampus of the other hemisphere.

15.2

A crescent-shaped area of pyramidal cells in the hippocampus, which is one of the areas where the cognitive map is located according to O'Keefe and Nadel. It is organized to provide the necessary associative links between various places in the environment. Destruction of this area should make spatial learning impossible.

15.3

In a research environment it refers to all the surrounding stimuli, excluding the manipulated stimuli to which the subject is to attend and respond.

15.4

First suggested to explain data on background firing in place cells. It states that the hippocampus records all environmental stimuli, emotions, drives, and responses that occurred during any one time episode. It then associates these events so that they form a memory of the context in which the primary stimulus and response occurred.

15.5

Employed in the study of working memory of primates. The animal is forced to make a choice between two stimulus objects. After the animal chooses, there is a delay, during which the animal must keep a memory of which of the stimulus objects was correct so that it can choose the alternate stimulus on the next trial.

15.11

medial septal nucleus

15.16

place cell

(599)

15.12

memory indexing system

(589)

15.17

radial arm maze

(598)

15.13

N_1

(594)

15.18

reference memory

(602)

15.14

N_2

(604)

15.19

theta rhythm

(602)

15.15

perforant path

(589)

15.20

working memory

(592)

(604)

15.16

A type of neuron found in the hippocampus of the rat. Apparently the receptive fields of these neurons are actually places in the rat's environment.

15.17

A maze that has a number of arms radiating out from a central circular platform like the spokes from the hub of a wheel.

15.18

That part of the memory that contains all the constant, stable engrams like the knowledge you learn in this course, the ability to recognize your car or notebook, and the words to a song.

15.19

Rhythmical EEG waves that have a frequency of about 4-5 Hz. These waves appear during the early stages of conditioning when the organism is still getting used to the situation and is orienting to the conditioned stimulus, unconditioned stimulus, and extraneous stimuli. This rhythm is associated with attention.

15.20

That part of the memory that is a short-lived record of events that need to be remembered only for a limited period of time. It would include the memory of having attended class today, or of having driven your car downtown.

Copyright 1990 by Wadsworth, Inc.

15.11

A group of cell bodies located in the septum. It provides part of the input for CA3. The lesioning of this nucleus mimics the effects of lesioning CA3. The nucleus is also the source of one type of theta rhythm in the hippocampus.

15.12

A context theory proposed by Teyler and DiScenna that views the hippocampus as a memory indexing system. It holds that the stimulus engrams are stored in portions of the cortex and subcortical brain devoted to a particular sense. The hippocampus contains a record of where engrams for any particular episode can be found in the rest of the brain.

15.13

The label given to the first negative wave of an evoked potential in an evoked response record. It is the product of the impulses from the entorhinal cortex arriving at the gyrus by way of the perforant path and the EPSPs they evoke in granule cell dendrites. They signal nonreinforcement experiences.

15.14

The label given to the second negative wave of an evoked potential in an evoked response record. It represents input to the granule cells of the dentate nucleus, which begins in the medial septal nucleus and signals a reinforcement experience.

15.15

A pathway consisting of axons of the entorhinal cortex cells. These axons synapse with the dendrites of the granule cells in the dentate gyrus.

CHAPTER SIXTEEN
MEMORY

READ-WRITE-REVIEW

Read pages 612-620 and summary statements 1-6 on pages 644-645, then answer each of the following questions in this section.
---

1. According to cognitive psychologists there is a significant amount of research data that suggest that the storage of a stimulus involves two distinct stages. List and briefly describe these two stages. (612)

    a. How is information usually transferred from the first to the second stage? (612)

    b. What is the implication of this idea of memory stages for physiological psychologists and their research in this area? (613)

2. Describe the activity of a reverberatory circuit. (613)

    a. Why is such a circuit ideally suited to serve as a basis for short-term memory? (613)

    b. Where might you find such a circuit? (613)

    c. What did Burns (1950) do to demonstrate the possible existence of reverberation? (613)

3. Why are reverberating circuits not used in describing long-term memory? (614)

    a. Assume that each engram is a different pathway in the nervous system. Now suppose that when you are first presented with a ball a neural circuit composed of neurons A, B, G, and HH fire. If you are to remember that ball the next time it is presented to you, some change in the circuit must occur. What must happen to make certain that the same collection of cells are activated the next time you see the ball? (614)

    b. According to Hebb, what brings this about? (614)

    c. Why is Hebb's explanation of what happens so difficult to demonstrate using standard research techniques (e.g., electrodes, stereotaxic instrument, and atlas)? (614)

    d. The hippocampal slice method has been used to circumvent these problems. Describe this method. (614)

349

e. What is long-term potentiation and why did its discovery generate so much excitement among memory researchers? (615)

f. In what ways are the experimental electrical stimulation of the perforant path and any natural stimulus the same? In what ways do they differ? (616)

g. What other findings do we have that strongly suggest that long-term potentiation is a part of the memory formation process? (615-616)

4. What is sprouting and how is it studied? (617)

   a. Discuss two possible explanations for how sprouting is triggered. (617)

   b. What is reactive synaptogenesis? (617)

   c. What reason is there for believing that reactive synaptogenesis is simply a continuation of the original growth process that produced the brain? (617-618)

   d. What reason do physiological psychologists interested in memory have for studying synaptogenesis? (618)

5. Rats trained in a series of mazes were found to have more dendritic branches on some types of cortical neurons than a control group. Parahippocampal gyrus neurons from elderly people with normal brains had markedly more dendritic branching than did such neurons in young adults. Suggest why these findings can be considered predictable. (618)

6. Rosenzweig and Bennett (1984) injected a drug called anisomycin directly into the brains of rats that had just learned a task. What effect does this produce when the animal is tested for retention later? (619)

   a. What explanation can you give for this result? (619)

   b. Suppose we modified this experiment such that we gave half of the rats 10 trials to master the task and the other half 20 trials. All rats are injected with anisomycin immediately after learning the task. Which group of rats will show the least effect of the anisomycin on retention? (619)

   c. Why? (619)

   d. How was this problem in the interpretation of protein-synthesis inhibition solved? (619)

   e. What did the findings of protein-synthesis inhibition studies employing this technique clearly demonstrate? (619)

   f. Now lets modify the protein-synthesis experiment again. Once again we will inject our control rats with a saline solution and inject our experimental animals with anisomycin just prior to learning the task. If we then test retention each hour after learning for the first six hours, what effect would be seen in the experimental group? (619-620)

g. What do such findings suggest? (620)

Read pages 620-631 and summary statements 7-10 on page 645, then answer each of the following questions in this section.

---

1. Why do some theorists argue for the existence of an "intermediate-term" memory linking short-term memory to long-term memory? (620)

    a. To be able to maintain the engram between the end of reverberation and the construction of new connections between neurons a hypothetical process would have to meet what two criteria? (620)

    b. In a study using goldfish, Shashoua (1985) discovered what two brain proteins that may serve as an intermediate but temporary template? (621)

    c. Where are these proteins normally concentrated? (621)

    d. Why was it necessary for Shashoua to carry out a second "protein-disablement" experiment? (621)

    e. What were the results of this "protein-disablement" study? (622)

    f. What similarities exist between protein synthesis-inhibition and "protein-disablement" experiments? (622)

    g. What role does the calcium ion play in Shashoua's hypothesis? (622)

2. Explain why some investigators in this area have focused attention on the shape of spines. (623)

    a. The induction of long-term potentiation in the hippocampus produced what kinds of changes in the dendrites in this area? (623)

    b. Why would such changes be likely candidates for intermediate-term memory? (623)

    c. What two interpretations have been given to the findings of such long-term potentiation studies? (624)

    d. The calpain-fodrin theory has been proposed by Lynch and Baudry (1984) to explain what? (625)

    e. What is the neurotransmitter for most of the major types of synapses in the hippocampus? (625)

    f. What is the role of the calcium ion in the calpain-fodrin theory? (626)

    g. What is calpain and what function does it have in the calpain-fodrin theory? (626)

h. What is fodrin and what role does it play in the calpain-fodrin theory? (626)

3. Nathanson and Greengard (1977) proposed the cAMP-kinase theory to explain what? (628)

   a. Explain how cyclic adenosine monophosphate is formed. (628)

   b. Once the cyclic adenosine monophosphate diffuses into the cytoplasm from the adenylate cyclase, it eventually encounters a molecule of _____. (628)

   c. This molecule is specialized to perform what function? (628)

   d. What is this process called? (628)

   e. There are two parts to the kinase molecule. What is the function of each part? (628)

   f. What is the function of a nuclear regulatory protein? (628)

   g. Describe how the gene is activated. (628)

   h. Once the gene is activated how are the proteins manufactured? (628)

   i. Explain how cAMP could be involved in long-term memory. (628)

   j. Explain how cAMP could be involved in short-term memory. (628)

   k. Are the cAMP-kinase mechanism and the calpain-fodrin theory competitors? Explain your answer. (630)

4. Associative learning would require what in terms of the nervous system? (630)

   a. What would be necessary for such linking to occur? (630)

   b. The arrangement would be called a(n) _____, and it has been suggested as the basis for associative learning. (630)

   c. Using the calpain-fodrin mechanism and glutamate synapses, explain how such an arrangement might work. (630)

Read pages 631-639 and summary statements 11-16 on page 645, then answer each of the following questions in this section.
---

1. What is amnesia? (631)

   a. What is concussive amnesia? (631)

   b. What is Korsakoff's syndrome? (631)

c. Distinguish between anterograde and retrograde amnesia. (632)

d. What is a lacuna? (633)

e. What is meant by the term "confabulation" and why is it sometimes resorted to by amnesia patients? (633)

2. Scoville's patient showed a dramatic loss of memory following brain surgery. What brain areas did Scoville remove? (634)

   a. In the case of Scoville's patient, which type of amnesia, anterograde or retrograde, was involved? (634)

   b. From an anatomical standpoint there may be two kinds of amnesia. List them. (634-635)

   c. Korsakoff's psychosis represents which of these types? (635)

   d. Scoville's patient represents which of these types? (634-635)

   e. At present what is the best working hypothesis concerning the anatomical regions destroyed in Korsakoff's syndrome? (635)

3. The process of shifting information from short-term to long-term memory is called _____, and having problems with this kind of information processing is characteristic of _____ amnesia. (635)

   a. Describe Hebb's (1949) two-stage theory of memory. (635-636)

   b. We now know that there is a problem with this early explanation. What was this problem? (636)

   c. In this early explanation of how memory works, at what point in the process was the engram most fragile, according to Hebb? (636)

   d. According to Hebb, what could happen to prevent consolidation at this point? (636)

   e. The two brain regions that are most likely to be very critical for consolidation are _____ and _____. (636)

   f. The consolidation-failure hypothesis places the role of creating long-term memories out of short-term memories in the _____. What is somewhat unusual about this? (636)

4. What is electroconvulsive shock therapy (ECT) and for what is it used? (637)

   a. What type of amnesia is experienced by patients who have undergone electroconvulsive shock therapy? (637)

   b. What is Ribot's law and how does it relate to the Squire (1977) study in which he had ECT patients learn some material either 18 hours or 10 minutes before receiving therapy? (637)

c. Explain Squire's (1977) results in terms of consolidation-failure theory. (637)

d. Describe the procedure researchers used in attempting to mimic the human electroconvulsive shock therapy effects with animal subjects. (637)

e. What is the procedure called and how successful were researchers in producing in animal subjects memory effects similar to those found in ECT patients? (637)

5. Describe the procedure employed by researchers in the reminder-cue studies. (637-638)

   a. What were the results obtained in such studies (e.g., Miller & Springer, 1972)? (638)

   b. How were such results interpreted? (638)

   c. Under what sort of experimental conditions do human amnesia patients show the same effects? (638)

   d. The explanation of these research findings helps to explain what phenomena associated with concussive amnesia? (638)

6. What major problems are there for the retrieval-failure hypothesis as an explanation for amnesia phenomena? (638-639)

   a. The original expression of the two-stage theory of memory suggested that short-term memory lasted only 15-20 seconds. What implication does this have for retrograde amnesia? (638)

   b. How well do these implications agree with data obtained on retrograde amnesia? (638)

   c. What must be done to make the consolidation-failure hypothesis better fit the retrograde amnesia data? (638)

   d. If this adjustment is made, can the consolidation-failure hypothesis explain the results of the reminder-cue studies? (638-639)

Read pages 639-644 and summary statements 17-19 on page 645-646, then answer each of the following questions in this section.
---

1. Bob Green is a 17-year-old who suffers from retrograde amnesia as a result of being hit in the head with a baseball. Yesterday he learned to throw a curve ball and today he practiced throwing this "new" pitch for three hours. What will he remember tomorrow? (640)

   a. What will he not remember? (640)

354

b. What is perceptual-motor learning? (640)

   c. Provide two other examples of memory sparing in amnesia. (640)

   d. What changes must be made in the primary task before amnesiacs do as well as normals at filling in the words from the list? (640)

   e. What do these findings suggest? (641)

2. According to Squire (1988) memory should initially be divided into two compartments. List and describe these compartments. (642)

   a. List and describe the two components of conscious memory. (642)

   b. There are several types of memory that are not available to the conscious mind. List and describe each of these. (642)

3. Distinguish between working memory and reference memory regarding permanence. (642-643)

   a. Distinguish between working memory and reference memory regarding brain location. (643)

   b. How does the distinction between working memory and reference memory help explain the results of the priming experiments? (643)

4. Why has there been so little data collected on reference memory amnesia? (644)

PRE-EXAM QUIZ

Multiple-Choice
Select the choice that best completes the stem in each question and indicate your selection in the appropriate space to the left of the question.

____ 1. During the 1950s, ____ was the most frequently suggested anatomical basis for short-term memory among physiological psychologists.
   a. sprouting
   b. long-term potentiation
   c. reverberatory circuits
   d. reactive synaptogenesis
   e. rehearsal

____ 2. The hippocampus slice method has been used to
   a. anatomically trace sprouting
   b. pinpoint possible short-term memory loci in the brain
   c. study reactive synaptogenesis
   d. study the changes in EPSPs before and after a synapse has been used
   e. none of the above

____ 3. Sprouting can occur as a result of
   a. a lesion
   b. the process of normal maintenance of the brain
   c. development during the prenatal period and infancy
   d. nerve impulse activity in the excited fibers
   e. more than one of the above

_____ 4. In the goldfish study by Shashoua (1985), in which the fish had to learn to swim upright once a float had been attached to it at the ventral midline, the experimenter found all but one of the following. Which of the following did he NOT find?
   a. the proteins produced in the brains of those fish who had learned the task were of a type found in high concentrations in the hippocampus
   b. he found only three types of protein that were in greater quantity in the brains of the trained experimental subjects than in the brains of the untrained controls
   c. in the "protein-disablement" portion of the study, he found that the fish injected with the antiserum were unable to retain what they had learned
   d. the proteins found in the initial part of the study were normal brain proteins that are manufactured by cells and then released into the extracellular fluid
   e. all of these were findings in the Shashoua study

_____ 5. According to the theory proposed by Lynch and Baudry (1984), what is the role of the calcium ion in the storage of an engram until the slower growth processes have had time to take place?
   a. they act directly on the glutamate receptors
   b. they serve to bind with and activate the enzyme calpain
   c. they break down the fodrin molecules
   d. they directly increase the ability of the dendrite to receive the neurotransmitter glutamate
   e. none of the above

_____ 6. Which of the following is best employed in explaining sensory memory?
   a. the development of an ependymin matrix
   b. AMP persistence
   c. changes in the shape of dendritic spines
   d. building of new terminals or dendrites
   e. reverberation

_____ 7. Korsakoff's syndrome is directly caused by
   a. brain trauma   d. psychological trauma
   b. alcohol abuse   e. electroshock therapy
   c. poor diet

_____ 8. Confabulation is
   a. a failure in retrieval
   b. an immediate-acting treatment to reduce depression that also produces retrograde amnesia
   c. the creation of pseudomemories to fill in the lacunae caused by amnesia
   d. the recovery of engrams lost in retrograde amnesia
   e. the moving of information from short-term to long-term memory

_____ 9. Currently the best working hypothesis concerning Korsakoff's syndrome is that such patients probably suffer anterograde amnesia because of the destruction of
   a. the lateral and medial geniculate nuclei of the thalamus
   b. the dorsomedial nucleus of the thalamus and the mammillary bodies of the hypothalamus
   c. the hippocampus and the mammillary bodies
   d. the supraoptic nucleus of the hypothalamus and the hippocampus
   e. none of the above

_____10. According to the consolidation-failure hypothesis the role of the hippocampus is to
   a. serve as the storage center for long-term memory
   b. serve as the storage center for short-term memory
   c. serve as the storage center for both long-term and short-term memory
   d. create long-term memories out of short-term memories, both of which are housed elsewhere in the brain
   e. move information from sensory storage to short-term memory

_____11. Which of the following can be explained by the retrieval-failure hypothesis?
   a. anterograde amnesia
   b. Ribot's law
   c. disappearance of much of retrograde amnesia in concussive amnesia
   d. reminder-cue studies
   e. more than one of the above

_____12. Studies of amnesia patients and their performances on mirror tracing and pursuit-tracking tasks forced the conclusion that there were two varieties of memory. Amnesia has an effect on
   a. both skill memory and event memory
   b. skill memory but not event memory
   c. event memory but not skill memory
   d. neither skill memory nor event memory
   e. these varieties of memory only if it is anterograde amnesia

_____13. Which of the following represents one of Squire's (1986) types of declarative memory?
   a. working memory
   b. skill memory
   c. primary memory
   d. classical conditioning memory
   e. none of the above

_____14. According to Squire's (1986) classification of memory, all your learned likes and dislikes and preferences for various stimuli are likely _____ memories.
   a. reference
   b. primary
   c. classical conditioning
   d. nondeclarative
   e. more than one of the above

_____15. The theoretical process of shifting information from short-term to long-term memory is called
   a. confabulation
   b. consolidation
   c. cued-recall
   d. retrieval
   e. none of these

True/False

_____ 1. Typically it is through rehearsal that information transfer from short-term to long-term memory is accomplished.

_____ 2. Synaptogenesis and sprouting represent two suggested ways in which structural changes occur at the synapse, thereby strengthening the connections between neurons in a circuit.

_____ 3. The fact that long-term potentiation cannot be demonstrated outside the hippocampus limits the usefulness of this phenomenon in explaining long-term memory.

_____ 4. Protein synthesis inhibition researchers began to use a passive-avoidance task so that the task could be completed before any new protein could be synthesized.

_____ 5. Shashoua's hypothesis hinges on the fact that if the extracellular fluid concentration of calcium ions is lower than normal the ependymins polymerize, and this clumping of proteins forms a matrix to guide the subsequent growth of the terminal.

_____ 6. Changes in the shape of the dendritic spine can occur within 10 minutes following stimulation; however, these changes seem to fade out within 2-3 hours.

_____ 7. The cAMP-kinase mechanism and the calpain-fodrin theory are competing theories used to explain an intermediate type of memory.

_____ 8. The inability to remember events that took place after the trauma is termed retrograde amnesia.

_____ 9. The patient described by Scoville had diencephalic amnesia.

_____10. Electroconvulsive shock with animal subjects has been used by researchers in an attempt to mimic the human electroconvulsive therapy effects.

_____11. One of the problems with the consolidation-failure hypothesis is that it does not explain Ribot's law.

_____12. Results of reminder-cue studies can be explained by the consolidation-failure hypothesis, but only if one makes the assumption that there are degrees of consolidation.

_____13. Priming task studies comparing amnesiacs and normals suggests that there are two kinds of memory: One that employs conscious retrieval and one that does not.

_____14. Of Squire's declarative and nondeclarative memories only the nondeclarative memory is available to the conscious mind.

_____15. The temporary nature of Squire's working memory is probably due to a greater opportunity for interference between similar memories.

16.1 adenylate cyclase (628)

16.2 amnesia (631)

16.3 anisomycin (619)

16.4 anterograde amnesia (632)

16.5 beta and gamma ependymin (621)

16.6 calpain (626)

16.7 classical conditioning memories (642)

16.8 concussive amnesia (631)

16.9 confabulation (633)

16.10 consolidation (635)

16.6

A group of proteinase enzymes that become active only after they react with calcium.

16.1

An enzyme located inside the membrane and in close association with the neurotransmitter receptor site. It reacts to the binding of transmitter with receptor site to become chemically active so that it can bind with adenosine triphosphate to strip two of its phosphate groups.

16.7

A type of nondeclarative memory. It consists of the automatic reactions to conditioned stimuli. Most of these are emotional or motivational.

16.2

Traumatic memory loss.

16.8

A form of memory loss caused by a blow to the head that throws the brain against the inside of the skull causing blood vessels to rupture and cells to die.

16.3

A protein synthesis inhibiting drug.

16.9

The creation of pseudomemories out of an amnesia patient's deductions about what must have happened during the forgotten episode.

16.4

The inability to remember events that took place after a brain trauma.

16.10

The theoretical process of shifting information from short-term to long-term memory.

16.5

Normal brain proteins found highly concentrated in the area of the midbrain called the zona ependyma. They are manufactured by cells and then released into the extracellular fluid that circulates between neurons and glia.

Copyright 1990 by Wadsworth, Inc.

16.11 consolidation-failure hypothesis (635)

16.12 cued-recall task (638)

16.13 cyclic AMP (cAMP) (628)

16.14 cytoskeleton (623)

16.15 declarative memory (642)

16.16 dendritic spines (623)

16.17 diencephalon (634)

16.18 dorsomedial nucleus of the thalamus (DMT) (635)

16.19 electroconvulsive therapy (ECT) (636)

16.20 fodrin (626)

16.16

Tiny protrusions that cover the dendrites of most cortical neurons and many hippocampal neurons. They come in a variety of shapes and sizes but fall into three major classes. Most of the excitatory synapses are made of these structures.

16.17

A region of the brain just above and anterior to the midbrain that consists chiefly of the thalamus, subthalamus, and hypothalamus.

16.18

A diencephalic structure that appears to be relevant to amnesia. Rats with lesions in this area had considerable difficulty in remembering from trial to trial what responses they had just made.

16.19

A form of therapy in which a series of shocks strong enough to produce convulsions is delivered to the brain. It is usually spread out over four or five sessions over two weeks. There is an immediate loss of consciousness that lasts for a number of minutes following the shock. The patient awakens feeling groggy and confused and often has some retrograde amnesia for the treatment.

16.20

The protein that appears to be altered in the dendritic spine as a result of the activity of the proteinase enzyme. It is one of the proteins making up the microtubules and microfilaments of the cytoskeleton.

Copyright 1990 by Wadsworth, Inc.

16.11

Hypothesis that suggests that anterograde amnesia is due to a breakdown in the process of shifting information from short-term to long-term memory.

16.12

A task employed in the study of amnesia in humans. Patients are asked to recall words that are chosen so that many different completions are possible and guessing would produce a very low score.

16.13

Results from the binding of adenylate cyclase with adenosine triphosphate. The latter loses two of its three phosphate groups. Once formed this molecule is released into the cytoplasm where, among other activities, it can initiate the opening of ion gates and effect both RNA and protein formation.

16.14

A network of protein fibers that holds the rather flimsy cell membrane into a stable shape.

16.15

Conscious memories that consist of events, facts, and general information about experiences.

16.21

glutamate

(625)

16.22

Hebbian synapse

(630)

16.23

hippocampal slice method

(614)

16.24

Korsakoff's syndrome

(631)

16.25

lacuna

(633)

16.26

long-term memory (LTM)

(612)

16.27

long-term potentiation

(615)

16.28

mammillary bodies

(635)

16.29

mirror tracing

(640)

16.30

NMDA receptors

(630)

16.26

The second stage in storing a stimulus in memory. If the stimulus is to be retained for any length of time it must be stored here. Transfer to this storage is usually accomplished by repeating the information a number of times.

16.27

The increase in EPSP size following extended use of the synapses. Some change has occurred at the synapses that allows the same number of presynaptic nerve impulses to produce a greater effect in postsynaptic cells. The effect has been observed to linger for as long as days or weeks.

16.28

Hypothalamic structures thought to be involved in amnesia. They receive one of the major outputs of the hippocampus via the fornix.

16.29

A task that requires the subject to trace a path with a pencil while viewing everything in a mirror.

16.30

Transmitter receptors that do not react to glutamate unless the membrane has already been polarized. It is a possible basis for a Hebbian synapse.

16.21

The neurotransmitter used for most of the major types of synapses in the hippocampus.

16.22

A synaptic arrangement named for its originator, David Hebb. It has been suggested as the basis for associative learning. It is an arrangement where the synapse could be used many times without strengthening it, but it must be able to grow stronger whenever the postsynaptic cell receives a simultaneous input from another synapse.

16.23

A technique that enables the electrophysiologist to guide electrodes to the correct sites with only the aid of a microscope. In this method the brain is removed and the hippocampus is dissected out and sliced into thick sections. The electrodes can now be placed into the zone of interest without the difficulty and imprecision of implanting them stereotaxically.

16.24

A form of memory loss produced by alcoholism. It seems to result from the poor diet of the chronic alcoholic rather than directly from the drug itself. Because the alcoholic obtains so many calories from the alcohol, he or she fails to eat foods that provide a sufficient supply of vitamin B_1. This deficiency is responsible for the brain damage and amnesia.

16.25

A memory gap that remains for a long time.

Copyright 1990 by Wadsworth, Inc.

16.31 nondeclarative memories (642)

16.32 nuclear regulatory protein (628)

16.33 perceptual-motor learning (640)

16.34 phosphorylation (628)

16.35 primary memory (642)

16.36 priming task (640)

16.37 protein kinase (628)

16.38 protein synthesis inhibitor (619)

16.39 pursuit-tracking task (640)

16.40 reactive synaptogenesis (617)

16.36

A memory task in which the subjects are presented with fragments of the original stimuli they are asked to recall.

16.31

Memories that are not available to the conscious mind. These memories are activated by the individual doing something rather than by consciously trying to remember.

16.37

An enzyme that specializes in transferring phosphate groups to protein molecules to bring about changes in their function. The kinase is kept inactive by a molecular fragment called an inhibitory subunit, which is removed by cyclic AMP. This activates the protein kinase, which then diffuses into the cell nucleus where it finds the protein on which it is to act.

16.32

A protein that is bound to a stretch of DNA, preventing that gene fragment from producing RNA until it is needed. It is acted on by cyclic AMP and removed from the gene fragment so that the latter can be activated to produce messenger RNA.

16.38

A drug that prevents the synthesis of proteins.

16.33

The acquisition of tasks that require perceptual skill learning such as pursuit-tracking or mirror-tracing tasks. Such learning is spared by amnesia.

16.39

A task in which the object is to hold a pointer on a moving target.

16.34

The process of transferring phosphate groups to protein molecules.

16.40

The production of new synapses to replace lost ones following damage to the nervous system.

16.35

The brief type of retention seen in a priming task; it is another type of nondeclarative memory.

Copyright 1990 by Wadsworth, Inc.

16.41 reference memory (642)

16.42 reminder-cue studies (637)

16.43 retrograde amnesia (632)

16.44 reverberatory circuit (613)

16.45 Ribot's law (637)

16.46 short-term memory (STM) (612)

16.47 skill memories (642)

16.48 sprouting (617)

16.49 synapse turnover (618)

16.50 working memory (642)

16.46

The first stage in storing a stimulus in memory. Storage in this stage is temporary.

16.47

A type of nondeclarative memory that contains the plans for making the movements involved in some skill. These are largely unconscious and very likely exist mostly within the basal ganglia.

16.48

The growth of new telodendria and/or terminals in the mature brain.

16.49

The periodic replacement of old synapses that have suffered from "wear and tear" through regular use. It is a normal "operation and maintenance" function of the brain.

16.50

A type of declarative memory. Such memory is episodic, a memory for events.

16.41

A type of declarative memory that contains all the constant, stable engrams.

16.42

Studies that yielded data contrary to retrieval-failure theory predictions. They begin by training rats to make avoidance responses and deliver ECS. After recovery the animal is taken to a new apparatus where a brief, unavoidable foot shock is given. This serves as a reminder of the original foot shock experience. Next day it is tested in the original apparatus.

16.43

The inability to remember events that preceded a brain trauma.

16.44

A circuit in which each cell can excite its postsynaptic cell so that activity in the loop will continue after the neuron has quit firing. This continued reverberation means that the circuit will provide an output to the rest of the nervous system after the original stimulus event is over. It is most frequently suggested as the basis for short-term memory.

16.45

Also referred to as the last-in first-out principle. It holds that the closer the experience is to the traumatic, amnesia-producing event, the greater the amnesia for that event.

Copyright 1990 by Wadsworth, Inc.

CHAPTER SEVENTEEN
BRAIN DYSFUNCTION

READ-WRITE-REVIEW

Read pages 650-656 and summary statements 1-4 on page 685, then answer each of the following questions in this section.
---

1. Explain why it is so difficult to understand many of the brain dysfunctions as compared to the dysfunctions of other body organs. (650)

2. What is the single outstanding symptom of psychosis? (650)

    a. What is an organic mental disorder? Provide several examples. (650-651)

    b. How do organic mental disorders and other psychotic disorders, such as schizophrenia, differ? (651)

    c. What is meant by the term "insanity"? (651)

3. Who is credited with the development of the concept of schizophrenia, and what did he or she believe was being split? (651)

    a. What differences exist between multiple personality and schizophrenia? (651-652)

    b. Describe the typical onset of schizophrenia. (652)

    c. When does the onset of schizophrenia typically occur? (652)

    d. Once the dysfunction has been established there are some clearly bizarre behaviors that become evident and that definitely signal the need for medical help. List and describe five such behaviors. (652)

    e. What are the chances for a full recovery? (652)

4. List and identify three major approaches researchers have taken in their attempt to discover a genetic factor in the causation of schizophrenia, and in each case summarize the general findings. (652-653)

    a. Although the overall evidence would strongly suggest that there is a genetic factor involved in schizophrenia, it also suggests we are dealing with something more complex than a single gene. How might you explain this complexity? (653)

b. The lack of concordance between monozygotic twins provides a strong argument for what? (653)

   c. What is proposed by Zubin and Steinhauer's (1982) vulnerability model of schizophrenia? (653)

   d. What is the role of the moderating factors in the vulnerability model? (653)

5. What is neuropathology? (654)

   a. Differentiate between neurological hard signs and neurological soft signs. (654)

   b. Which type of neurological sign is more abundant in schizophrenia and what are some of these signs? (654)

   c. What two signs of neuropathology are fairly consistently found in the brains of schizophrenic patients on autopsy? (654)

   d. Explain how each of these autopsy findings might be related to specific neurological soft signs seen in the schizophrenic patient. (654)

6. PET-scan studies of schizophrenia have produced what general findings? (654-655)

   a. What, if anything, might these findings have to do with dopamine? (655)

   b. What contributions to the general understanding of the functioning of the schizophrenic brain have been made by regional cerebral blood flow scan studies? (655)

   c. What are the possible implications of the results obtained using radiological techniques to study the schizophrenic's brain function? (656)

Read pages 656-663 and summary statements 5-7 on page 685, then answer each of the following questions in this section.

---

1. Describe the Crow (1982) categorization of schizophrenia. (656-657)

   a. What is a prognosis? (656)

   b. What does Crow mean by the term "positive" symptoms of schizophrenia? (656)

   c. What does Crow mean by the term "negative" symptoms of schizophrenia? (656)

   d. According to Crow, which of his two types of schizophrenia probably arises from a chemical error in the system? (656)

   e. According to Crow, which of his types of schizophrenia responds best to the antipsychotic drugs? (657)

2. What general behavioral evidence can you cite that supports the notion that schizophrenics suffer an impairment in attention? (657)

   a. What is the continuous performance task? (658)

   b. Using this task with hospitalized schizophrenics and neurotics, Stammeyer (1983) obtained what results? (658)

   c. How can averaged evoked potentials be used to reveal attention deficit? (658)

   d. What is the Yerkes-Dodson law? (658)

   e. How might hyperarousal explain the attention deficit so characteristic of schizophrenics?

   f. Combining the results of CT scan and regional cerebral blood flow studies with the Yerkes-Dodson law provides what possible further explanations of schizophrenic behavior? (659)

3. There is considerable evidence now to suggest that besides the midbrain reticular formation there is another midbrain area that is malfunctioning in schizophrenics. Identify this other area. (660)

   a. This area is just medial to another nucleus, and the two appear to overlap. Name this structure. (660)

   b. Together these two areas contain the cell bodies of the two most important dopaminergic projection systems in the brain. List these two projection systems and identify the major tract by which they send their axons forward to the anterior structures of the brain. (661)

   c. To where do each of these pathways project? (661)

   d. Distinguish between the limbic striatum and the neostriatum in terms of their composition. (661)

   e. What findings have been reported as a result of ventrotegmental area stimulation? (662-663)

   f. What is paranoia and how is it related to the ventrotegmental area? (663)

Read pages 663-667 and summary statements 8-10 on page 685, then answer each of the following questions in this section.
---

1. What are amphetamines and what is their major effect? (663-664)

   a. Provide three examples of amphetamines. (664)

   b. List some of the other effects produced by amphetamines. (664)

c. What are some of the withdrawal effects following prolonged use of amphetamines? (664)

   d. What is amphetamine psychosis and what comparison, if any, exists between this drug-induced psychosis and schizophrenia? (664)

   e. Describe what happens when amphetamines are given to a schizophrenic. (664)

   f. What effect, if any, do amphetamines have on the catecholamines, and how is this effect brought about? (665)

   g. On what grounds did researchers believe that dopamine is the neurotransmitter of greatest importance in the neural response to amphetamines? (665)

   h. What effect does amphetamine administration have on serotonin? (665)

   i. What do these findings suggest about the role of serotonin in some cases of schizophrenia? (665)

2. What is the dopamine hypothesis of schizophrenia?

   a. Chlorpromazine is one of a large class of antipsychotic drugs known as phenothiazines. How do these drugs have their effect on dopamine? (666)

   b. What simple interpretation of such findings was first suggested? (666)

   c. What basic problem does this interpretation have? (666)

   d. What findings were provided by autopsy studies of schizophrenic brains? (666)

   e. How were these autopsy findings interpreted? (666)

   f. What do these autopsy findings suggest about the function of antipsychotic drugs? (666)

   g. Based on these autopsy findings why might one consider amphetamine psychosis to be a good model of schizophrenia? (666)

3. Identify three major problems that plague the dopamine hypothesis. (666-667)

Read pages 667-675 and summary statements 11-18 on pages 685-686, then answer each of the following questions in this section.
---

1. What are grief reactions? (667)

   a. How do grief reactions differ from mood disorders? (667)

   b. What are the two types of mood disorders currently recognized by psychiatry? (667)

   c. In depressive disorders what range of activation can we expect? (667)

d. Describe the symptoms one might see in an individual in a depressed period. (667-668)

e. What is the relationship between the onset of a depressive episode and any environmental, psychosocial factor? (668)

f. What does this suggest about a cause for depressive disorder? (668)

g. What is a bipolar disorder? (668)

h. In addition to the depressive symptoms what other symptoms are we likely to observe in the patient suffering from a bipolar disorder? (668)

2. What role does heredity appear to play in mood disorders? (668)

   a. What evidence is available to support your answer? (668)

   b. Do these results leave any room for other possible causative factors? (668)

   c. What would be the most likely way for a genetic difference to be expressed in a different pattern of emotional disorder? (668)

   d. In relation to bipolar and depressive disorders what do the results of such studies show? (668)

   e. What conclusions have geneticists reached concerning the relationship between these two mood disorders? (668)

3. What is reserpine? (669)

   a. If you were a physician in the 1950s, for what would you probably have prescribed reserpine? (669)

   b. What problems did reserpine have as a therapeutic drug? (669)

   c. What was isoniazid being used for in the 1950s? (669)

   d. What was the major side effect of isoniazid? (669)

   e. What effects did these drugs have on the monoamine neurotransmitters? (669)

4. Locate the locus coeruleus. (669)

   a. What two factors make the locus coeruleus an ideal place to look for the physiological disruptions underlying depression? (669)

   b. What was the earliest and most simplistic version of the catecholamine theory? (669)

5. What is monoamine oxidase and what effect does it have on norepinephrine? (669)

   a. At what point in the synaptic transmission process is norepinephrine most vulnerable to monoamine oxidase? (669)

b. What rationale can you provide for the use of MAO inhibitors in the treatment of depression? (669-670)

c. Besides the MAO inhibitors what other class of drugs provided not only further support for the catecholamine theory of depression but also another group of therapeutic drugs for depression? (670)

d. What is the best guess as to how the drugs in this class produce their effect on norepinephrine? (670)

6. What is the effect of the amphetamines on norepinephrine levels, and how is this effect accomplished? (670)

   a. Why do amphetamines pose a problem for the catecholamine theory of depression? (670)

   b. What explanation can you give for this finding? (670)

   c. Such an explanation, if correct, would help to provide answers for what three questions? (670)

   d. What problem does tricyclic antidepressant drug therapy pose for the catecholamine theory? (670)

   e. What possible explanation can you give for this phenomenon? (670)

7. What is the function of the alpha presynaptic receptors? (670)

   a. Why are these receptors frequently referred to as autoreceptors? (670)

   b. What additional kinds of receptor sites are typically found at catecholamine synapses? (670)

   c. How do beta and alpha autoreceptors respond once an impulse arrives at the presynaptic terminal? (670)

   d. If we now add a tricyclic antidepressant such as amitriptyline, what should happen? (671)

   e. In order for this scenario to be correct what assumption do we have to make concerning the alpha receptors? (671)

   f. How does this information concerning the autoreceptors and the role they play explain the fact that tricyclic antidepressant drug therapy reduces norepinephrine levels almost immediately but takes one to two weeks of continuous treatment to alleviate depression? (671)

   g. If this explanation is correct what are we forced to conclude? (671)

   h. Explain how the synaptic mechanism that produces both up-regulation and down-regulation might work to control the amount of norepinephrine in the synapse. (671)

i. How does this mechanism help to explain how tricyclic antidepressant therapy can slowly increase the amount of norepinephrine in the synapse? (671)

   j. What research support can you offer for this hypothesis? (672)

   k. What might we predict would happen in postsynaptic cells as norepinephrine levels drop during depression? (672)

   l. What is produced at the postsynaptic cells as a result of chronic tricyclic antidepressant drug therapy? (672)

   m. Describe the timing of events that occur at the pre- and postsynaptic cells as a result of tricyclic antidepressant drug therapy. (672)

8. What evidence can you give for suspecting that the neurotransmitter serotonin might be involved in depression? (672-673)

9. What is lithium? (673)

   a. What is it used to treat? (673)

   b. How long does it take for lithium to be fully effective? (673)

   c. What two effects does lithium have in the brain? (673)

   d. How does lithium produce its therapeutic effect? (673)

10. With what type of mood disorder is electroconvulsive shock therapy (ECT) widely employed? (673)

    a. What was Meduna's rationale for using ECT with schizophrenic patients in the 1930s? (674)

    b. Compare early electroconvulsive shock therapy techniques with those of today. (674)

    c. What are the side effects of electroconvulsive shock therapy? (674)

    d. What feature do ECT and the antidepressant drug and lithium therapies have in common? (674-675)

Read pages 675-677 and summary statements 19-22 on page 686, then answer each of the following questions in this section.
---

1. What are the major symptoms associated with senility? (675)

   a. Until the 1970s what was the prevalent explanation for senility? (675)

   b. What would cause a stroke to occur? (675)

   c. What evidence can you site that suggests that the mini-stroke theory of senility is not definitive? (675)

d. How might EEG activity be used to explain senility? (675)

2. Describe the development of Alzheimer's disease in a typical patient. (675-676)

   a. When (agewise) is it most likely to begin? (675)

   b. What differences in EEG activity are likely to be observed when comparing the records of a normal 70-year-old and a 70-year-old with early Alzheimer's disease? (676)

   c. Postmortem examination of the brain of an Alzheimer's disease victim is apt to reveal what gross changes? (676)

   d. At the microscopic level what differences are apt to be seen in such an examination? (676)

   e. From where does the abnormal protein β-amyloid come, and theoretically how is it formed? (676-677)

3. What reason is there to suspect that the neurotransmitter acetylcholine may also be involved in Alzheimer's disease? (677)

   a. Locate the nucleus basalis of Meynert. (677)

   b. Why might the finding of a loss of cells in this small area be an important clue to understanding Alzheimer's disease? (677)

   c. Why has the use of cholinergic agonists been unsuccessful as a drug therapy for Alzheimer's disease? (677)

   d. What other drug therapy may be more promising? (677)

4. What is the connection between Down syndrome and Alzheimer's disease? (677)

Read pages 677-682 and summary statements 23-24 on pages 686-867, then answer each of the following questions in this section.
---

1. If it is true that epilepsy is not a disease, then what is it? (678)

   a. What is the most outstanding feature of the seizure activity seen in epilepsy? (678)

   b. How might this feature be caused? (678)

   c. Interpret the large EEG waves that are seen both in epilepsy and in coma so as to account for the lack of consciousness observed. (678)

2. Distinguish between partial and generalized seizures. (679)

   a. In what two areas of the brain will you never find epileptic activity? (679)

   b. To most people, the term "epilepsy" evokes the image of what type of seizure activity? (679)

c. Trace the development of such seizure activity from the beginning until after the patient regains consciousness. (679)

d. Tonic and atonic seizures are two kinds of generalized seizures. How do they differ? (680)

e. Absence attacks, also known as _____, involve only a loss of _____ and last for about _____. What kind of behavior might we expect to see in the individual during such a seizure? (680)

f. What is characteristic of the EEG activity during an absence attack? (680)

3. What are the two major differences between simple and complex partial seizures? (681)

   a. What kinds of symptoms are likely to be experienced in simple partial seizures? (681)

   b. List three common examples of automatic behaviors that might occur during complex partial seizures. (681)

   c. What is a fugue state? (681)

   d. In the rare case of Julia, where was the focal point of her seizures? (681)

Read pages 682-684 and summary statements 26-29 on page 687, then answer each of the following questions in this section.
---

1. Describe the phenomenon of kindling. (682)

   a. What brain area is most sensitive to this process? (682)

   b. What is the anatomical relationship between this structure and the hippocampus? (682)

   c. What is long-term potentiation? (682)

   d. Using both the phenomenon of kindling and long-term potentiation, explain how a series of seizures might make the brain more seizure prone. (682)

2. What reason can you give for assuming that two factors must be present to cause a seizure? (682)

   a. List and describe these two general factors. (682)

   b. How is an animal model of epilepsy produced? (683)

   c. Using such a model and recording from an individual cell located in the epileptic focus during a seizure, what kind of electrical activity will we see? (683)

   d. What is this phenomenon called? (683)

e. Ribak et al.(1982) reports that cells within the epileptic focus have been stripped of their GABA end bulbs. What implications might this have concerning the underlying factor in epilepsy? (683)

   f. Identify four possible triggering mechanisms for an epileptic seizure. (683)

3. In terms of drug therapy, for many years the drug of choice for epilepsy was what? (684)

   a. What is the current status of that drug in the treatment of epilepsy? (684)

   b. What is currently the drug of choice for the treatment of grand mal seizures? (684)

   c. What is currently the drug of choice for the treatment of petit mal seizures? (684)

   d. What condition must be presented for surgery to be a viable option in the treatment of epilepsy that has not responded to drug therapy? (684)

   e. What is the strategy of such surgery? (684)

   f. Under what rare condition might some portion of the corpus callosum be cut in the treatment of epilepsy? (684)

PRE-EXAM QUIZ

Multiple-Choice
Select the choice that best completes the stem in each question and indicate your selection in the appropriate space to the left of the question.

_____ 1. Schizophrenia is a(n)
   a. organic brain disorder
   b. form of multiple personality disorder
   c. psychotic disorder
   d. synonym for insanity
   e. none of the above

_____ 2. Regional cerebral blood flow scans of schizophrenics typically evidence
   a. enlarged ventricles
   b. increased blood flow throughout the cerebral cortex
   c. hyperactivity in both the prefrontal cortex and the striatum
   d. hypofrontality
   e. more than one of the above

_____ 3. According to Crow all but one of the following is characteristic of Type 1 schizophrenia. Which is NOT a characteristic of this type of schizophrenia?
   a. usually shows a good response to antipsychotics
   b. typical symptoms include affect flattening, loss of speech and movement, and a loss of drive
   c. most frequently seen in acute cases
   d. good prognosis
   e. little or no intellectual impairment

_____ 4. The dopamine theory of schizophrenia holds that schizophrenia is the result of excessive dopamine transmission at the terminals of the _____ neurons where they synapse on neurons in the _____.
   a. nucleus accumbens, septal area, and prefrontal cortex; caudate and striatum
   b. nucleus basalis of Meynert; areas of the limbic system
   c. ventral tegmental area; caudate and putamen
   d. ventral tegmental area and midbrain reticular formation; temporal and frontal cortex
   e. none of the above

_____ 5. Researchers have found at least one major difference between amphetamine psychosis and schizophrenia. It is that
   a. amphetamine psychosis is due to excessive serotonin transmission, whereas schizophrenia is caused by excessive dopamine transmission
   b. symptoms are much less severe in amphetamine psychosis than in schizophrenia
   c. amphetamine psychosis is caused by excessive release of dopamine, whereas schizophrenia is the result of too many dopamine receptors
   d. amphetamine psychosis is due to excessive levels of both dopamine and serotonin, whereas schizophrenia is due to excessive levels of dopamine and norepinephrine
   e. none of the above

_____ 6. Genetic research strongly suggests that
   a. the two types of mood disorders represent the expression of two separate genetic defects
   b. depression is caused by a genetic defect that results in a missing enzyme
   c. although there may be a weak genetic component in depression, family environment and rearing are far more important determinants
   d. the lack of 100% concordance between monozygotic twins can be attributed to poor diagnostic techniques
   e. none of the above

_____ 7. Which of the following classes of drugs are used in the treatment of depression?
   a. monoamine oxidase inhibitors   d. amphetamines
   b. antipsychotics   e. more than one of the above
   c. lithium

_____ 8. Current theory suggests that tricyclic antidepressants most probably produce their effect on depression by
   a. blocking but not activating norepinephrine postsynaptic receptor sites
   b. increasing the number of alpha presynaptic receptor sites
   c. decreasing the number of beta presynaptic receptor sites
   d. decreasing the number of alpha presynaptic receptor sites while blocking norepinephrine reuptake
   e. increasing the number of beta presynaptic receptor sites

_____ 9. Which of the following neurotransmitters other than norepinephrine may also be involved with depression?
   a. dopamine   d. acetylcholine
   b. gamma aminobuteric acid   e. endorphin
   c. serotonin

_____10. Which of the following brain alterations is NOT characteristic of Alzheimer's disease?
   a. significant increase in both acetylcholine and the enzyme responsible for its production, choline acetyltransferase
   b. presence of an abnormal protein, β-amyloid, which is found in clumps squeezed in between neurons and glial cells of the cortex
   c. cellular degeneration in the hippocampus and the cerebral cortex
   d. presence of neurofibrillary tangles
   e. all of the above are characteristic of Alzheimer's disease

_____11. Alzheimer's patients have which of the following in common with Down syndrome patients?
   a. an extra chromosome 21
   b. a gene located in the same place on the same chromosome that is responsible for producing β-amyloid precursor protein in Down's patients
   c. neuritic plaques
   d. neurofibrillary tangles
   e. none of the above

_____12. The most outstanding feature of EEG activity during an epileptic seizure is
   a. desynchrony   d. hypersynchrony
   b. hyposynchrony   e. none of the above
   c. synchrony

_____13. Which of the following is NOT one of the symptoms commonly found in grand mal seizures?
   a. involvement of entire cortex
   b. complete rigidity accompanied by cessation of breathing
   c. flexors and extensors are out of phase with one another so that the convulsions become an alternation of the two
   d. loss of consciousness
   e. all of the above

_____14. These seizures result in a particular, semiconscious condition in which the person responds only to those external stimuli that fit into the automatic behavior that is being executed. These seizures are
   a. complex partial seizures   d. tonic seizures
   b. absence attacks   e. none of the above
   c. simple partial seizures

_____15. Some research suggests that the neuropathological result of the initial brain damage may be some sort of malfunction in the _____ system in the cortex, which allows neurons to become hyperactive.
   a. dopaminergic inhibitory   d. serotonin excitatory
   b. cholinergic excitatory   e. none of the above
   c. GABA inhibitory

True/False

_____ 1. The accumulated evidence for a genetic factor in schizophrenia is extremely strong and few researchers today bother to challenge the idea.

_____ 2. The lack of 100% concordance between monozygotic twins strongly argues for some kind of interaction between the genetic factor and environmental variables in the production of schizophrenia.

_____ 3. One fairly consistent finding when brains of schizophrenic patients are studied in autopsy is atrophy in both the cerebral cortex and the cerebellar cortex.

_____ 4. A common thought disorder that is characteristic of schizophrenics is the tendency to include all sorts of mental associations in their speech that most people suppress as irrelevant to the conversation.

_____ 5. The mesolimbic system, which includes the dopaminergic neurons of the ventrotegmental area, the mesolimbic path, and all the neurons to which they send their axons in limbic sites, is involved in the hallucinatory problems of schizophrenia.

_____ 6. Antipsychotic drugs appear to have no effect on the problem of attention in schizophrenia.

_____ 7. The neurons of the locus coeruleus employ serotonin as their neurotransmitter.

_____ 8. Both lithium and electroconvulsive therapy are treatments of choice for bipolar disorders.

_____ 9. It is clear from recent studies that lithium has its effect by blocking the release of norepinephrine, thereby substantially decreasing its level.

_____10. It is the seizure and not the electricity that is therapeutic when electroconvulsive therapy is used to treat mood disorders.

_____11. Neuritic plaques are more prevalent in senile dementia, whereas neurofibrillary tangles are more prevalent in Alzheimer's disease.

_____12. The aura normally signals the onset of any of the partial seizures.

_____13. β-amyloid is found in the brains of both Alzheimer's patients and Down's patients.

_____14. Petit mal seizures are most frequent in children.

_____15. Both some forms of brain damage brought about by the primary cause and some type of triggering process must be present to cause a seizure.

17.1 absence attacks (680)	17.6 atonic seizures (680)
17.2 alpha presynaptic receptors (670)	17.7 atrophy (654)
17.3 Alzheimer's disease (675)	17.8 aura (679)
17.4 amphetamines (663)	17.9 autoreceptors (670)
17.5 antipsychotic drugs (666)	17.10 β-amyloid (676)

17.6

Generalized type of seizure that seems to involve a loss of all muscle tone, especially in the "antigravity" muscles of the back and legs. The result of the seizure is a fall to the floor with no effect on consciousness.

17.7

A condition in the brain in which the tissue is shrunk because of a loss of cells.

17.8

A conscious experience that occurs at the beginning of a grand mal seizure.

17.9

Receptor sites located on the membrane of the presynaptic cell that releases the neurotransmitter to which they respond.

17.10

An abnormal protein consisting of only 39 amino acids that has been cleaved from a molecule called β-amyloid precursor protein. It is found in clumps, around which are clusters of peculiar dendrite and axon tips.

Copyright 1990 by Wadsworth, Inc.

17.1

Generalized type of seizure that involves only a loss of awareness and lasts for about 10 seconds. Rare in individuals over the age of 15. Also known as petit mal. The EEG of such patients is quite distinctive, with each wave consisting of a large, slow "dome" with a sharp spike added.

17.2

A type of autoreceptor found on norepinephrine-using presynaptic neurons. It serves as the trigger for an inhibitory feedback mechanism that limits the release of norepinephrine.

17.3

Although it rarely strikes before the age of 60, Alzheimer's disease is not equivalent to aging. Its progress is faster in people who contract it earlier in life and slowest when it begins after age 70. There is no cure for this disease. Prognosis is a slow decline into total loss of mental functions and death.

17.4

A class of drugs whose major effect is arousal. Called "speed," they are commonly used both as stimulants and as diet pills. Examples include destroamphetamine, methamphetamine, and dextroamphetamine. Other effects include irritability, pupil dilation, sweating, elevated heart rate, insomnia, loss of appetite, and increased blood pressure.

17.5

Those drugs that are used in the treatment of schizophrenia.

17.11 β-amyloid precursor protein (676)

17.12 bipolar disorder (668)

17.13 carbamazepine (684)

17.14 catatonia (652)

17.15 chlorpromazine (666)

17.16 complex partial seizures (681)

17.17 continuous performance test (CPT) (658)

17.18 convulsions (674, 679)

17.19 delusions (652)

17.20 depressive disorder (667)

17.16

In this type of seizure consciousness is affected but is not entirely lost. The result is a semiconscious state in which the person responds only to those external stimuli that fit into the automatic behavior being executed. Typical automatic behaviors are chewing, picking at clothing, lip smacking, assuming a bizarre posture.

17.17

One way of measuring attention in which the subject must monitor a series of stimuli for periods of up to 20 minutes and be scored for those he or she fails to report or reports incorrectly.

17.18

Intense muscle spasms.

17.19

Incorrect beliefs frequently involving feelings of persecution, or sometimes involving feelings of grandeur.

17.20

A type of mood disorder in which the person often enjoys a normal range of activation but has periods during which the activation level gradually falls to a depressed level and stays there for days or weeks before it rises again.

Copyright 1990 by Wadsworth, Inc.

17.11

A protein molecule from the abnormal protein, β-amyloid, found in the cortex of Alzheimer's patients. It also contains another part, a chemical that can inhibit the enzyme that cleaves out the β-amyloid.

17.12

A mood disorder in which episodes of extremely high activation (mania) are involved, usually alternating with periods of depression, which is much like the depression seen in the depressive disorder.

17.13

Currently the drug of choice in the treatment of grand mal seizures.

17.14

An extreme posture that involves remaining absolutely motionless and speechless for hours at a time.

17.15

The trade name is Thorazine. This drug was the first of the phenothiazines to be developed and is the best known.

17.21

dizygotic twins

(653)

17.22

down-regulation

(671)

17.23

Down syndrome

(677)

17.24

electroconvulsive therapy (ECT)

(673)

17.25

epilepsy

(678)

17.26

epileptic focus

(679)

17.27

ethosuximide

(684)

17.28

flattened effect

(652)

17.29

fugue state

(681)

17.30

GABA

(683)

17.26

The small area of the brain in which a seizure starts.

17.21

Also called fraternal twins. In this case each twin comes from a different ovum and sperm and has different genes.

17.27

Currently the drug of choice in the treatment of petit mal seizures.

17.22

The decrease in receptor density during periods when transmitter is scarce.

17.28

A loss of appropriate emotional responses, often seen in schizophrenia.

17.23

A congenital brain disorder characterized by mental retardation. One of the abnormalities of Down syndrome is the presence of an extra copy of chromosome 21. It is on this chromosome that β-amyloid precursor protein is found.

17.29

A condition involving travel to a different location in a trance-like state with amnesia for the episode after the seizure ends.

17.24

A widely employed treatment of mood disorder, especially with the depressive disorder cases in which it is most effective. Electric shock is administered through the brain to produce convulsions under controlled conditions.

17.30

An inhibitory neurotransmitter that may be depleted in an area of the brain subject to seizures.

17.25

A collection of different brain dysfunction symptoms, all of which involve seizure activity.

Copyright 1990 by Wadsworth, Inc.

17.31

generalized seizures

(679)

17.32

genetic factor

(653)

17.33

grand mal seizure (tonic-clonic seizure)

(679)

17.34

grief reactions

(667)

17.35

hallucination

(652)

17.36

hypersynchrony

(678)

17.37

hypofrontality

(655)

17.38

insanity

(651)

17.39

kindling

(682)

17.40

limbic striatum

(661)

17.36

The most outstanding feature of seizure activity. It is a condition in which there is too much stimulus facilitation so that there are too many excitatory postsynaptic potentials at the same time. This is seen in the EEG record as very large amplitude slow waves.

17.37

A pattern of blood flow in the cortex seen in regional cerebral blood flow scan studies of some schizophrenic patients. Such a test will typically reveal an unusually low blood flow activity in the frontal lobe combined with an increased blood flow in the sensory and sensory related areas of the parietal, occipital, and temporal lobes.

17.38

A legal term that is used to categorize people who are mentally and emotionally incapable of being held responsible for their actions. It is not a psychological or psychiatric term.

17.39

Phenomenon that occurs as a result of providing the amygdala with low-intensity brief electrical stimulation daily until seizure activity suddenly appears in the EEG during the second week. It begins as a small focal seizure but grows to a full-blown generalized seizure with clonic convulsions.

17.40

Includes the septal area and the nucleus accumbens, which is different from but related to the evolutionarily newer neostriatum. The dopaminergic fibers of the ventrotegmental area project to the limbic system.

Copyright 1990 by Wadsworth, Inc.

17.31

Seizures that include the entire cortex.

17.32

A factor that creates a predisposition or vulnerability for developing a disease.

17.33

The generalized type of seizure that strongly invades the motor areas of the cortex and produces patterns of muscular contractions called convulsions. Its onset is signaled by an aura, which is followed by a loss of consciousness and the beginning of convulsions, consisting of both a tonic phase and a clonic phase.

17.34

Normal reaction to life event that is characterized by a temporary depression lasting anywhere from one to six months.

17.35

Strange, incorrect sensory perceptions such as hearing voices that are not there and feeling worms crawling under the skin.

17.41 lithium (673)

17.42 locus coeruleus (669)

17.43 long-term potentiation (LTP) (682)

17.44 MAO inhibitors (669)

17.45 mesolimbic system (661)

17.46 moderating factors (653)

17.47 monoamine oxidase (MOA) (669)

17.48 monoamine transmitters (669)

17.49 monoamines (665, 669)

17.50 monozygotic twins (652)

17.46

Factors that either help or hinder the development of the disease. These factors were posited by the Zubin and Steinhauer vulnerability model.

17.47

An enzyme that destroys norepinephrine.

17.48

A group of neurotransmitters that include the indolamines, serotonin, and the catecholamines, dopamines, norepinephrine, and epinephrine.

17.49

A class of neurotransmitters that includes both the catecholamines and serotonin.

17.50

Also called identical twins. In this case one fertilized ovum splits to form two embryos, both having the same set of genes.

Copyright 1990 by Wadsworth, Inc.

17.41

A basic element used in the form of lithium carbonate to treat bipolar disorder.

17.42

A small cluster of norepinephergic neurons located near the pontine-midbrain border that sends its axons up the base of the brain through the hypothalamus and eventually branches and rebranches in the cortex, particularly in the region of the forebrain.

17.43

An increase in sensitivity at the hippocampal synapses produced by a stimulus consisting of a brief train of electrical pulses. It lasts for some hours after the brief stimulus that initiated it and may serve as part of the explanation for kindling.

17.44

A class of drugs that interferes with the enzyme activity of monoamine oxidase, thereby increasing norepinephrine levels. These drugs are used in the treatment of depression. Isoniazid is an example of an MOA inhibitor.

17.45

The dopaminergic neurons of the ventrotegmental area (VTA), the mesolimbic path, and all the neurons to which they send their axons in the nucleus accumbens, septal area, prefrontal cortex, and other limbic sites as well as the descending pathways from the limbic structures back to the VTA.

17.51 mood disorder (667)	17.56 neurofibrillary tangle (676)
17.52 multiple personality (651)	17.57 neurological soft signs (654)
17.53 negative symptoms (656)	17.58 neuropathological factors (in epilepsy) (682)
17.54 neostriatum (661)	17.59 neuropathology (654)
17.55 neuritic plaque (676)	17.60 nucleus accumbens (661)

17.56

A dense thicket of strange filaments that fill some of the surviving cortical cells in the brain of Alzheimer's patients.

17.57

Neuropathology signs that are less specific than we would like and that provide only weak clues about the type and location of a particular malfunction in the nervous system.

17.58

Those factors involved in the cause of a nervous system disease.

17.59

The physical deformities or damage, either structural or chemical or both, to the brain that has been produced by disease, infection, or trauma.

17.60

A limbic system cell group just lateral to the septal area.

Copyright 1990 by Wadsworth, Inc.

17.51

Disorders in which the episodes occur repeatedly and fail to correlate with any discernible change in the person's environment. The preponderance of evidence suggests that the causes of mood disorders are mainly within the physiology of the nervous system. Two kinds are recognized: depressive disorder and bipolar disorder.

17.52

An emotional disorder in which the patient's personality has fragmented into two or more distinct persons that compete for control of conscious processes, with the loser lying latent at an unconscious level until the next opportunity to emerge. Multiple personality is not a psychosis and bears no resemblance to schizophrenia.

17.53

These are symptoms of schizophrenia that include flattened affect, refusal to speak, catatonia, and loss of motivation. Such symptoms are termed negative because they are symptoms associated with a negative prognosis.

17.54

The name given to the caudate and putamen to differentiate them from an evolutionarily older but related group of structures that are known as the limbic striatum. The dopaminergic fibers of the substantia nigra project to the neostriatum.

17.55

A tangled mass squeezed in between some of the cortical cells and glial cells of an Alzheimer's patient's brain. It consists of intrusive clusters of peculiar dendrite and axon tips gathered around central clumps of β-amyloid.

17.61 nucleus basalis of Meynert (677)

17.62 organic mental disorders (650)

17.63 overinclusion (659)

17.64 P300 (658)

17.65 paranoia (663)

17.66 paroxysmal depolarization shift (PDS) (683)

17.67 partial seizures (679)

17.68 phenothiazines (666)

17.69 phenytoin (684)

17.70 positive symptoms (656)

17.66

The activity of cells within the focus of a seizure. Consists of a shift in membrane potential toward depolarization, on top of which is a train of nerve impulses that it has triggered.

17.67

Seizures that are localized to a particular area of the cortex.

17.68

The largest category of antipsychotic drugs. It includes the drug chlorpromazine. (Trade name: Thorazine)

17.69

Sold under the trade name Dilantin, this was the drug of choice in the treatment of epilepsy for many years.

17.70

These symptoms of schizophrenia include hallucinations, delusions, and thought disorders and are termed positive because they are symptoms associated with a positive prognosis.

17.61

A small region adjacent to the medial septal nucleus at the ventromedial boundary of the globus pallidus. Its neurons project to the entire cerebral cortex as a part of an arousal system involved in memory and attention. There is a loss of cholinergic cells in this area in Alzheimer's patients.

17.62

A type of psychosis that has readily identifiable causes. These are the disorders in which there is some clear evidence of brain damage or disruption.

17.63

A thought deficit that is characteristic of schizophrenics in that they show a tendency to include all sorts of mental associations in their speech that most people suppress as irrelevant to their conversation.

17.64

The large positive wave of an averaged evoked potential that occurs 300-400 ms after the beginning of the stimulus. It has been found to be correlated with the degree of attention to the stimulus.

17.65

A set of delusional beliefs, usually of persecution. The individual having such delusions is deeply suspicious of his or her whole environment, believing that everything relates to himself and every behavior of the other people around him is all part of a plot to do him some harm. It is often a symptom of schizophrenia.

17.71 prognosis (656)	17.76 septal area (661)
17.72 psychotic (650)	17.77 simple partial seizures (681)
17.73 seizure (674)	17.78 stress factor (653)
17.74 senile dementia (675)	17.79 thought disorder (652)
17.75 senility (675)	17.80 tonic seizures (680)

17.76

A limbic system cell group anterior to the hypothalamus and ventral to the septum.

17.71

The chances of the patient's recovery or improvement in symptoms.

17.77

Type of seizure characterized either by sensory symptoms such as auditory distortions, shrinking vision, taste hallucinations, and severe abdominal pain, or by motor symptoms including paralysis or twitching in one or more limbs on one side of the body. There is no loss of consciousness.

17.72

A person whose behaviors are strange and socially inappropriate, whose thoughts are disordered, and who may sometimes hallucinate and suffer from delusions. The chief symptom of psychosis is a loss of contact with reality.

17.78

A factor that can act as the agent that triggers the actual development of the disorder.

17.73

A condition in which large numbers of brain cells fire together in massive volleys.

17.79

Strange, wild mental associations that are often characteristic of schizophrenia.

17.74

A loss of mental functions in old age. As a syndrome it includes memory loss, inability to reason, slow reaction time, poor motor control, and sensory loss.

17.80

Generalized type of seizure in which the convulsion is limited to a sudden stiffening of all muscles, frequently accompanied by impairment of consciousness.

17.75

The loss of mental functions and motor control with aging.

17.81

tricyclic antidepressants (TADs)

(670)

17.82

triggering process (in epilepsy)

(683)

17.83

Type I schizophrenia

(656)

17.84

Type II schizophrenia

(656)

17.85

up-regulation

(671)

17.86

ventrotegmental area (VTA)

(660)

17.87

vulnerability model

(653)

17.88

Yerkes-Dodson law

(658)

17.86

A ventral midbrain area found in close proximity to the reticular formation and medial to the substantia nigra. Its cells project via the dopaminergic mesolimbic path to the nucleus accumbens, septal area, and prefrontal cortex. The VTA has been implicated in the hyperarousal and attentional problems of schizophrenics.

17.87

A model of schizophrenia that proposes that there must be at least two causal factors at work to produce the disorder: a genetic factor, which creates a predisposition or vulnerability for developing schizophrenia, and a stress factor, which can act as the agent that triggers the actual development of the disorder.

17.88

States that the capacity of an organism to perform well increases as arousal increases, up to a point, and then further increases in arousal produce worse and worse performance.

17.81

A class of antidepressant drugs that may have their action by blocking the reuptake of catecholamines. Examples include amitriptyline and imipramine.

17.82

The factor that actually starts a seizure.

17.83

One of Crow's two types of schizophrenia. It is characterized by positive symptoms and a good prognosis. Such patients typically show an absence of intellectual impairment, normal radiographic scans, and a good response to antipsychotics.

17.84

One of Crow's two types of schizophrenia. It is characterized by negative symptoms and a poor prognosis. Such patients may show some intellectual impairment, hypofrontality, ventricular enlargement in radiographic scans, and a poor response to to antipsychotics.

17.85

The increase in receptor density during periods when transmitter is scarce.

Copyright 1990 by Wadsworth, Inc.

CHAPTER EIGHTEEN
NEUROPSYCHOLOGY OF CORTICAL FUNCTION

READ-WRITE-REVIEW

Read pages 692-697 and summary statements 1-2 on page 741, then answer each of the following questions in this section.
---

1. What two medical specialties come into play when the brain suffers physical damage? (692)

    a. What are the roles of each of these special when the brain suffers physical damage? (692)

    b. What is neuropsychology? (692)

    c. What is the role of the neuropsychologist when the brain suffers physical damage? (692)

    d. Neuropsychological practice and research focuses on what part of the brain? (693)

    e. More recently those neuropsychologists with strong interest in basic research on language, attention, and hemispheric differences have formed a subfield known as what? (693)

2. What are the five major divisions of the frontal lobes? (693)

3. The data collected by a neuropsychologist on a patient will probably be used for what? (693)

    a. Describe the makeup and administration of the Prisco delayed-comparison task. (694)

    b. If your patient has frontal lobe damage, what kinds of results might you expect on the Prisco delayed-comparison task? (694)

    c. What are the specific implications of such a performance on the Prisco delayed-comparison task? (694)

    d. Describe the makeup and administration of the Corsi recency-discrimination task. (694)

    e. If your patient has frontal lobe damage, what kinds of results might you expect on the Corsi recency-discrimination task? (694-695)

    f. What are the specific implications of such a performance on the Corsi recency-discrimination task? (695)

g. Suppose that your patient had temporal lobe damage rather than frontal lobe damage. What kinds of results would you expect on the Corsi recency-discrimination task? (694-695)

h. Describe the makeup and administration of the Stroop test. (695)

i. If your patient had frontal lobe damage, what kinds of results would you expect on the Stroop test? (695-696)

j. What are the specific implications of such a performance on the Stroop test? (695)

k. Describe the makeup and administration of the Wisconsin card-sorting tasks. (696)

l. If your patient has frontal lobe damage, what kinds of responses might you expect on the Wisconsin card-sorting task? (696)

m. What is the name generally given this sort of behavior? (696)

n. The fact that such behavior frequently seems to embarrass the patient when he or she is told about it should suggest what to the neuropsychologist? (696)

o. Describe the makeup and administration of the maze-learning tasks. (696)

p. What kind of behavior might you expect on the maze-learning task if your patient has frontal lobe damage? (696-697)

q. Despite the fact that frontal lobe patients acknowledge that they have made an error and are embarrassed, what two expected behaviors will you not see with such patients? (697)

r. Given these findings what suggestions can you make concerning the occupational rehabilitation of such a patient? (697)

Read pages 697-702 and summary statements 3-4 on page 742, then answer each of the following questions in this section.
---

1. Describe the delayed-response task. (697)

   a. Describe the behavior you would expect to see in the prefrontal monkey when faced with a delayed-response task? (698)

   b. What does such behavior indicate? (698)

   c. List and describe two other similar tasks that have been found to be sensitive to the prefrontal lesions. (698-699)

2. A number of experimenters have proposed that the most fundamental ability of the prefrontal cortex is what? (699)

   a. Explain how this fits with what we know about the evolution of the prefrontal cortex. (699-700)

   b. What are the two steps involved in the act of "willing" or "intending" to do something? (700)

c. How does this hypothesis explain the behavior of the homemaker who failed to buy every item on her supermarket shopping list? (700-701)

d. How does this hypothesis help to explain the patient's inability to follow the rules or even her comprehension of the rules in performing a task? (701)

e. Based on the symptoms it would seem that goal sets serve three functions. List them. (701)

3. Anatomically locate the orbitofrontal cortex. (701)

a. This area provides information about what to the planning mechanism of the prefrontal cortex? (701)

b. Why is it necessary to think of this connection from limbic system to prefrontal cortex as a two-way street? (701-702)

c. What symptoms are you likely to see in a frontal lobe personality? (703)

Read pages 702-709 and summary statement 5 on page 742, then answer each of the following questions in this section.
---

1. What is the visual field of an eye? (703)

a. What is the relationship between the visual fields of the adult human eyes? (703)

b. What is the result of the fact that as the light image of the visual field passes through the lens of the eye it is reversed, right and left and upside down? (703)

c. What happens at the optic chiasm? (703)

d. To where do the optic fibers in both bundles project from the optic chiasm? (703)

e. Distinguish between contralateral and ipsilateral projections. (703)

f. Imagine that you see a dollar bill in the left visual field and indicate where it would fall in:

(1) the retina (703)
(2) the lateral geniculate nucleus (703)
(3) the occipital lobe (703)

g. What benefit is derived from having a visual system that provides us with overlapping images? (704-705)

2. Describe the resultant loss of vision if:

a. fibers at the optic chiasm are all destroyed. (705)

b. fibers of the right optic nerve are all destroyed. (705)

c. there is a loss of fibers in the optic radiations on the left side. (705)

d. fibers of the left tract are all lesioned. (705)

3. Identify the visual analyzer areas that make up the visual cortex. (705)

   a. Why is the V1 area considered to be the crucial area of the occipital cortex? (705)

   b. Suppose that the entire V1 area in the right hemisphere is lost. What visual loss would the patient experience? (705-706)

   c. What causes a scotoma and how might it be caused? (705)

   d. What is a visual agnosia and how might it be caused? (705)

   e. Describe briefly the kinds of attentional deficits one might expect to see in visual agnosia cases. (706-707)

   f. How might the attentional problems of agnosia be related to visual scanning problems? (708)

4. Describe two strategies for dealing with specific loss of visual function in agnosia. (708-709)

Read pages 709-713 and summary statement 6 on page 742, then answer each of the following questions in this section.
---

1. Locate S1 and S2 anatomically and identify the perceptual abilities for which they are responsible. (709)

2. Lesions in the area of the postcentral gyrus may produce what kind of deficit? (710)

   a. Describe each of the following conditions:

      (1) apraxia (710)

      (2) anosognosia (710)

      (3) autotopagnosia (710)

      (4) pain asymbolia (710)

   b. Research results suggest that what general principle may be emerging concerning parietal cortex injury? (711)

   c. What kind of input is required in spatial orientation? (711)

   d. Describe the makeup and administration of the Weinstein maps. (711)

e. What is visuospatial agnosia? (711)

f. What is unilateral neglect and what causes it? (712)

g. How do anosognosia and unilateral neglect differ? (712)

h. How would you interpret the finding that right hemisphere symptoms of unilateral neglect differ from those of left hemisphere unilateral neglect? (712)

i. What is covert orienting? (712)

j. What three processors are deemed necessary in covert orienting? (712)

k. Which processor is located in the parietal lobe, according to Posner (1984)? (712)

Read pages 713-716 and summary statement 7 on page 742, then answer each of the following questions in this section.
---

1. Language comprehension is controlled by _____ of the brain, whereas speech is controlled by _____ of the brain. (713-714)

    a. Anatomically locate each of these two structures. (713-714)

    b. Identify the deficit that would occur if:

        (1) the speech production area was damaged. (714)

        (2) the language comprehension area was destroyed. (714)

2. What problem does one encounter in attempting to classify various cases of aphasia into clear-cut types? (714)

    a. Expressive aphasia is also known by what other names? (714)

    b. List and identify three major symptoms of expressive aphasia. (714)

    c. What is the difference between phonemic and semantic paraphrasia? (714-715)

3. Another name for Wernicke's aphasia is what? (715)

    a. How does this form of aphasia differ from expressive aphasia? (715)

    b. What is neologism? (715)

    c. What reasons can you give for the occurrence of neologisms and paraphrasias in Wernicke's aphasia? (715)

    d. What is meant by word salad? (715)

Read pages 716-723 and summary statements 8-9 on page 742, then answer each of the following questions in this section.
---

1. Identify each of the following types of aphasia based on a description of symptoms:

    a. Loss of language comprehension, word salad, but with ability to repeat with great accuracy whatever is heard or read. (715-716)

    b. Good comprehension of speech and writing, adequate fluency, but lacks the ability to repeat what is heard or read. (715)

    c. A complete absence of spontaneous speech. (715)

    d. Dysarthria, paraphrasias, telegraphic speech, and circumlocution location. (714-716)

    e. Comprehends language well and is capable of repeating what is said to him and can read out loud but lacks spontaneous speech. (715)

    f. The major problem seems to be a loss of reference memory for words. The person's only real difficulty is in naming things, thus speech is peppered with semantic paraphrasias and circumlocutions. (715)

    g. Symptoms include neologisms and paraphrasias, word salad, good word fluency but poor comprehension. (715)

2. What is a cardiovascular accident (CVA)? (716)

    a. Why is there some loss of brain tissue following a CVA? (716)

    b. What artery is usually involved in cases where an aphasia is produced by a stroke? (716-717)

    c. Describe the extent of damage seen in Leborgne's brain as observed using CAT scanning. (717)

    d. What was the probable reason for Broca's choosing to ignore the reduction in size of the temporal lobe of Leborgne's brain? (718)

    e. Poeck et al.(1984) did CAT scans of the brains of eight aphasia patients. What did they find? (718)

    f. Electrically stimulating Broca's area in connection with surgery, Lesser et al.(1984) observed what kinds of activity, and what does this tell us about the function of Broca's area? (718)

    g. What important discovery did Metler and Rowland (1948) make when they removed Broca's area in two catatonic schizophrenic patients who had not spoken in 20 years? (719)

3. Where does Broca's area lie relative to the premotor cortex. (720)

    a. What is the function of the premotor cortex? (720)

b. A major symptom of expressive aphasia is the slow, halting nature of the speech. How might this symptom be interpreted as a result of damage to the premotor area? (720)

c. What do these anatomical findings and symptomatology suggest concerning the function of Broca's area? (720)

d. What is the basic reason the patient with expressive aphasia has difficulty with cause-and-effect arrangements, according to Bradley and his colleagues (1980)? (720)

e. Describe the type of sentences Bradley et al.(1980) employed in the test they constructed. (720)

f. When they tested their hypothesis, what did Bradley et al. find? (720)

4. What is the rough rule of thumb concerning lesion location and the type of aphasia? (720)

   a. What reasons can you give for the finding of so much variability between the location of the lesion and the type of aphasia? (720-721)

   b. Both the speech production circuits and the speech comprehension circuits appear to be intact in the patient with conduction aphasia. What then is the problem? (721)

   c. Identify and locate the primary auditory projection area. (721)

   d. Anatomically locate Wernicke's area. (721)

   e. Trace the path of the arcuate fasciculus. (721)

   f. In conduction aphasia what area is damaged? (721)

   g. The difficulty in the initiation of speech that is seen in transcortical motor aphasia can be caused by damage to what two areas? (721)

   h. Identify precisely what is lost when each of these areas is damaged. (721)

   i. What kind of lesion is necessary to produce the condition known as transcortical sensory aphasia? (722)

Read pages 723-724 and summary statement 10 on page 742, then answer each of the following questions in this section.
---

1. What is agraphia?

   a. According to Margolin and Binder's (1984) study, agraphia is more than an inability to perceive what one is writing. What did they find to suggest this? (723)

   b. What is the probable site of lesion in cases of agraphia? (723)

   c. What is alexia? (723)

   d. Distinguish between developmental dyslexia and acquired alexia. (723)

e. Pure alexia is associated with lesions in what area of the brain? (723)

f. Most cases of acquired alexia involve a lesion that effectively does what? (723)

g. Where would such a lesion lie? (723)

Read pages 724-728 and summary statements 11-12 on **page 742,** then answer each of the following questions in this section.

---

1. Clinical experience suggests that speech lateralization exists in humans. What does this mean? (724)

    a. What area of the brain is usually larger on one side of the brain than on the other side? (725)

    b. The fact that this structure exists on both sides of the brain suggests what? (725)

2. What makes it difficult to restrict the initial visual input to one hemisphere or the other? (727)

    a. What is a tachistoscope? (727)

    b. What is the advantage of presenting a visual stimulus with a tachistoscope when you wish to restrict the initial input to one hemisphere? (727)

    c. What is this procedure called? (727)

    d. What are the results of studies using this procedure? (727)

    e. What is the limitation of this procedure? (727)

3. What problem is presented by the anatomy of the auditory system when the researcher tries to present the stimulus to only one hemisphere? (727)

    a. What is the difference between ipsilateral and contralateral projections in the auditory system? (727)

    b. Identify and describe the experimental procedure designed to take advantage of this fact. (727)

    c. What findings are obtained when this procedure is employed? (727)

    d. What conclusions did Kimura (1964) arrive at based on her dichotic listening studies using short melodic segments? (728)

    e. What conclusions have been reached from more recent studies concerning hemispheric lateralization of music processing? (728)

    f. What problem do researchers using the dichotic listening technique encounter? (728)

Read pages 728-735 and summary statements 13-15 on pages 742-743, then answer each of the following questions in this section.
---

1. The surgical severing has been used medically for what purpose? (728)

    a. With the severing of the corpus callosum, what connections remain between the hemispheres above the level of the brain stem? (728)

    b. Describe the deficits in everyday behavior in patients who have had such surgery. (728)

    c. Describe the experimental arrangement employed by Sperry (1961) in testing such patients. (728)

    d. How would you explain Sperry's results using this experimental procedure? (728-729)

    e. What results are typically obtained when the subject is asked to identify objects from touch? (731-732)

    f. What is intermanual conflict? (732)

2. Because of a brain tumor in the left hemisphere, Jamie lost a large portion of that area known as the speech centers. This happened when she was 9 months old. Predict what we can expect from her in speech by age 15. (732)

    a. How did Zaidel (1985) attempt to circumvent the problem of speaking to one side of the brain without the other side listening? (732-733)

    b. Describe the token test. (733)

    c. What conclusions has Zaidel (1985) reached concerning right hemispheric speech? (733)

    d. What limitations exist concerning Zaidel's (1985) findings? (733)

    e. What reason does Gazzaniga (1983) offer for being so cautious about interpreting experimental results to mean that the right hemisphere of a patient possesses language ability? (733)

    f. What is this phenomenon called? (733)

    g. What is the Wada test? (734)

    h. The research use of the Wada test in language lateralization has produced what conclusions? (734)

    i. What is meant by the term "prosody"? (734-735)

    j. Which brain hemisphere is thought to contribute prosody to speech production? (735)

Read pages 735-740 and summary statements 16-19 on page 743, then answer each of the following questions in this section.
---

1. Two major theoretical views concerning whether we are born with our brains fully lateralized or acquire hemispheric specialization have developed. Identify each theory by proponent and state the basic premise of each. (735-736)

   a. Describe the time-sharing technique. (736-737)

   b. What results did White and Kinsbourne (1980) obtain when they applied this technique to children? (737)

   c. What conclusion did they make on the basis of these results? (737)

   d. What problem is common to these time-sharing experiments? (737)

   e. The findings of Kelly and Tomlinson-Keasey (1981) using children with severe hearing impairments support which of the two major theories? (737)

2. Distinguish between a sinistral individual and a dextral individual. (738)

   a. What is the contralateral rule? (738)

   b. What is meant by the term "hemispheric dominance"? (738)

   c. What results have been obtained by testing the contralateral rule using the Wada test? (738)

   d. What usually accompanies a lack of lateralization for language in sinistrals? (738)

3. Evidence from Springer and Deutch (1981) suggests that there are a large group of individuals who are clearly right-handed and have left-hemisphere speech. What about the lateralization of the smaller group of individuals who have neither? (739)

   a. How does Bakan (1977) account for left-handedness? (739)

   b. What is the difference between familial sinistrals and pathological sinistrals? (739)

   c. State Annett's (1981) right-shift theory. (739)

   d. What two differences in brain structures are seen when sinistral and dextral brains are compared? (739-740)

PRE-EXAM QUIZ

Multiple-Choice
Select the choice that best completes the stem in each question and indicate your selection in the appropriate space to the left of the question.

_____ 1. Which of the following tests consists of a page of color names not printed in the color named but in a different color?
   a. Stroop test
   b. Corsi recency-discrimination task
   c. Prisco delayed-comparison task
   d. maze-learning task
   e. Wisconsin card-sorting task

_____ 2. Perseveration is
   a. the establishment of a particular way of performing
   b. the inability to employ a concept to control behavior even though the concept is verbally comprehended
   c. the inability to recall stimulus sequences
   d. the inability to shift from one operation to another
   e. more than one of these

_____ 3. Delayed-response tasks are used with animals to test for
   a. short-term memory deficits
   b. perseveration
   c. the inability to disregard interfering stimuli
   d. the inability to maintain a behavioral set
   e. the inability to give up an out-of date set

_____ 4. Which of the following does not appear to be a part of the frontal lobe personality?
   a. blunted feeling
   b. callous unconcern
   c. unrestrained and tactless behavior
   d. mood changes
   e. all of the above are characteristic of this personality

_____ 5. A lesion in which of the following areas would cause you to lose the entire left visual field of each eye?
   a. left optic tract   d. right optic tract
   b. right optic nerve   e. right optic radiations
   c. optic chiasm

_____ 6. Damage to which of the following would be likely to cause visual agnosia?
   a. V1   d. MT
   b. V2   e. more than one of the above
   c. V3

_____ 7. A(n) _____ is an inability to perform some set of movements despite a lack of paralysis or any other obvious damage to the motor system.
   a. autotopagnosia   d. anosognosia
   b. aphasia   e. asymbolia
   c. apraxia

411

_____ 8. Unilateral neglect is caused by damage to
   a. the posterior parietal cortex in one hemisphere
   b. the anterior parietal cortex in one hemisphere
   c. the occipital cortex in one hemisphere
   d. the anterior temporal cortex in one hemisphere
   e. a combination of two of the above in the same hemisphere

_____ 9. According to Posner and colleagues (1984, 1987), covert orienting, the ability of the individual to attend to another part of the visual field despite keeping his eyes and head fixed, requires at least at least three processors. For which of the following does Posner et al. claim to have evidence that it exists in the parietal cortex?
   a. an engage mechanism that allows one to focus on the new location
   b. a disengage mechanism that allows one to stop paying attention to some previous stimulus
   c. a shift mechanism that allows the movement of the eyes from the previous stimulus to the new stimulus
   d. a shift mechanism that calculates where in visual space the current locus of attention is and where the new locus will be
   e. none of the above

_____ 10. Which of the following would you not expect to find in expressive aphasia?
   a. telegraphic speech   d. paraphrasia
   b. inability to comprehend speech   e. none of the above
   c. dysarthria

_____ 11. This patient suffers from an inability to comprehend language. Her spontaneous speech is a disorganized word salad; however the patient is able to repeat with great accuracy whatever is heard or read. This patient most probably suffers from which of the following?
   a. receptive aphasia   d. conduction aphasia
   b. transcortical sensory aphasia   e. expressive aphasia
   e. mutism

_____ 12. Which of the following is used to explain why so much variability seems to occur between the type of aphasia and the site of the lesions?
   a. researchers have often failed to consider the extent to which subcortical damage exists
   b. there are individual differences between brains
   c. researchers have often failed to look at the extent of the cortical damage
   d. researchers are forced to deal with experimental data obtained from naturally occurring accident victims not from controlled research-produced lesions
   e. more than one of the above

_____ 13. Which of the following techniques has been employed in an effort to present a stimulus to only one hemisphere of the brain?
   a. Weinstein's maps   d. token task
   b. hemifield tachistoscopy   e. none of the above
   c. dichotic listening

_____14. Which of the following represents a possible brain difference between dextrals and sinistrals?
   a. the left hemisphere of most dextrals has larger posterior regions than those of the right hemisphere, a bias that is not seen in most sinistrals
   b. the planum temporale is larger on the left side in dextrals but larger on the right side in sinistrals
   c. The operculum in the left hemisphere of dextrals is larger than it is in the left hemisphere of sinistrals
   d. the corpus callosum is larger in sinistrals than in dextrals
   e. more than one of the above

_____15. Which of the following research techniques has been used by Kinsbourne to gather data in support of his invariance hypothesis?
   a. Wada test   d. Weinstein's maps
   b. cross cueing   e. token task
   c. time sharing

True/False

_____ 1. The Corsi task tests the patient's ability to use verbal concepts to command behavior sequences.

_____ 2. Both the Wisconsin card-sorting task and the maze-learning task are designed to reveal perseveration in the patient.

_____ 3. A number of experimenters have suggested that the most fundamental ability of the prefrontal cortex is to provide the organism with goal sets.

_____ 4. Hemianopsia of the left visual field can be observed in individuals whose left occipital lobe has been destroyed.

_____ 5. Voluntary eye movements are directed by the frontal eye fields of the occipital cortex.

_____ 6. A patient suffering from autotopagnosia appears to have lost the location of his body part.

_____ 7. Generally, the farther back the lesion is in the parietal lobe, the more the defect is directly related to the body part and the less such damage has to do with perceiving the space around the body.

_____ 8. Damage to the arcuate fasciculus will most probably result in Wernicke's aphasia.

_____ 9. Broca's decision to locate the entire speech center in the third frontal convolution was probably influenced greatly by the phrenologists' belief that the prefrontal cortex was the latest evolutionary development and therefore it must contain the most human of the brain functions.

_____10. Studies such as those by Metler and Rowland (1948) using cadaver heads and later two schizophrenic patients strongly suggest that receptive aphasia is not caused by damage to Broca's area.

_____11. The inability to read produced by brain damage is termed development dyslexia.

_____12. The planum temporale exists only in the left hemisphere.

_____13. According to Lenneberg speech lateralization is acquired slowly through experience.

_____14. The fact that the right hemisphere can follow verbal instructions implies that the right hemisphere must have some sort of language ability.

_____15. A stimulus to one ear reaches both hemispheres; however the contralateral projection is always considerably weaker than the ipsilateral projection system.

18.1 acquired alexia (723)	18.6 anosognosia (710)
18.2 agraphia (723)	18.7 apraxia (710)
18.3 alexia (723)	18.8 arcuate fasciculus (721)
18.4 angular gyrus (723)	18.9 autotopagnosia (710)
18.5 anomic aphasia (715)	18.10 Broca's aphasia (714)

18.6

The inability to recognize a defect in some part of the body, which occurs in some cases of right-side parietal injury.

18.1

The adult loss of the ability to read because of brain damage.

18.7

A disorder in which there is an inability to perform some set of movements despite lack of paralysis or any other obvious damage to the motor system.

18.2

Loss of ability to write spontaneously.

18.8

A tract that takes an almost loop-like path out of Wernicke's area and runs forward through the white matter to connect with the frontal lobe speech area, including Broca's.

18.3

The inability to read.

18.9

A disorder in which the patient appears to have lost the location of his or her body parts. The difficulty is not a language problem but rather an inability to think in terms of body "geography."

18.4

The part of the left parietal lobe just behind Wernicke's area.

18.10

A language loss that is usually more expressive than receptive.

18.5

Type of aphasia in which there is good language comprehension, and speech is intact except for the absence of many nouns. Speech is consequently full of semantic paraphrasias and circumlocutions.

Copyright 1990 by Wadsworth, Inc.

18.11 Broca's area (713)

18.12 circumlocution (715)

18.13 conduction aphasia (715)

18.14 contralateral projection (703, 727)

18.15 contralateral rule (738)

18.16 Corsi recency-discrimination task (694)

18.17 covert orienting (712)

18.18 cross cueing (733)

18.19 delayed-alternation task (698)

18.20 delayed matching-to-sample task (699)

18.16

Patient views a series of cards with two pictures. Some are repeated on other cards paired with different pictures. Some cards have a question mark telling him to say if either picture has been shown before and which was more recent. Failure on the second part and success on the first shows memory deficit for sequence of stimuli.

18.17

The process of directing one's attention to another part of the visual field despite keeping the head and eyes fixed.

18.18

A phenomenon identified by Gazzaniga and Hillyard in which the left hemisphere gets clever at picking up subtle cues from the behavior controlled by the right brain and using them to correctly infer what was shown to the right.

18.19

Task in which the animal must choose to respond to either the right button or the left button, wait through a delay, and then choose the alternate button.
This task is sensitive to prefrontal damage.

18.20

Task in which the display of the S+ (the correct stimulus) is shown first followed by a delayed period. Next both S+ and S- are displayed and the monkey must choose S+ in order to receive food.

Copyright 1990 by Wadsworth, Inc.

18.11

An area of the cortex in the frontal lobes just anterior to the precentral gyrus that has to do with speech production.

18.12

A symptom of aphasia in which rough description or phrase is substituted for the missing word.

18.13

The type of aphasia in which there is good comprehension of speech and writing and reasonably good speech with adequate fluency. The major problem is that the patient cannot repeat what he or she reads or hears. This of aphasia involves damage to the arcuate fasciculus tract.

18.14

Projection in which the fibers cross over to the side of the brain opposite their side of origin (i.e., left retina to right geniculate nucleus).

18.15

A notion that the speech hemisphere is always the one contralateral to the preferred hand.

18.21 delayed-response task (697)

18.22 developmental dyslexia (723)

18.23 dextral (738)

18.24 dichotic listening (727)

18.25 dysarthria (714)

18.26 expressive aphasia (714)

18.27 familial sinistrals (739)

18.28 fovea (707)

18.29 frontal eye field (708)

18.30 frontal lobe personality (702)

18.26

The language disorder that results from a loss of an area of cortex in the left frontal lobe just anterior to the precentral gyrus, which results in a speech production deficit.

18.27

Left-handers who have a number of sinistrals in their immediate family, suggesting that sinistrality can be inherited.

18.28

Tiny central area of the retina where detailed vision is accomplished.

18.29

Area of the frontal cortex just posterior to the prefrontal cortex. It directs voluntary eye movements.

18.30

Syndrome due to prefrontal and orbitofrontal cortex damage. Symptoms include unrestrained, tactless behavior; mood changes; blunted feelings; callous unconcern; boastfulness; and grandiose, obstinate, and egocentric behavior.

Copyright 1990 by Wadsworth, Inc.

18.21

A type of memory task in which the animal subject is shown a piece of food being placed under one of two stimulus objects. A screen is then moved in front of the stimulus object for a brief time, then taken away to allow the animal to make its choice.

18.22

Disorder that refers to difficulties in learning to read seen in some children. The loss is partial and not total.

18.23

Right-hander.

18.24

An experimental technique in which the subject wearing earphones hears a separate string of digits in each ear and tries to repeat them.

18.25

A symptom of expressive aphasia in which the problem lies in production and fluency. Speech is choppy and halting and the lips and tongue may not respond properly to form the syllables.

18.31 goal set (699)

18.32 hemianopsia (706)

18.33 hemifield tachistoscopy (727)

18.34 hemispheric dominance (738)

18.35 Heschl's gyrus (721)

18.36 intermanual conflict (732)

18.37 invariance hypothesis (736)

18.38 ipsilateral projection (703, 727)

18.39 lateral geniculate nucleus (LGN) (703)

18.40 lateralization (724)

18.36

A transitory symptom often seen in split-brain patients in which one hand opposes what the other is doing.

18.37

Kinsbourne's hypothesis that lateralization is present at birth and does not increase with experience.

18.38

Projection in which the fibers stay on the same side as their origin (i.e., left retina to left lateral geniculate nucleus).

18.39

Portion of the thalamus where the optic tract terminates.

18.40

Specialization of a hemisphere of the brain.

Copyright 1990 by Wadsworth, Inc.

18.31

A neural mechanism that prepares a set of response circuits for action.

18.32

Loss of vision in one visual field.

18.33

A method in which a visual stimulus is presented for 100 ms, which is short enough to be over before an eye movement can be made but long enough that the visual system can perceive the stimulus if attention is focused.

18.34

Holds that the hemisphere containing language and the motor area for the preferred hand is in some way stronger than the other hemisphere and dominates brain function.

18.35

A strip of the cortex that forms the floor of the lateral fissure. It is the location of the primary auditory projection area and provides the input for Wernicke's area.

18.41 maze-learning task (696)	18.46 optic nerve (705)
18.42 mutism (715)	18.47 optic radiations (705)
18.43 neologisms (715)	18.48 optic tract (705)
18.44 neuropsychology (692)	18.49 pain asymbolia (710)
18.45 optic chiasm (703)	18.50 paraphrasia (714)

18.46

The section of the optic fibers between their origin in the retina and the optic chiasm.

18.47

The axons of lateral geniculate nucleus cells that run from the lateral geniculate nucleus to the visual cortex.

18.48

The section of optic fibers between the chiasm and the lateral geniculate nucleus.

18.49

A disturbance of body image in which the patient seems to be unable to appreciate painful stimuli in a particular body part, which usually results in neglect, carelessness, and injury to the "disowned" limb.

18.50

The substitution of one word for another.

18.41

Neuropsychological task in which the subject is required to push a metal stylus along a metal-lined groove in a wooden board hidden from view. When a blind alley is entered, an error buzzer sounds. This task tests for perseveration in frontal lobe patients.

18.42

Lack of spontaneous speech.

18.43

The substituted words in the type of paraphrasia in which the patient creates her own word to fill the blank in her word memory.

18.44

Branch of clinical psychology aimed at diagnosing brain damage and studying dysfunctions of the nervous system from the viewpoint of a psychologist.

18.45

Point in optic tract at which one half of the fibers of each optic nerve cross to the opposite side of the brain.

Copyright 1990 by Wadsworth, Inc.

18.51

pathological sinistrality

(739)

18.52

perseveration

(696)

18.53

phonemic paraphrasia

(714)

18.54

planum temporale

(721)

18.55

Prisco delayed-comparison task

(694)

18.56

prosody

(734)

18.57

receptive aphasia

(714)

18.58

right-shift theory

(739)

18.59

scotoma

(705)

18.60

semantic paraphrasia

(715)

18.56

The intonation of speech that gives it a rhythm or a musical quality.

18.51

Left-handedness based on brain damage.

18.57

The loss of language comprehension that results from loss of an area of cortex in the posterior end of the left temporal lobe.

18.52

A symptom of prefrontal damage in which the patient is unable to make a shift from one task to another.

18.58

Theory proposed by Annett, who postulates that there is no gene for handedness itself, but rather one that creates a left-hemisphere advantage for language, and the bias for left-hemisphere hand control is an accidental by-product.

18.53

A paraphrasia in which the substituted word simply sounds similar to the desired word, although the meaning may be very different.

18.59

An area of blindness that is experienced by the patient as a black area in a zone of vision. It is caused by a loss of a part of V1.

18.54

A cortical area hidden within the lateral fissure that contains a part of Wernicke's area.

18.60

Symptom in which the substituted word is similar to the blocked word in meaning, such as "lizard" for "frog."

18.55

A neuropsychological test. The patient is asked to determine whether two series of light flashes presented at different rates were the same or different. Then the flash stimuli are replaced with nonsense figures. Success on the second part after failure on the first indicates trouble handling interference between stimuli.

Copyright 1990 by Wadsworth, Inc.

18.61 sinistral (738)

18.62 sodium amytal (734)

18.63 spatial orientation (711)

18.64 stroke (716)

18.65 Stroop test (695)

18.66 tachistoscope (727)

18.67 telegraphic speech (714)

18.68 time sharing (736)

18.69 token test (733)

18.70 transcortical motor aphasia (715)

18.66

An instrument that allows one to view a stimulus for a limited amount of time.

18.61

Left-hander.

18.67

A symptom of expressive aphasia in which the speech omits many of the linking words of grammar and syntax. It consists mainly of nouns, verbs, and short common phrases.

18.62

A very short-acting barbiturate.

18.68

An experimental technique used by Kinsbourne to explore language lateralization in children. The subject is given two tasks to perform simultaneously, one involving speech and the other involving something else such as tapping.

18.63

The ability to perceive where objects are in space in relation to self and in relation to other objects.

18.69

A test designed by Zaidel to examine language functions more complex than simple word recognition. The subject must must follow complex instructions. A contact lens and viewer are used to throw the entire image from right to left visual fields onto just one half of the retina--the half that projects through the right hemisphere.

18.64

Brain damage resulting from loss of blood supply to a part of the brain; a "cardiovascular accident."

18.70

A type of aphasia in which the patient comprehends language well and is capable of repeating most of what is said to her. The major symptom is that left on her own the patient will say nothing at all.

18.65

Neuropsychological test designed to measure the patient's ability to minimize interference and maintain a response set. It consists of a page of color names printed in different colors but not the ones that they name.

Copyright 1990 by Wadsworth, Inc.

18.71 transcortical sensory aphasia

(715)

18.72 unilateral neglect

(712)

18.73 visual agnosia

(706)

18.74 visual field

(703)

18.75 visual scanning

(709)

18.76 visuospatial agnosia

(711)

18.77 Wada test

(734)

18.78 Weinstein maps test

(711)

18.79 Wernicke's aphasia

(715)

18.80 Wernicke's area

(714)

18.76

Loss of the spatial orientation ability that allows you to guide yourself from one location to another.

18.77

A test made prior to surgery to see if language is in this patient's right or left hemisphere. Sodium amytal is injected directly into the external carotid. This artery serves only one half of the brain, so the drug puts only one side of the brain to sleep.

18.78

Test for the loss of a form of spatial orientation that probably resides closer to the postcentral gyrus than to the occipital lobes. One hand is placed into a flat box in order to feel a raised line on a board inside. The object is to use the turns the line makes to guide himself through an identical series of turns painted on the floor.

18.79

A form of aphasia in which the greater part of the deficit is in the ability to comprehend language rather than its expression.

18.80

A cortical area that serves as the language comprehension center of the brain. It is located in the posterior end of the left temporal lobe.

18.71

A type of aphasia similar to receptive aphasia in that language comprehension has been lost. Spontaneous speech is disorganized word salad, but the patient can repeat with great accuracy whatever is heard or read.

18.72

A condition in which the patient forgets the side of his body contralateral to the lesion. The condition results from damage to the posterior parietal lobe on one side of the brain, especially in the right hemisphere

---

18.73

A loss of visual abilities such as the ability to identify an object visually without blindness. Caused by damage to occipital cortex areas other than V1.

18.74

The area of the environment visible to the eye at any one moment.

18.75

The sequence of eye movements used in constructing a visual image.

Copyright 1990 by Wadsworth, Inc.

18.81

Wisconsin card-sorting task

(696)

18.82

word salad

(715)

18.81

Neuropsychological task in which the subject is presented with four cards with colored figures and asked to place each of the remaining cards in the deck in the correct pile while not defining "correct." Following 10 successful responses under one unspoken matching rule, the rule is changed. This is a test for perseveration.

18.82

The jumble of words produced by receptive aphasia patients that results from the lack of comprehension and subsequent misuse of words like conjunctions and adjectives.

PRE-EXAM ANSWERS

CHAPTER 1

Multiple-Choice
1. E (3); 2. B (4); 3. D (5); 4. D (6); 5. B (6); 6. C (8); 7. A (10); 8. C (10); 9. C (12); 10. (14)

True/False
1. F (3); 2. F (2); 3. F (3); 4. T (5); 5. F (6); 6. T (6); 7. F (8); 8. T (10); 9. F (12); 10. T (14)

CHAPTER 2

Multiple-Choice
1. B (25); 2. B (39-40); 3. D (38); 4. C (43); 5. C (20); 6. C (39); 7. A (36); 8. E (31); 9. C (23); 10. B (37-38); 11. D (41, 43); 12. B (33); 13. E (23); 14. E (24); 15. D (27)

True/False
1. T (22); 2. F (24); 3. F (27); 4. T (29); 5. F (24); 6. F (37); 7. F (40); 8. T (43); 9. F (30); 10. F (24); 11. T (21-28); 12. T (35); 13. F (43); 14. F (43); 15. F (20)

CHAPTER 3

Multiple-Choice
1. A (72); 2. C (77); 3. B (88); 4. B (87); 5. A (59); 6. E (62); 7. D (68-69); 8. C (85); 9. E (66); 10. B (67); 11. C (82); 12. E (79); 13. A (84); 14. D (96); 15. B (64)

True/False
1. F (90); 2. T (84); 3. T (79); 4. F (68); 5. F (69); 6. T (100); 7. F (55); 8. F (72); 9. T (53); 10. F (53); 11. F (63); 12. T (76); 13. T (79); 14. T (85); 15. T (62)

Chapter 4

Multiple-Choice
1. A (133); 2. D (115); 3. D (121); 4. C (128); 5. D (142); 6. D (111); 7. C (121); 8. D (117); 9. A (119); 10. E (130); 11. C (133-134); 12. D (136); 13. C (145); 14. B (145); 15. C (139-140)

True/False
1. T (115); 2. F (114); 3. F (145); 4. T (111); 5. T (111); 6. T (113); 7. F (131-132); 8. F (121); 9. T (137-138); 10. T (115); 11. F (117); 12. F (127); 13. T (128); 14. T (128); 15. T (122-123)

CHAPTER 5

Multiple-Choice
1. B (155);   2. C (157);   3. B (162);   4. D (164);   5. E (167);   6. E (171);
7. B (166);   8. A (174);   9. C (175);   10. C (176);   11. A (177);   12. B (178);
13. D (177);   14. D (184-185);   15. C (190)

True/False
1. T (153);   2. F (155);   3. F (155-156);   4. F (157);   5. T (158);   6. F (160);
7. F (160);   8. T (169-170);   9. T (167);   10. T (174);   11. T (174);   12. F (176);
13. T (177);   14. T (180);   15. F (185)

CHAPTER 6

Multiple-Choice
1. D (201);   2. A (201);   3. E (208);   4. C (203);   5. B (214);   6. D (214);
7. A (216);   8. E (210);   9. B (239);   10. C (232);   11. C (224);   12. E (226-227);
13. C (239);   14. C (245);   15. B (243-244)

True/False
1. T (210);   2. F (206);   3. T (204);   4. T (207);   5. F (214);   6. T (218);
7. F (219);   8. F (219);   9. T (219);   10. F (222);   11. F (224);   12. T (225);
13. F (229);   14. T (230);   15. F (237)

CHAPTER 7

Multiple-Choice
1. C (280);   2. E (281);   3. D (272);   4. B (275);   5. B (267);   6. D (281);
7. C (281);   8. C (257);   9. C (283);   10. E (259);   11. B (259);   12. D (272);
13. A (281);   14. E (283);   15. B (260)

True/False
1. F (281);   2. T (281);   3. T (258);   4. F (280);   5. T (258);   6. F (272);
7. T (273);   8. F (277);   9. F (271-272);   10. F (290-291);   11. T (281);   12. F (258);
13. F (277);   14. F (281);   15. T (260)

CHAPTER 8

Multiple-Choice
1. A (300);   2. D (309);   3. E (307);   4. B (309);   5. E (309);   6. C (310);
7. C (317);   8. E (312-313);   9. A (325);   10. A (324);   11. D (327);   12. A (328);
13. D (329);   14. E (333);   15. C (331)

True/False
1. T (301);   2. F (302);   3. F (303);   4. T (308-309);   5. F (310);   6. F (311);
7. F (311);   8. F (313);   9. T (319);   10. F (320);   11. F (323);   12. T (320);
13. F (325);   14. T (326);   15. T (329)

CHAPTER 9

Multiple-Choice
1. D (343);   2. C (345);   3. B (347);   4. A (350);   5. E (353);   6. B (352-353);
7. B (354);   8. C (359);   9. E (363);   10. E (365, 369);   11. B (371);   12. D (377);
13. C (379);   14. E (389-390);   15. A (393)

True/False
1. F (342);   2. T (345);   3. F (347);   4. T (348);   5. T (350);   6. F (352);
7. F (354);   8. T (358);   9. T (359);   10. T (361-362);   11. F (362);   12. F (377, 379)
13. F (380);   14. T (386);   15. T (387)

CHAPTER 10

Multiple-Choice
1. D (401-402); 2. C (402); 3. E (410-411); 4. C (404); 5. B (410); 6. C (416-417);
7. E (418-419); 8. D (422); 9. B (424); 10. C (424); 11. E (424-425); 12. D (428);
13. E (430); 14. D (433-434); 15. E (432)

True/False
1. F (402); 2. T (401); 3. F (410); 4. F (406); 5. F (408); 6. F (410);
7. T (411); 8. F (413); 9. F (413); 10. T (414); 11. F (419); 12. F (425);
13. T (425); 14. T (426); 15. F (433)

CHAPTER 11

Multiple-Choice
1. B (441,443); 2. E (444); 3. D (447); 4. B (451); 5. C (453-454); 6. D (456);
7. D (457); 8. A (463); 9. C (464); 10. E (469); 11. D (470); 12. D (471);
13. C (471); 14. B (472-473); 15. C (475)

True/False
1. F (440); 2. F (441); 3. F (444); 4. T (445); 5. F (445); 6. T (447);
7. F (451); 8. F (455); 9. F (458); 10. F (462); 11. F (470); 12. F (468);
13. T (471); 14. T (475); 15. F (475)

CHAPTER 12

Multiple-Choice
1. E (485); 2. C (488); 3. E (492); 4. B (494); 5. D (498); 6. B (498);
7. C (499); 8. A (504); 9. C (488); 10. E (483-484); 11. C (494); 12. B (498);
13. C (503); 14. E (483); 15. B (489)

True/False
1. F (493); 2. T (485-486); 3. F (490); 4. T (494); 5. T (485); 6. F (498);
7. T (492); 8. F (500); 9. F (504); 10. T (505); 11. F (508-509); 12. T (489-490);
13. T (504); 14. F (485); 15. F (487)

CHAPTER 13

Multiple-Choice
1. E (513); 2. B (515-516); 3. D (517-518); 4. A (521); 5. C (524); 6. A (525);
7. D (527); 8. C (527); 9. B (535-536); 10. B (540); 11. D (515); 12. B (523);
13. D (536); 14. E (538); 15. E (539-540)

True/False
1. T (534); 2. F (535); 3. F (522); 4. F (515); 5. T (517); 6. F (518);
7. T (521); 8. T (523); 9. F (529); 10. T (525); 11. T (529); 12. F (536);
13. T (537); 14. F (538); 15. F (538)

CHAPTER 14

Multiple-Choice
1. A (567); 2. C (562); 3. B (574-575); 4. E (570); 5. D (549); 6. B (572);
7. C (552); 8. D (578); 9. B (547); 10. E (564); 11. C (548); 12. A (564);
13. D (567); 14. D (581); 15. B (563)

True/False
1. T (571); 2. F (547-548); 3. T (548); 4. F (570); 5. T (562-563); 6. T (554-555);
7. T (570-571); 8. T (577); 9. F (563-564); 10. T (551-552); 11. F (557);
12. F (550); 13. F (579); 14. T (559); 15. F (549)

CHAPTER 15

Multiple-Choice
1. D (588-589); 2. B (589); 3. E (590); 4. B (592); 5. D (595); 6. C (597);
7. E (599); 8. A (600-601); 9. E (600); 10. D (604); 11. E (605); 12. D (602-603);
13. A (595); 14. C (598); 15. E (589)

True/False
1. T (589); 2. T (589); 3. T (589); 4. T (591); 5. F (593); 6. F (593);
7. T (594); 8. T (595); 9. F (599); 10. T (599-600); 11. T (601); 12. F (602);
13. F (607); 14. F (608); 15. T (603-604)

CHAPTER 16

Multiple-Choice
1. C (613); 2. D (614); 3. E (617-618); 4. A (621); 5. B (626); 6. E (631);
7. C (631); 8. C (633); 9. B (635); 10. D (637); 11. D (637-638); 12. C (640);
13. A (642); 14. C (642); 15. B (635)

True/False
1. T (612); 2. T (617-618); 3. F (616); 4. T (619); 5. T (622); 6. T (623);
7. F (630); 8. F (632); 9. F (635); 10. T (637); 11. F (637); 12. T (638-639);
13. T (640-641); 14. F (642); 15. T (642-643)

CHAPTER 17

Multiple-Choice
1. C (650); 2. D (655); 3. B (656-657); 4. E (661); 5. C (666); 6. E (668);
7. A (669); 8. D (671); 9. C (672); 10. A (677); 11. C (677); 12. D (678);
13. E (679); 14. A (681); 15. C (683)

True/False
1. T (652); 2. T (653); 3. F (654); 4. T (659); 5. F (661); 6. T (667);
7. F (669); 8. F (673); 9. F (673); 10. T (674); 11. F (676); 12. F (679);
13. T (677); 14. T (680); 15. T (682-683)

CHAPTER 18

Multiple-Choice
1. A (695); 2. D (696); 3. C (698); 4. E (702); 5. D (705); 6. E (706);
7. C (710); 8. A (712); 9. B (712); 10. B (714); 11. B (715-716); 12. E (721);
13. A (726-727, 732); 14. A (739-740); 15. C (736-737)

True/False
1. F (694-695); 2. T (696); 3. T (699); 4. F (706); 5. F (708); 6. T (710);
7. F (711); 8. F (721); 9. T (718); 10. T (719-720); 11. F (723); 12. F (725);
13. T (735); 14. T (732); 15. F (727)